American Pendulum

A VOLUME IN THE SERIES

Cornell Studies in Security Affairs

Edited by Robert J. Art, Robert Jervis, and Stephen M. Walt

A list of titles in this series is available at www.cornellpress.cornell.edu

American Pendulum

*Recurring Debates in
U.S. Grand Strategy*

CHRISTOPHER HEMMER

Cornell University Press

Ithaca and London

The views expressed here are those of the author alone and do not necessarily represent the official policy of the United States Government, Department of Defense, or Air War College.

First published 2015 by Cornell University Press

Library of Congress Cataloging-in-Publication Data

Hemmer, Christopher M. (Christopher Michael), 1969– author.
    American pendulum : recurring debates in U.S. grand strategy / Christopher Hemmer.
        pages cm. — (Cornell studies in security affairs)
    Includes bibliographical references and index.
    ISBN 978-0-8014-5424-0 (cloth)
    1. United States—Foreign relations—20th century.   2. United States—Foreign relations—21st century   I. Title.

    E183.7H416 2015
    327.73009'04—dc23

                                                        2015015949

Cornell University Press strives to use environmentally responsible suppliers and materials to the fullest extent possible in the publishing of its books. Such materials include vegetable-based, low-VOC inks and acid-free papers that are recycled, totally chlorine-free, or partly composed of nonwood fibers. For further information, visit our website at www.cornellpress.cornell.edu.

Cloth printing   10 9 8 7 6 5 4 3 2 1

For Sandy, Kyle, and Paige

Contents

Acknowledgments

My first thanks properly belong to my students at the Air War College, especially those who took my U.S. Grand Strategy elective and those who signed up for the Grand Strategy Program/Seminar. Virtually all the ideas contained in this book were first tried out, developed, expanded upon, and refined in our class discussions. I always walked out of seminar smarter than I was when I walked in. My fellow faculty members at the Air War College, especially those in the Department of International Security Studies, also deserve thanks for sitting through more lectures and faculty workshops on this topic than many of us would care to count.

While I hope that my debts to others working in this field are well represented in the footnotes, I would also like to thank some of the best teachers I have had, whose influence may be less apparent but no less important including Tim Borstelmann, Tom Christensen, Jim Goldgeier, Peter Katzenstein, Steven Livingston, and Shibley Telhami.

I would also like to thank everyone at Cornell University Press, including Susan Barnett and especially Roger Haydon, who was enthusiastic about this project from the beginning and expertly shepherded it through to publication. The copy editing skills of Michael Bohrer-Clancy, Sara Ferguson, and Therese Malhame saved me from many errors and greatly improved the prose throughout the book. Thanks as well to the reviewers of the book from the press, especially Robert Jervis who waived anonymity to better provide constructive comments. Unknown to him, this is the second intellectual debt I owe him. When I was an undergraduate struggling to find a topic for my senior thesis, my adviser tried to get me started by asking which of the books in the field had the greatest influence on me. My answer was Jervis's *Perception and Misperception in International Politics*, a book that provided the launch point for my thesis as well as for many subsequent efforts. Now, many years later, it has been especially gratifying to receive such generous, specific, and helpful comments from him on the draft of this book. My final and most important thanks go to Sandy, Kyle, and Paige. I hope they know why.

American Pendulum

Introduction

Recurring Debates in U.S. Grand Strategy

With the coming to power of each presidential administration, observers of U.S. foreign policy often dispute how novel the new team's approach to foreign policy is.[1] Although compelling, such discussions can also be frustrating. No U.S. grand strategy will be completely novel. New presidential administrations never start from a blank slate, so it is always possible to see similarities between an administration and its predecessors. Conversely, because each administration faces novel problems and operates in a unique context, no U.S. foreign policy strategy will be an exact replica of its predecessors. Thus, analysts will be able to identify both continuity and change in U.S. foreign policy. In addition, these debates have little bearing on the substance of foreign policy strategy. Whether a strategy is deemed to be revolutionary, new, modified, or traditional tells us nothing about the merit of that policy. Even if a strategy has a distinguished historical pedigree, that does not mean it is the correct one in current circumstances. Similarly, a revolutionary strategy can be appropriate or inappropriate for the current challenges a country faces.

This book attempts to limit these frustrations by examining the grand strategic choices of the United States through the lens of four recurring debates in U.S. foreign policy. The first debate focuses on how the United States should balance the trade-offs between working alone (unilaterally) and working with other states and international organizations (multilaterally). The second debate focuses on the proper place of U.S. values in U.S. foreign policy. The third debate is about where the strategic perimeter of the United States lies: what parts of the world and what issues must the United States be deeply concerned with and what parts of the world and what issues can it safely ignore? The final debate focuses on the question of whether time is on the side of the United States or that of its enemies. These four debates were chosen on pragmatic rather than theoretical grounds. They represent a manageable number of distinct debates that have run throughout U.S. history and still animate arguments about U.S. foreign policy today. If a better understanding of these four debates, what is at stake in each, and how they have recurred throughout U.S. history, offers a useful way of thinking about the current and future strategic choices of the United States, then the principal aim of this book will have been met.

The history of U.S. foreign policy is not a settled tradition against which one can usefully judge the faithfulness or originality of a given policy. Instead, that history consists of fierce debates regarding the proper course for the United States with policy choices being only a temporary resolution of those debates. This approach shifts the focus from a discussion of how similar or dissimilar a policy is to one of its predecessors to a discussion of how previous debates in the history of U.S. foreign policy might help to illuminate current choices. The key benefit of this altered focus is that it moves the discussion of current U.S. strategy toward substantive issues and away from the perceived degree of fidelity to a historical tradition. The issue is not, for example, how similar the 2002 National Security Strategy is to the foreign policy of John Quincy Adams, but what we can learn from the debates on U.S. foreign policy that took place in the 1820s and the results of the policies that flowed from those debates, which can help us think more clearly about the challenges facing the United States today.

The purpose of this book is not to offer a diplomatic history of U.S. foreign relations.[2] Several significant foreign policies will remain unaddressed or be mentioned only in passing. Furthermore, the book does not aim to closely examine the process by which U.S. foreign policy is made.[3] The purpose of this book is to examine some of the fundamental debates that have recurred in U.S. foreign policy history, to explore how the temporary resolutions of those debates have shaped previous attempts of the United States to make itself more secure, and to analyze what can be taken from those policies and their results to better evaluate what U.S. grand strategy should be today and in the future.[4]

What Is Grand Strategy?

As Barry Posen phrases it, grand strategy is "a state's theory about how it can best 'cause' security for itself."[5] Grand strategy is distinct from other types of strategy both in the objectives it seeks and the resources it has at its disposal. For objectives, grand strategy should focus on goals that are national, comprehensive, and long term. The ends a grand strategy seeks should not be the objectives solely of a particular ruling group, party, class, or ethnic group, but should focus instead on advancing some conception of a state's national interests as a whole. Whereas the concept of the national interest is notoriously fuzzy, for the purposes of defining grand strategy, intent is more important than content. If the intent of a strategy is to advance only the interests of a substate group, regardless of how those interests are defined, the strategy does not merit the title "grand." Conversely, if the intent of a strategy is to advance a state's overall interests, regardless of how those interests are defined in practice, then the term "grand strategy" is appropriate.

A state's grand strategy should also be comprehensive. Grand strategy should not focus on a specific issue or a relationship with a particular state; it should focus on how a state wants its place in the world to look. Most states are more concerned with their immediate region than with distant parts of the globe, and more powerful states have a wider purview than weaker states, but a state's grand strategy should address every area in which a state sees itself as having important interests.

Grand strategy should also have a long-term focus. It should not just be a plan for today or tomorrow, but a plan that looks to the future. As with national interests, the definition of long term can vary from state to state. One stereotype of the United States is that, either because of temperament or electoral cycles, it wants everything done tomorrow (or even better, yesterday) and it is thus unable to sustain policies over the long term. This stereotype can be misleading: U.S. policymakers have been able to think in terms beyond the next election. In thinking about grand strategy, U.S. policymakers have tended to define the proper grand strategic time horizon in terms of decades.

Grand strategy is also distinct in the means at its disposal. It should focus on all the resources at, or even potentially at, a state's disposal. A grand strategy is not a strategy for using a state's military resources, economic resources, or ideological resources; instead, it should attempt to combine all of a country's instruments of power into a coherent whole.

Given these criteria, grand strategy should delineate a country's fundamental national interests, offer an assessment of the principal threats to those interests, and present a plan to use all instruments of national power to ward off those threats and advance those interests in the long term.

Grand strategy can be both implicit and explicit. Since World War II, analysts of U.S. foreign policy have had the benefit of access to formal written documents that attempt to encapsulate U.S. grand strategy. During the Cold War, George Kennan's X-Article and the National Security Council Report 68 (once it became declassified) served as summary documents encapsulating the overall thrust of U.S. grand strategy. Since the passage of the Goldwater–Nichols Defense Reorganization Act in 1986, Congress has required each president to regularly submit to Congress an overarching statement regarding the administration's approach to U.S. foreign policy, known as the National Security Strategy (NSS). Because the subject of this book is the United States, I will use the terms "grand strategy" and "national security strategy" interchangeably.[6] Theoretically, everything the United States does in the international arena is supposed to flow out of the arguments contained in the

NSS, and all of the executive agencies involved in implementing U.S. foreign policy are supposed to look to it for guidance.

The absence of a summary document does not necessarily mean that a grand strategy does not exist. Indeed, from a historical and comparative perspective, having such a summary document might be the exception rather than the norm. Similarly, the presence of such a summary document is also no guarantee that what is expressed in it is an accurate and comprehensive account of a state's grand strategy, especially in the case of the current National Security strategies, which are documents intended for worldwide public consumption. Thus, even when such summary documents are offered, the analyst's job in discerning grand strategy is still to piece it together by looking at a series of statements and actions to try to understand what overarching vision lies behind any state's various acts, without ignoring the fact that grand strategy is only one influence on state policy.[7]

Thinking explicitly in terms of grand strategy can offer policymakers several potential benefits. First, grand strategy can offer guidance on how to prioritize limited resources. No country has unlimited means, and no matter how clever policymakers are in figuring out innovative ways to use those means, eventually states have to decide where to focus their resources. Should a state invest more in its armed forces, its health-care system, the education of its young, its economic infrastructure, or its diplomatic apparatus? Which regions of the world, issues, or potential threats merit the most attention? Grand strategy is the basis for making these allocations.

Grand strategy can also help various state policies cohere across time and across organizations. If policymakers simply reacted to each individual event as it occurred, without any overarching framework to knit their choices together over time, the resulting policies would be disconnected at best and contradictory at worst. Having an enduring national security strategy to inform those choices would allow each decision to contribute to a larger whole, or at least minimize fratricide between policies. Moreover, the foreign policy of any country is typically carried out by large organizations, and grand strategy helps those discrete bureaucracies determine how they can contribute to the greater whole. For example, a country's defense establishment is charged with determining how to best use the military resources at its disposal to advance the national interest. In short, it must determine what the national defense strategy should be. A national security strategy offers a place to start, by discussing what the country's leadership expects of the military and how the military fits into the broader whole. Without a grand strategy, these organizations would be operating in a strategic vacuum. If all of the foreign policy bureaucracies are attempting to implement the same grand strategy, their actions are more likely to be in tune than if they were all working independently. Similarly, if organizational goals do conflict, grand strategy can offer a basis for adjudicating these conflicts. An added benefit for democracies is that explicit grand strategy also helps to keep elected policymakers in control by offering guidance to the bureaucrats in foreign policy organizations.

Grand strategy also guides policymakers about how to react to new developments. When an unexpected crisis arises, the presence of a grand strategy means that policymakers do not have to start from scratch every time they are taken by surprise because their national strategy offers them a starting point for thinking about how these unforeseen developments might upset their plans. President Dwight D. Eisenhower was fond of quoting Helmuth von Moltke the Elder's aphorism: "The plan is nothing, but planning is everything."[8] Strategies, grand strategies in particular, can never be implemented exactly as formulated. Rather than making grand strategies useless, however, this makes them vital because they educate policymakers about how to adapt their strategies when unexpected events inevitably arise.

Grand strategies can also help build morale across a government by offering a common sense of mission and a standard by which to judge a state's or an administration's progress in meeting its goals. Grand strategy can also serve as a signaling function, for example, by letting other states know where a state stands so allies can be reassured and enemies deterred.

Grand strategy poses some potential pitfalls as well. One is the danger of oversimplification and rigidification. For critics of the entire enterprise of thinking in terms of grand strategy, foreign policymaking is a place not for grandiose theory but for intelligent people making informed case-by-case judgments. For example, after George Kennan wrote the X-Article, he immediately regretted it and spent much of the rest of his life trying to correct what he saw as the misinterpretations, simplifications, and overapplications of his arguments. Because the foreign policy situations a state confronts are constantly evolving, grand strategy poses the danger of locking a state into policy ruts that may no longer be as relevant or effective as they were at their initial design. In short, there is always the danger that a grand strategy can become a substitute for judgment rather than an aid to it.

By telegraphing a state's intent, grand strategy can also give ammunition to an administration's enemies both abroad and at home. When a state knows what another's plan is, it can design a strategy to react, undermine, or counter that plan. Domestically, once a strategy is outlined, an administration can be criticized for its content or for failing to live up to it sufficiently.

A final danger is that a state's grand strategy may simply be wrong. A clearly defined and articulated national plan will not help your state if that plan is foolish. A state would be better off going in circles than marching off smartly in the wrong direction.

In executing policy, some notion of a grand strategy may be unavoidable. Unless policymakers simply spin a roulette wheel or find some other means of making their decisions randomly, the trade-offs inherent in policy choices have to be made on some basis, whether explicit or implicit. Because having some standards is inevitable, policymakers are better served if they make their assumptions, reasoning, and principles as explicit as possible. On the other hand, mechanical, slave-like devotion to a given document as the embodiment of a state's grand strategy can easily lead to disaster.

To balance these pluses and minuses, it is useful to think about grand strategy as a living document. This is what Fred Kagan is getting at when he characterizes grand strategy as "a process of continuous adaptation"; or what Andrew Krepinevich and Barry Watts mean when they say that strategies are not solutions to problems but "always works in progress."[9] For this reason, if there is a written grand strategy document, such as the National Security Strategy, it is important to update it regularly. According to the relevant legislation, the president is supposed to issue a National Security Strategy every year, but, in reality, these documents have been produced less frequently. For example, George W. Bush issued one during his first term (2002) and another in his second term (2006). President Obama is also following this model, having released only one National Security Strategy in his first term (2010). A formal reconsideration of the National Security Strategy in every presidential term provides a regular mechanism for course correction, additions, and deletions, which can help ward off the danger of the strategy's becoming calcified and out of touch with emerging global trends.

It is also important to think of a grand strategy as offering guidance, not directives. The goal of a grand strategy should not be to eliminate the need for expertise in determining how to respond to specific events.[10] The aim should be to offer guidance on the overall goals sought and the thinking about potential problems and trade-offs. Leaving discretion to those entrusted with implementing grand strategy will diminish the need for oversimplification, allow for flexibility in execution, and minimize the chances for others to anticipate and perhaps work against a state's actions.[11]

Those responsible for implementing foreign policy should see grand strategy as an aid to judgment, not as an instruction manual, a cookbook, or a checklist. During a crisis, no one should expect policymakers to reread the National Security Strategy to figure out what they should do that afternoon. Indeed, the first formal National Security Strategy produced in the United States stressed that the objectives it outlined were "not intended to be applied mechanically or automatically, but constitute a general guide for policy development in specific situations."[12] Applying grand strategic principles to specific situations requires thought and knowledge about the given problem. Grand strategy is a starting point for thinking about policies, not an ending point. It is an aid for judgment, not a substitute for it.

Balancing Unilateralism and Multilateralism

One recurring debate throughout the history of U.S. foreign policy revolves around the question of how much the United States should rely on other countries, international organizations, and international law in its foreign policy. Both unilateral and multilateral approaches to foreign policy offer advantages and disadvantages for the United States and, as a result, the country is often torn between wanting to work alone and wanting to work with others. Although this is often characterized as a bipolar choice, it is more useful to think of this debate as a discussion about what point along that continuum does the best job of managing the trade-offs between more unilateral and more multilateral approaches.

The debate between unilateralism and multilateralism is a more useful way of understanding U.S. foreign policy than is the conventional split between isolationism and internationalism. According to the latter view, the U.S. approach to the world has alternated between periods of intense involvement in international affairs and periods of trying to shut the world out and revert to a fortress America.[13] The problem with using the internationalist versus isolationist divide as a lens to analyze U.S. foreign policy is that little substantial debate exists on this issue because the United States has consistently pursued an internationalist foreign policy.[14] Even before the United States declared its independence it decided to invade Canada, something it repeated in the War of 1812 (neither invasion went well because policymakers mistakenly believed that U.S. forces would be greeted as liberators). Throughout the 1800s, the United States marched across North America defeating the French, the Spanish, the British, the Mexicans, and the Native Americans standing in its way. The young republic was also heavily involved in international trade and early on was eager to claim the entire hemisphere as its sphere of influence. After the United States succeeded in stretching from "sea to shining sea," it went overseas, where it acquired islands in the Pacific and the Atlantic. It fought in World Wars I and II while continuing to build up its foreign trade and investments. It emerged from World War II as the most powerful state on earth, a title that it still holds. This is not the history of a country with consequential isolationist tendencies. The debate between isolationism and internationalism is not a particularly useful way of looking at U.S. foreign policy because internationalism has dominated.

The crucial debate is not about whether to be internationally involved but about how to be internationally involved? Are international agreements and organizations the path to a safer and more prosperous world, or are they dangerous because they tie America's hands or risk dragging it into foreign quarrels? Multilateral actions, especially through formal institutions like the United Nations (UN) or the North Atlantic Treaty Organization (NATO), are going to require set-up costs to build and maintain these organizations and the United States might have to go more slowly or offer side-payments (otherwise known as bribes) to get support. It could also create gridlock or cause U.S. involvement in a problem that it would prefer to stay out of, and there is always the possibility that the other members of the organization might just say no. On the positive side, if the United States works multilaterally it gains international legitimacy, it tends to bolster domestic support, it allows for burden sharing with allies, and it gives itself access to capabilities and expertise it might not otherwise possess. Furthermore, in keeping with the wisdom of the founders regarding the importance of checks and balances in any political system, having allies in a position to question the judiciousness of U.S. policy might provide the United States with salutary opportunities for constructive second thoughts.[15] The balance between working alone and working with others is a continuous source of debate in U.S. foreign policy.[16]

Perhaps the most famous and eloquent statement of the case for unilateralism in U.S. foreign policy comes from George Washington's farewell address, where the first U.S. president attempted to sum up the lessons he had learned about the principles on which he thought U.S. foreign policy should be based: "The great rule of conduct for us in regard to foreign nations is in extending our commercial relations, to have with them as little political connection as possible. . . . Our detached and distant situation invites and enables us to pursue a different course. . . . Why forego the advantages of so peculiar a situation? Why quit our own to stand upon foreign ground? . . . It is our true policy to steer clear of permanent alliances with any portion of the foreign world . . . we may safely trust to temporary alliances for extraordinary emergencies."[17]

Thomas Jefferson, in his inaugural address, similarly warned his countrymen about the dangers of "entangling alliances."[18] Note that neither Washington nor Jefferson calls for isolationism, only for unilateralism. Washington approved commercial relations and temporary alliances if necessary, and Jefferson called for "commerce and honest friendship with all nations." Whereas supporters of unilateralism in U.S. foreign policy prefer to portray the warnings of Washington and Jefferson about multilateralism as a timeless U.S. tradition, it was an open question from the start as to how appropriate their advice on this point would remain as circumstances developed. Even Washington's original draft of his farewell address, for example, stressed that his discussion of the benefits of unilateralism might be good for only about twenty years, at which time the United States might be strong enough to profitably form formal alliances.[19]

Indeed, in just a little over twenty years after Washington's farewell address, the issue of finding the right balance between unilateralism and multilateralism came to the fore again, this time in the context of policy toward Spain's rebellious colonies in the Western Hemisphere and the fear that Paris, in alliance with Madrid, would attempt to reassert Spanish control over its possessions in the Western Hemisphere. In 1823, the British foreign secretary, George Canning, approached the U.S. ambassador in London, Richard Rush, with a proposal to issue a joint statement that neither Britain nor the United States would permit France or Spain to try to retake any of Spain's

American possessions. As a demonstration of disinterest in the matter, Canning also suggested that the joint pledge include a statement that neither Britain nor America desired to take any of Spain's possessions in the hemisphere themselves.

When Rush forwarded Canning's proposal to Washington, President Monroe as well as former presidents Madison and Jefferson were initially inclined to accept. Despite worries about entangling alliances, cooperation with the most powerful state on earth, a state that remained the greatest threat to the United States, had significant attraction to the United States. Ultimately, however, Madison and his cabinet were persuaded by the arguments of the secretary of state, John Quincy Adams, among others, to reject the proposal. Adams believed that such a pledge would be "inconvenient" for two key reasons, both dealing with the trade-offs between unilateralism and multilateralism. The first had to do with fears of tying one's hands. In the future, the United States might want to annex some of these Spanish territories, so why limit the country's options by renouncing such claims now? As Adams put it in his account of the cabinet discussions, "Without entering now into the enquiry of the expediency of our annexing Texas or Cuba into our Union, we should at least keep ourselves free to act as emergencies may arise, and not tie ourselves down to any principle which might immediately afterwards be brought to bear against ourselves." The second reason focused on the political sensitivities of a small state cooperating with a great power. "The President," Adams assessed, "was averse to any course which should have the appearance of taking a position subordinate to that of Great Britain. . . . It would be more candid as well as more dignified, to avow our principles explicitly to Russia and France, than to come in as a Cock-boat in the wake of a British man of war."[20] In short, the United States had no desire to be seen as Britain's poodle.

As a result, instead of Canning's joint declaration, the United States opted to make a unilateral declaration that the countries of the Western Hemisphere are "henceforth not to be considered as subjects for future colonization by any European powers." Although enforcement of what would become known as the Monroe Doctrine remained at the time more in the hands of the British Navy than the United States, by issuing the statement unilaterally, the United States avoided tying its hands to a pledge that would have proved inconvenient given future U.S. acquisitions and minimized the perception that it was Britain's junior partner.[21]

The purpose of these brief examples is not to make a case for a supposed U.S. tradition in favor of unilateralism. By choosing different examples, such as the U.S. decisions to create NATO and the UN, proponents of greater multilateralism in U.S. foreign policy could proffer a countertradition in favor of formal international cooperation. The point, instead, is that in each of these cases policy was contested. Washington and Jefferson were arguing for greater unilateralism in U.S. foreign policy. Monroe's cabinet debated the trade-offs involved in working with England versus working independently. Although they might be rhetorically useful, appeals to any unitary traditions in U.S. foreign policy to justify current policies offer little analytical leverage. To better grapple with the grand strategic choices the United States faces today, analysts would be better served to examine the recurrence of debates about how to balance the trade-offs between unilateralism and multilateralism rather than declaring one a more legitimate tradition than the other.

Values and Interests in U.S. Foreign Policy

Determining a state's core national interests is a fundamental part of grand strategy. The United States, in making that determination, has had to figure out how U.S. values, such as supporting democracy, individual rights, and free markets, fit within its conception of its interests.[22] One traditional way of analyzing this issue is to characterize the debate as one between realism and idealism, with realists preferring the pursuit of U.S. material interests and idealists advocating for the advancement of U.S. values.[23] The problem with this characterization of the debate for U.S. grand strategy, however, is that it presents a dichotomy that most U.S. policymakers have rejected. The consensus position in the United States is that there is no way to choose material interests over values or vice versa, but that the United States has to pursue both at the same time because its values and interests are inherently intertwined. U.S. policymakers believe that the advancement of U.S. material interests inevitably promotes the spread of U.S. values, and the spread of U.S. values simultaneously advances U.S. material interests. When pushed to think in terms of end states for failing states, potential enemies, or the international system as a whole, U.S. policymakers see the spread of U.S. values as the default aspiration. Stephen Krasner goes as far as arguing that, outside of democracy, the United States has "no alternative objective toward which policy might be oriented."[24] Whereas trade-offs between interests and values might be necessary in specific cases over the short term, for U.S. grand strategy it is never a question of interests versus values but one of how best to simultaneously pursue U.S. interest and its values.

In capturing the perennial debates about how to best protect U.S. interests and its values, Walter McDougall's distinction between those who see the United States as a "Crusader State" and those who see it as the "Promised Land" is particularly enlightening.[25] Should the United States act as a Crusader State and attempt to actively impose its values on others, or should it instead act as the Promised Land and simply serve as a model for its values that others would seek to emulate? The debate is not about whether the United States should spread its values or advance its interests, but about which of two potential roles it should adopt in the pursuit of its values and interests. As McDougall summarized it, "while America the Promised Land had held that to try to change the world was stupid (and immoral), America the Crusader State held that to *refrain* from trying to change the world was immoral (and stupid)."[26]

Adherents of America as the Promised Land believe that the United States can best protect its interests and advance its values by not actively pushing those values onto others. Instead, the United States should focus on perfecting democracy at home, thus making it a model that others want to emulate. The way a magnet attracts metal, the United States as exemplar will attract others to its values by serving as a model of a well-functioning, progressive, strong, and prosperous democracy. From this perspective, an attempt to impose U.S. values on others is seen as too costly and ultimately futile; furthermore, it would violate the very values that the United States stands for. There is clearly something self-contradictory about an outside power forcing democracy onto another state. Proponents of America as the Promised Land tend to see U.S. values as ideals toward which the United States itself has to ceaselessly toil and aspire to live up to but can never reach. The first line of the U.S. Constitution talks not about forming a perfect union, but a "more perfect union." This sentiment also led Abraham Lincoln to refer to Americans as God's "almost chosen people" to stress how the struggle to live up to U.S. ideals continues.[27] For the Promised Landers, it is in recognizing its faults and striving to move closer to those ideals that the United States is a model for others. This striving for domestic improvement, however, often remains cautious and slow because many Promised Landers tend to be skeptical of all calls for drastic and sudden reforms, whether domestic or international.

Conversely, proponents of America as a Crusader State believe that the best way to protect U.S. interests and values is to actively strive to get others to adopt U.S. principles. It is not enough to be good at home; America has to spread the word as a missionary, either converting or defeating those who reject core U.S. values like democracy. Crusaders tend to see U.S. values as something the country embodies and can therefore potentially bequeath to others. Rather than be distracted by domestic imperfections, crusaders prefer to recognize what the United States has already accomplished and to maintain that those values need to be protected and exported. If significant domestic problems are identified, however, the same zeal that leads crusaders to act decisively overseas might be applied by them at home as well.

Even before America was America, its values were seen as closely entwined with its interests. Talking to the Puritans as they were about to leave England in 1630, John Winthrop, who would become the first governor of the Massachusetts Bay Colony, told these nascent Americans that if they act in line with their values: "The Lord will be our God and delight to dwell among us, as his own people, and will command a blessing upon us in all our ways. So that we shall see much more of his wisdom, power, goodness, and truth than formerly we have been acquainted with. We shall find that the God of Israel is among us when ten of us shall be able to resist a thousand of our enemies."

Beyond linking American values with earthly success, Winthrop also argued that America's experience would serve as a model for others. God, Winthrop continued, "shall make us a praise and glory that men shall say of succeeding plantations, 'the lord make it like that of New England.' For we must consider that we shall be as a city on a hill, the eyes of all people are upon us." These promises, however, were paired with a warning about what would happen if America failed to live up to its values. "If we shall deal falsely with our God in this work we have undertaken, and so cause him to withdraw his present help from us, we shall be made a story and a by-word through the world. . . . We shall shame the faces of many of God's worthy servants, and cause their prayers to be turned into curses upon us till we be consumed out of the good land whither we are a going."[28]

From Winthrop forward, Americans have tended to see their values as universal and America as having an important role to play in spreading those values. As Thomas Paine concisely put it, "We have it in our power to begin the world over again."[29] Similarly, the last words Thomas Jefferson wrote expressed his hope that the American Revolution would be "to the world what I believe it will be (to some party sooner, to others later, but finally to all); a signal arousing men to burst chains."[30]

It is not surprising that Winthrop and Jefferson, as spokesmen for a small and relatively weak country struggling to come into being and maintain its independence, used imagery to describe America's role that focuses more on the force of America's example than on any overt American policies designed to spread its values. America at the time had few capabilities to directly advance its values even if it wanted to. As the United States grew in power, however, should it have done more than just serve as a city on a hill?

John Quincy Adams offered one prominent answer to this question. The problem that spurred Adams to grapple with this issue was U.S. policy toward Spain's colonies in the Western Hemisphere as they attempted to break free of Madrid's control. If these independence movements were fighting for the same principles that lay at the heart of the American Revolution, was it in U.S. interests and was it in accord with U.S. values to support them? Adams answered no to both questions.

Wherever the standard of freedom and Independence has been or shall be unfurled, there will her [America's] heart, her benedictions and her prayers be. But she goes not abroad in search of monsters to destroy. She is the well-wisher to the freedom and independence of all. She is the champion and vindicator only of her own. She will commend the general cause by the countenance of her voice, and the benignant sympathy of her example. She well knows that by once enlisting under other banners than her own, were they even banners of foreign independence, she would involve herself beyond the power of her extrication. . . . She might become dictatress of the world. She would no longer be the ruler of her own spirit.[31]

This quote remains perhaps the most eloquent statement of the Promised Land position in U.S. foreign policy. Adams does not reject any U.S. role in spreading its values overseas, but sharply limits that role to the "countenance of her voice and the benignant sympathy of her example," explicitly rejecting the argument of would-be crusaders that it is the job of the United States to go "abroad in search of monsters to destroy."

Adams based his conclusion on an appeal to U.S. material interests and values. Materially, if the United States took direct action to spread its values overseas, Adams feared that it "would involve herself beyond the power of her extrication." In modern terms, Adams is warning about the dangers of mission-creep, quagmires, and imperial overstretch. The secretary of state also warned that such a policy would violate and potentially destroy U.S. values. "She might be dictatress of the world. She would no longer be the ruler of her own spirit." Thus, even if the United States possessed the power to force its values onto others, it should be leery of doing so, according to Adams.

Some may be tempted to dismiss as propaganda all discussion of the proper role of U.S. values in its foreign policy. Perhaps it is true that some advocates of America as the Promised Land are simply isolationists looking to cloak their preference for a modest foreign policy by speaking of the United States only as an example. Conversely, perhaps some crusaders are simply expansionists disguising their preference for an activist foreign policy by talking about the mission of the United States to spread its values. Rather than dismiss all invocations of America as the Promised Land or as a Crusader State as empty and cynical rhetoric, this book argues that it is more useful, as Robert Kagan has phrased it, to see U.S. values as "a super-ego looming in judgment of US egoistic pursuits," which forces the United States into a "ceaseless effort to reconcile universal principles with selfish interests."[32] Moreover, once the United States finds itself involved in events outside its borders, the positions of crusaders and exemplars are likely to converge in favor of actively promoting U.S. values because even exemplars will find it unpalatable to avoid attempting to destroy the monsters that the United States does encounter. The debate in the United States is not about interests versus values with a predominant victor emerging, but about determining whether acting as the Crusader State or the Promised Land is the best way to advance U.S material interests and values.

Where Is the U.S. Strategic Perimeter?

Another key question that any grand strategy has to answer is: what are the most significant threats a state faces? For the United States, which regions and issues must Washington be deeply concerned about and which can be safely ignored? Assessing and prioritizing the threats against which the United States has to place its limited foreign policy resources, in essence defining the U.S. strategic perimeter, has also been a continuous source of debate in U.S. foreign policy.

One commonly held view of U.S. foreign policy is that traditionally the United States has not had to worry about severe international threats. Surrounded by weak neighbors and fish, in this view, the United States has historically enjoyed what C. Vann Woodward has called "free security."[33] Typically, arguments about the secure past of the United States are contrasted with what is now seen as the country's insecure present and future. When Woodward was writing about the era of free security, his purpose was to declare it over. Consider the following similar quotes:

> America is no longer protected by vast oceans. We are protected from attack only by vigorous action abroad, and increased vigilance at home.

> The ocean barrier which defended us in 1776 and 1812 no longer exists . . . [technology has] destroyed it.

> It should be remembered [that these new weapons] . . . are easily made, and that . . . the commerce of entire cities [can be] destroyed by an infuriated people with means carried with perfect safety to themselves in the pockets of their clothing.

All three of these quotes appeal to a secure past, declare that era to be over, and argue that the United States now faces a set of threats far worse than anything the country had previously faced. These quotes however, span more than 120 years of U.S. history. The first comes from President George W. Bush's State of the Union Speech of January 29, 2002, responding to the terrorist attacks of September 11, 2001.[34] Almost eighty-five years before Bush declared the era of free security to be over, Senator Henry Cabot Lodge made a similar declaration, and the technologies he is referring to in the second quote are the steam engine and electricity.[35] The final quote predates Bush's speech by about 120 years. It comes from a report of General Philip Sheridan in 1884, and the weapon of mass destruction he is talking about is dynamite.[36]

It cannot be denied that as global neighborhoods go the United States is in a good one and that technological developments can change the threat picture a state faces, but the argument that the United States has now reached the end of its era of free security is of limited usefulness as a guide to understanding U.S. grand strategic choices because it simultaneously overstates the security that the United States had in the past and understates the extent to which it is still secure today. Starting with the past, U.S. foreign policymakers have never seen the country's security as free. As Alexander Hamilton warned in *The Federalist Papers*: "Though a wide ocean separates the United States from Europe, yet there are various considerations that warn us against an excess of confidence in our security. On the one side of us, and stretching far into our rear, are growing settlements subject to the dominion of Britain. On the other side, and extending to meet the British settlements are colonies and establishments subject to the dominion of Spain. . . . The savage tribes on our Western frontier ought to be regarded as our natural enemies, their natural allies."[37]

As the United States expanded its borders westward, growth did not alleviate its security concerns but instead served to enlarge what it included within its strategic perimeter. When John Quincy Adams negotiated the Adams–Onís Treaty with Spain in 1819, the United States agreed to recognize Spain's claims to Texas in return for Madrid's cession of Florida to the United States. Before signing the treaty, Adams asked Andrew Jackson whether he thought the trade was worth it. In response, Jackson told President Monroe: "With the Floridas in our possession, our fortifications complete, Orleans, the great emporium of the West is secure. The Floridas in possession of a foreign power, you can be invaded, your fortifications turned, the Mississippi reached, and the lower country reduced. From Texas an invading enemy will never attempt such an enterprise."[38]

Thus, from Jackson's perspective in 1820, the trade was worth it. Whereas Florida was in the U.S. strategic perimeter, Texas was not. Approximately twenty-five years later, however, Jackson revised his definition of the U.S. strategic perimeter, concluding that Texas is "of the utmost importance to the safety of the United States and particularly the safety of New Orleans."[39] What had been peripheral was now deemed vital as the U.S. population grew and continued to move westward.

With regard to the future of U.S. grand strategy, the declaration that U.S. free security is once again at an end can also mislead by implying that the threats the United States faces today are completely unprecedented or significantly worse than the threats the country faced in the past. Instead of comparing current dangers with a mythically secure past, it is more useful to recognize that the United States has consistently faced potential threats from abroad and had to prioritize some of those threats and allocate its limited resources accordingly. In short, all previous generations of policymakers had to ask: Where does America's strategic perimeter lie? What parts of the world and what issues are vital and need defending?

Is Time on America's Side?

The final debate used throughout this book as a lens through which to examine U.S. grand strategy involves the question of whether time is working for or against the United States. Are the threats facing the United States best confronted immediately, lest they grow stronger, or is it more prudent to contain certain threats in the expectation that they will wither over time? Similarly, do opportunities need to be seized immediately, lest they be lost, or is it wiser to forgo certain opportunities in the present in the expectation that more promising ones will be forthcoming?

One common criticism of U.S. foreign policy is that the United States tends to focus too much on the short term. U.S. policymakers rarely think beyond the next election and consequently, in this view, the United States demands immediate results and is unable to sustain any foreign policy stance that requires a protracted commitment. Niall Ferguson, for example, worries that the United States is a superpower that suffers from attention deficit disorder.[40]

This characterization of the United States as an impatient power, however, is difficult to square with much of the history of U.S. foreign policy. For instance, rather than risk war or make important concessions in order to acquire what would later become the Louisiana Purchase, Thomas Jefferson believed patience to be the better policy. As Jefferson put it, he was "confident in the policy of putting off the day of contention for it, till we are stronger in ourselves, and stronger in our allies, but especially till we shall have planted such a population" in the area.[41] The country's rapidly growing population, which would later be called the "American multiplication table," meant that time was on the side of the United States and it would benefit from patience in its expansion.[42] As John C. Calhoun phrased it, this time regarding the possible acquisition of Oregon, "There is only one means by which it can be done; but that, fortunately is the most powerful of all—*time*. *Time* is acting for us; and if we shall have the wisdom to trust its operation, it will assert and maintain our right with resistless force."[43]

Instead of attempting to characterize U.S. foreign policy as inherently impatient (or patient), it is more useful to recognize this as an area where U.S. policies have varied. What that variation depends on, to a large extent, are calculations regarding whether time is working for or against the United States. When convinced that time is on America's side, the United States can be a patient great power. Impatience is far more likely in cases where evidence of progress is scarce and worries multiply that time is not working for the United States. Determining whether time is on America's side or that of its enemies is thus a crucial grand strategic consideration and one that has been a source of debate throughout U.S. history.

Organization of the Book

The rest of this book aims to examine U.S. grand strategy through the lens of the four debates introduced in this chapter. Chapter 1 covers the initial attempts of the United States to find its place on the world stage as a great power and examines the competing but partly complementary alternatives offered by Theodore Roosevelt and Woodrow Wilson, the grand strategy pursued by the Republican presidents in the 1920s, and Franklin Delano Roosevelt's attempt to forge a grand strategy for the United States prior to the onset of the Cold War. Chapter 2 examines the origins of the containment era in U.S. grand strategy under the Truman administration and the debates answered and raised by containment. Chapter 3 looks at ongoing debates about how to implement containment under presidents Eisenhower, Kennedy, and Johnson. Chapter 4 explores two largely failed attempts to move beyond containment under the Nixon and Carter administrations. Chapter 5 explores the Reagan administration's grand strategy and the role played by it and containment as a whole in ending the Cold War. Chapter 6 examines attempts by both George H. W. Bush and Bill Clinton to find a replacement for containment after the disappearance of the Soviet threat. Chapter 7 looks at the rise and fall of the War on Terror in U.S. grand strategy and examines the foreign policy of the George W. Bush administration both before and after the terrorist attacks of September 11, 2001, and before and after the difficulties encountered in Iraq. Chapter 8 brings the story of U.S. grand strategy up to the beginning of 2015 assessing the debates over the grand strategic choices of the Obama administration. The conclusion looks to the future of U.S. grand strategy and offers an assessment of how the United States, based on its past approaches to these questions, should think about addressing the grand strategic debates covered in this book.

Finding a Place on the World Stage

From Roosevelt to Roosevelt

At the outset of the twentieth century, following the economic growth of the United States as well as the strengthening of the federal government as a result of the Civil War and Reconstruction, the United States was poised to take its place as a major power on the global stage. No longer just a regional power, the United States now had to approach its grand strategy as a world power. Using the four debates discussed in the introduction as a framework, this chapter explores the evolution of initial attempts by the United States to construct a grand strategy as a great power, tracing developments from Theodore Roosevelt, through Woodrow Wilson and the Republican presidents of the 1920s, to Franklin Roosevelt.

This approach to the study of American grand strategy cuts against some traditionally offered accounts of the country's early experiences as a great power. For instance, a stark divide between a purportedly realist Teddy Roosevelt and the liberal Woodrow Wilson is a conventional way of discussing early debates over the proper role of the United States as a world power.[1] By widening the focus to include the four debates used in this book, however, these two central figures are seen less as polar opposites and more as allies in the effort to find a place for the United States on a global stage. Both favored greatly expanding America's conception of its security perimeter and both shared a strong conviction that time was on America's side. Although they differed on the proper place of values in U.S. foreign policy, their positions even on this issue, as will be argued below, contain an important amount of overlap. The one area where the two disagreed most sharply was on the relative merits of unilateral versus multilateral approaches to U.S. foreign policy.

Another bit of conventional wisdom regarding the early years of the United States as a great power is that disappointment stemming from the meager results of World War I led the United States to turn inward and adopt an isolationist grand strategy. Using the four debates outlined in the introduction as a lens, however, a more varied and richer story emerges. The Republican presidents of the 1920s pursued a global strategy to advance U.S. values and interests, but contrary to Wilson, they attempted to privatize America's crusade rather than multilateralize it. This strategy collapsed with the onset of the Great Depression because economic collapse undermined a key component of that strategy, which was the conviction that time was on America's side. Rather than accept this historical pessimism, however, Franklin Roosevelt attempted a new synthesis of the policies of Theodore Roosevelt and Woodrow Wilson that put a concert of great powers at its center, rather than the unilateralism of his familial ancestor, or the more egalitarian international institutions favored by his political ancestor, Woodrow Wilson. This chapter explores the successes and failures of these attempts at constructing U.S. grand strategy, attempts that should not be reduced to a single debate between idealism and realism or dismissed as a misguided turn to isolationism.

The Expanding Security Perimeter of a Confident and Growing Power

The central question that both Theodore Roosevelt and Woodrow Wilson attempted to answer was: What should the overall foreign policy of the United States be now that it was a growing world power? This common question ensured an important degree of overlap in their grand strategies because the question itself contained certain assumptions that had important implications for U.S. foreign policy. That the United States was now a world power meant that its security perimeter had to be defined more broadly than it had been in the past. This expanding security perimeter took institutional form in 1898 when President William McKinley created a "war room" in the White House equipped with global maps and telegraph connections to oversee expanded U.S. activities overseas. These activities included the annexation of Hawaii; the acquisition of the Philippines, Guam, and Puerto Rico in the war with Spain; a treaty splitting Samoa with Germany; and military participation in putting down the Boxer Rebellion in China.[2] Whereas the U.S. Navy prior to 1890 was focused on issues of coastal defense and contained not a single battleship, by 1905 the fleet had twenty-five blue-water battleships.[3] Looking to the future, as long as America's economic expansion continued, time was on America's side as a growing power.

Whereas most of the founders would have shared the latter assumption that time was on America's side (provided the issue of slavery did not permanently divide the Union), the move to a global rather than a regional security perimeter marks an important break in U.S. grand strategy, although that break was probably more seamless in the Pacific than in the Atlantic.

As Walter McDougall noted regarding the Monroe Doctrine, "the watery boundary where America stopped and Asia began was never defined."[4] Greater involvement in European politics, however, required a more direct challenge to the Monroe Doctrine. Although he declared that the growing American republic considered the entire Western hemisphere to be its sphere of influence, President Monroe had also pledged that "In the Wars of the European powers in matters relating to themselves we have never taken any part, nor does it comport with our policy to do so."[5]

Theodore Roosevelt later added a corollary to the Monroe Doctrine that furthered the proclaimed U.S. role in the Western Hemisphere, arrogating for the United States the right to exercise what he called "international policy power" throughout the region.[6] As it grew in power, however, did the United States want to keep the second half of Monroe's pledge, forswearing U.S. involvement with issues outside the hemisphere? Roosevelt's secretary of state, Elihu Root, in justifying the continued inclusion of South America within the ambit of the Monroe Doctrine, did so in expansive terms that implied that America's strategic perimeter had no logical geographical endpoint. According to Root, "Undoubtedly as one passes to the south and the distance from the Caribbean increases, the necessity of maintaining the rule of Monroe becomes less immediate and apparent. But who is competent to draw the line? Who will say, 'To this point the rule of Monroe should apply; beyond this point, it should not'? Who will say that a new national force created beyond any line that can be drawn will stay beyond it and will not in the long course of time extend itself indefinitely?"[7]

Root was quick to affirm his commitment to keeping the separation between Europe and the Americas "as absolute and complete as possible,"[8] but the logic of his argument provided no basis for such a separation. Instead, the security perimeter of the United States, a rising power, was likely to "extend itself indefinitely." Moreover, as Frank Ninkovich notes, the Roosevelt Corollary fundamentally altered the nature of the Monroe doctrine. The United States was no longer pledging to protect the states of Latin America against the Europeans; instead, it was pledging to police the area in the interest of both the United States and the Europeans.[9]

Wilson too believed that the U.S. security perimeter had expanded, and by the coming of World War I he was explicitly speaking of America's interests in global terms. As a result of the Spanish-American war, the United States had "stepped forth into the open arena of the world" in Wilson's estimation. No matter how much the United States may have historically preferred to stay aloof from European wars, Wilson maintained that "nothing that concerns the whole world can be indifferent to us" and that "the interests of all nations are our own also. We are partners with the rest. What affects mankind is inevitably our affair."[10] In short, the security perimeter of the United States had been universalized.

Does Can Imply Ought? Values in American Foreign Policy

The increasing power of the United States also raised questions about the proper place of American values in its foreign policy. When John Quincy Adams warned his country about the dangers of going abroad in search of monsters to destroy, he was speaking as the representative of a young and weak nation. Even if the United States had wanted to do more to help independence movements in Latin America or democratic movements in Greece, the country Adams spoke for lacked the capabilities to make a significant contribution. Was Adams's course still the right one for a stronger American republic? As early as 1851, Senator Robert Stockton argued that the policy of husbanding the resources of "the infant Hercules" was sound only to the point where "he should be able to encounter, on more equal terms, the monsters he was destined to overthrow."[11] That impulse was stronger at the start of the twentieth century. As President William McKinley confidently assessed the situation, "It is not possible that 75 millions of American freemen are unable to establish liberty and justice and good government in our new possessions."[12] In the even more expansive language of Senator Albert Beveridge in 1898:

> God has not been preparing the English-speaking and Teutonic peoples for a thousand years for nothing but vain and idle self-contemplation and self-admiration. No. He has made us master organizers of the world to establish system where chaos reigned. He has given us the spirit of progress to overwhelm the forces of reaction throughout the earth. He has made us adept in government that we may administer government among savage and senile people. Were it not for such a force as this the world would relapse into barbarism and night. And of all our race He has marked the American people as His chosen nation to finally lead in the redemption of the world.[13]

If, in moral reasoning, ought implies can, the growing power of the United States raised the question of whether, politically, can implies ought. Did the greater power possessed by the United States at the outset of the twentieth century mean that the United States had a greater responsibility to see the spread of its values overseas? Woodrow Wilson's answer has often led to his classification as the epitome of an idealist in American foreign policy. Consider the following excerpt from a speech Wilson made after returning from the Versailles Peace Conference:

> America is the hope of the world. And if she does not justify that hope, the results are unthinkable. . . . All nations will be set up as hostile camps again; . . . We set up this nation to make men free, and we did not confine our conception to America, and now we will make men free. If we did not do that, all the fame of America would be gone, and all her power dissipated. She would then have to keep her power for those narrow, selfish, provincial

purposes which seem so dear to some minds that have no sweep beyond the nearest horizon. . . . Think of the picture, think of the utter blackness that would fall upon the world. America has failed. . . . America said, "Here is our power to vindicate right," and then the next day said, "Let right take care of itself and we will take care of ourselves." . . . Think of the world that we would leave.[14]

With the emphasis on American ideals and the rejection of "narrow, self-ish, [and] provincial" interests, Wilson's classification as an idealist is certainly justified. Leaving the issue there, however, misses a great deal about Wilson's grand strategy. What it misses, moreover, is indicative of the drawbacks of using the lens of realism versus idealism to study U.S. foreign policy.[15] The divide between pursuing values or pursuing interests that is at the heart of the realist/idealist debate is a dichotomy that does not exist for Wilson. As he put it, if America did not actively fight for the spread of its values overseas, "all the fame of America would be gone, and all her power dissipated." To abandon the active pursuit of American values would not protect American power, for Wilson; it would destroy it.

Wilson certainly believed that the United States had a unique role to play in the world in advancing its values. Wilson rejected any simple dichotomy between realism and idealism, and believed that the United States could most effectively play that historical role by attempting to advance its interests and its values at the same time. Neither of these beliefs, moreover, distinguishes Wilson from many of his predecessors, including some, like John Quincy Adams, who would probably reject much of Wilson's foreign policy agenda. Woodrow Wilson does not see his policy as unrealistic any more than John Quincy Adams saw his policy as contrary to the advancement of American values. The debate between John Quincy Adams and Woodrow Wilson is not one between interests and values. Both support policies that they believe jointly advance the material and ideological interests of the United States. Both reject the trade-off at the center of the realist/idealist schism. For Wilson, actively encouraging the spread of American values is one key way to ensure that the material interests of the United States are protected. Similarly, John Quincy Adams did not see his admonition against "going abroad in search of monsters to destroy" as undermining the potential spread of American values in favor of the country's more material national interests. Instead, he too believed he was advancing American values along with more particular national interests.

The core of the debate between Wilson and Adams, therefore, is not about interests versus values; instead, it is a question of the best way to promote American interests and values at the same time. For understanding this debate, Walter McDougall's distinction between America as the Promised Land and America as the Crusader State is far more enlightening than the distinction between realism and idealism.[16] John Quincy Adams viewed

America as the Promised Land—as an example, a magnet, a city on the hill, a light in the darkness. If the United States can serve as an example of a well-functioning and prosperous democratic society, others will gravitate to American values on their own, which would further the country's values and interests. Trying to compel others to accept these values would be too costly, it would fail, and it would undermine those values at home. Let other states choose to join America in the Promised Land rather than attempting to force them to accept American values.

For Wilson, the United States must be more than an example. It must also be a Crusader State, actively seeking to vindicate and spread its values. As the United States would be safer and more prosperous in a world where its ideals were more widely accepted, the best way to advance U.S. interests is to act as a missionary, perhaps even a well-armed missionary, to ensure the advancement of American values. While in power Wilson acted on these impulses, famously declaring his ambition "to teach the South American Republics to elect good men," and pursuing that policy with armed interventions in Mexico, Haiti, and the Dominican Republic.[17] Why let monsters roam freely, vindicators like Wilson ask, if the United States has the power to defeat them?

Categories like Crusaders and Promised Landers are ideal types, and no presidency is likely to purely represent one of these endpoints on the spectrum. Wilson himself was far more likely to act as a crusader in areas where the United States had overwhelming power, such as in Latin America, than he was in Europe, when facing other great powers.[18] Further, the costs and relatively meager results of America's military forays into Mexican politics, in particular, led Wilson to better understand the limits of unilaterally seeking to export democracy through force of arms,[19] even if they did not fully extinguish that impulse.[20]

How does Theodore Roosevelt fit within this framework? Roosevelt is often painted as the quintessential realist in American foreign policy, one who worried deeply about the balance of power and famously advised America to "carry a big stick." Just as there is evidence for Wilson's classification as an idealist, there is also justification for Teddy Roosevelt's identification as a realist. However, to limit the discussion of Roosevelt's grand strategy simply to power and realism would miss a great deal.[21] Indeed, in comparing Roosevelt and Wilson with much of what came before them in U.S. foreign policy, Roosevelt comes much closer to the progressive imperialism of his contemporary than to the restraint of their predecessors. Roosevelt agreed with Wilson that promoting self-governance abroad would help make the United States more secure by warding off threats that could come from ungoverned or poorly governed areas.[22] Moving beyond Thomas Jefferson's hope that the American Revolution would be "a signal arousing men to burst chains," Teddy Roosevelt asserted that, "It is our duty to the people living in barbarism to see that they are freed from their chains."[23]

Like Wilson, Roosevelt was also seeking to expand America's power and principles at the same time. War with Spain and the acquisition of Cuba would advance the material interests of the United States, but a key part of Roosevelt's justification for the war focused on what he saw as the immorality of Spanish policy on the island. As Roosevelt summarized his combination of ideals and interests in American foreign policy: "Our chief usefulness to humanity rests on our combining power with high purpose; and high purpose by itself is utterly useless if the power to put it into effect is lacking."[24]

This was how Teddy Roosevelt attempted to balance ideals and interests throughout his political career. In approaching problems like sweatshops that arose as a result of industrialization, rather than declare his intention, like Thomas Paine, to "begin the world anew," Roosevelt concluded more moderately, "We have it in our power to partially abate the misery and wrongdoing of a peculiarly flagrant kind which bears with peculiar heaviness upon the most helpless class of our population and which results in danger to all classes."[25]

Applied to foreign policy, this view lent itself to limited crusading. In his 1904 Message to Congress, Roosevelt started by talking as a proponent of America as the Promised Land. "Ordinarily it is very much wiser and more useful," he asserted, "for us to concern ourselves with striving for our own moral and material betterment here at home than to concern ourselves with trying to better the condition of things in other nations." The United States, Roosevelt continued, has "plenty of sins of our own to war against, and under ordinary circumstances we can do more for the general uplifting of humanity by striving with heart and soul to put a stop to civic corruption, to brutal lawlessness and violent race prejudices here at home than by passing resolutions about wrongdoing elsewhere."

"Nevertheless," Roosevelt concluded,

> there are occasional crimes committed on so vast a scale and of such peculiar horror as to make us doubt whether it is not our manifest duty to endeavor at least to show our disapproval of the deed and our sympathy with those who have suffered by it. The cases must be extreme in which such a course is justifiable. There must be no effort made to remove the mote from our brother's eye if we refuse to remove the beam from our own. But in extreme cases action may be justifiable and proper. What form the action shall take must depend upon the circumstances of the case; that is, upon the degree of the atrocity and upon our power to remedy it. The cases in which we could interfere by force of arms as we interfered to put a stop to intolerable conditions in Cuba are necessarily very few.[26]

For example, Roosevelt strongly advocated for American intervention against Turkey in World War I largely on moral grounds as a result of its actions against the Armenians, a crusade that even Wilson was hesitant to join.[27]

The difference between Wilson and Roosevelt, unlike the difference between both men and John Quincy Adams, for example, is simply a debate
over which crusades to undertake. Roosevelt did not object to America's values directly informing its foreign policy; he just reserved such actions for
stopping the most heinous violations of human rights overseas and in cases
where the United States had the physical power to do something about it.
As he put it, he did not want America "to go to war every time a Jugoslav
wishes to slap a Czecho-slav in the face."[28]

The division between Wilson and Roosevelt and earlier American policymakers like John Quincy Adams on this point mirrors developments in religion in the United States at the turn of the century. Many of the religious
practices of the early settlers fit within a "sinners in the hands of an angry
God" model.[29] This approach stressed the inherent depravity of man and the
need to accept that fact and to live one's life in such a way as not to increase
God's anger. The progressive era of Wilson and Roosevelt corresponded to
the growing influence of a religion of social uplift that focused more on actively striving to make the world a better place. Rather than stressing man's
inherent depravity, the focus was on trying to make the world less depraved.
The move from the Promised Land view of John Quincy Adams to the more
crusading views of Woodrow Wilson and Theodore Roosevelt closely parallels this religious development.[30] This new crusading spirit was not limited to foreign policy elites but was also characteristic of other important actors in American society at the time, such as organized labor and religious
missionaries.[31]

The League of Nations and the Divide over Multilateralism

The most significant foreign policy divide between Teddy Roosevelt and
Woodrow Wilson focused on the value of multilateralism. Wilson went beyond democratization and the spread of free markets, and was also a champion of the third part of the liberal triad with his support for international
law and international organizations.[32] Indeed, Wilson's proposal for a League
of Nations was perhaps the most distinctive part of his grand strategic
agenda. Just as internal checks and balances are designed to help states avoid
or correct mistakes domestically, the league's "capacity for self-correction
under the pressure of world opinion" was similarly central to Wilson's international program.[33]

Roosevelt, in contrast, saw international organizations as playing only a
peripheral role in global security. The compulsory arbitration treaties that
Roosevelt had signed as president, for example, specifically exempted from
consideration cases the United States deemed pertinent to its vital interests,
its national honor, or its independence. "Sound internationalism," as Roosevelt saw it, required states to promise only what they had the power and

interest to fulfill. The pressure of world opinion or the "moral obligation" that Wilson argued was at the heart of America's commitment to the League of Nations was too weak a foundation for a sound U.S. grand strategy in Roosevelt's estimation. Whereas limited and specified commitments among the great powers could play a useful role in U.S. grand strategy, even for Roosevelt, universal legal commitments were likely to be pernicious rather than helpful. "In international matters," Roosevelt explained, "the declaration of a right, or the announcement of a worthy purpose, is not only aimless but is a just cause for derision, and may even be mischievous, if force is not put behind the right or purpose."[34]

The Senate's refusal to consent to America's joining the League of Nations was a victory for the unilateralists. As Senator William Borah (R-ID) explained, "What we want is a free, untrammeled Nation . . . not isolationism but freedom to do as our own people think wise and just."[35] This victory, however, was only temporary. Although it was defeated on this front, Wilson's multilateral vision of American foreign policy has repeatedly reemerged, leading some analysts to conclude that Wilson more than anyone else defined the agenda for U.S. foreign policy in the twentieth century.[36]

Although it was less cited as a model for future statesmen, Theodore Roosevelt's more unilateral vision of American foreign policy has also had a continuing influence. Given George W. Bush's emphasis on the spread of democracy and free markets in his foreign policy, many analysts have been tempted to link his policies back to Wilson. Bush may have adopted Wilsonian ends, but he simultaneously rejected the Wilsonian means of international law and international organizations. The policies of George W. Bush have thus been described as "Wolfish Wilsonianism"[37] or "Wilsonianism in Boots."[38] A more direct line to the foreign policies of George W. Bush, however, can probably be drawn from Theodore Roosevelt,[39] who also combined a strong commitment to the spread of American values with an emphasis on military power and a distrust of international institutions. Roosevelt and Wilson would therefore continue to influence U.S. foreign policy as a great power, in areas where they agreed as well as disagreed.

The Republican Grand Strategy of the 1920s

When U.S. foreign policy in the 1920s and 1930s comes up in current political debates over U.S. grand strategy, it is typically used as a rhetorical cudgel to condemn opponents for being shortsighted and insufficiently internationalist. For example, when the Senate was debating the Comprehensive Nuclear Test-Ban Treaty and it became clear that the treaty was about to be defeated, President Clinton complained that this "would be the first time the Senate has rejected a treaty since the Treaty of Versailles." To signal his disdain for the defeat of the treaty, Clinton concluded, "We all know what

America's walking away from the world after World War One brought us."[40] When the treaty failed to gain the necessary votes, Clinton warned about what he called "signs of a new isolationism."[41] The coming to power of the George W. Bush administration kept comparisons with the interwar years in the public debate, except then it was typically those outside the administration hurling charges at the White House for foolishly frittering away U.S. ties with the rest of the world, like the policymakers of the twenties and thirties, by denigrating the United Nations or not ratifying the Kyoto Accord or failing to embrace the International Criminal Court.

Whereas all caricatures are by necessity simplifications, this simplification of American foreign policy in the 1920s and 1930s as isolationist is dangerously misleading. It distorts the past because neither the foreign policy pursued by the Republican occupants of the White House in the 1920s nor the foreign policy pursued by Franklin Delano Roosevelt in the 1930s can properly be called isolationism. Moreover, this historical distortion obscures potentially enlightening historical parallels between this era and other eras in U.S. foreign policy, including the present, by simply dismissing this period as one of myopic isolationism. Looking at U.S. foreign policy in the interwar years through the lens of the four debates discussed in the introduction demonstrates that this era was far more than a misguided turn to a historically nonexistent isolationism.

On the diplomatic front, the United States in the 1920s retained, rather than dismantled, much of the diplomatic establishment it had built up in the years preceding and during World War I. The Department of State in Washington employed 91 people in 1900, a number that jumped to 234 in 1910, and then soared to 708 in 1920. This growth stagnated in the 1920s as the department ended the decade with only 714 employees, but these numbers suggest a sustained investment in foreign policy rather than a sharp retraction. Tellingly, one area where a sharp retraction did take place was in the number of Foreign Service Officers employed overseas, where the numbers dropped from over 1,000 in 1910 to just over 500 in 1920.[42] Together, these figures are more suggestive of a desire for unilateralism than isolationism. Indeed, far from embracing the nascent multilateral institutions of the era, the Department of State remained reluctant even to answer any correspondence it received from the League of Nations.[43] Instead, the diplomatic corps of the United States acted mostly as commercial agents for U.S. traders and investors abroad. This was a continuation of a trend already well-established under President William Howard Taft's earlier "dollar diplomacy," where, as his secretary of state put it, "diplomacy works for trade."[44]

On the military front, the postwar years saw the development of a permanent system of chiefs of staff for planning as well as an air force, settling in after the war with approximately ten thousand men and three thousand planes, whereas before the war the United States possessed a mere handful of planes. Here technology furthered the universalization of America's security perimeter; as Billy Mitchell, an early advocate for air power, put it, "aircraft are able to go anywhere on the planet . . . [and] have set aside all ideas of frontiers."[45] The U.S. Navy also continued to be one of the strongest in the world, building more warships in the first three years after World War I than the rest of the world combined.[46] Such numbers do not square with the popular image that after the war the United States simply let its military resources wither. With regard to missions, the navy was tasked with its traditional duty of keeping the sea-lanes of communication open, and whereas the army was not given a major overseas role, the marine corps continued to engage in quasi-policing duties throughout Latin America.

It is in the economic arena, however, that the conventional view of the United States as an isolationist power after World War I is most misleading. World War I saw the transition of the United States from being a debtor to a creditor nation and its growth to become the largest trading nation in the world. The United States, far from turning inward economically, more than doubled its overseas investments during the 1920s.[47]

It is also in the economic arena that the Republican grand strategy of the 1920s is perhaps most distinctive; U.S. policymakers saw private business rather than governmental institutions as the preferred means of implementing U.S. grand strategy. As President Warren G. Harding phrased it in his inaugural address, one of the overall goals of his administration was to cut back on "interference of Government with business . . . and for more efficient business in Government administration."[48] In this more privatized grand strategy, as Reinhold Niebuhr characterized it, the "legates of our empire are not admirals or proconsuls, but bankers."[49] In Latin America, for example, the United States attempted to scale back the commitments of the marine corps in favor of relying on friendly local strongmen backed by and supportive of close economic ties with the United States.[50] In addition to U.S. businesses, U.S. missionary activity also expanded overseas as a key component of America's privatized crusade to spread its values across the globe.[51]

Even under privatization, the goals of U.S. foreign policy remained ambitious. The idea was that, operating with faith in what Akira Iriye calls "business civilization," the spread of private business and trade was the key to advancing U.S. interests and U.S. values abroad.[52] The underlying belief was that the rationality of private business would bring peace and prosperity where international politics as usual had failed. The more expansive military and diplomatic resources possessed by the United States in the 1920s as opposed to a generation earlier was in many ways beside the point for American grand strategy. The question of U.S. membership in international organizations like the League of Nations was similarly beside the point. If the spread of private business was the key to a more prosperous and peaceful world, then all the military and diplomatic instruments of state power had to do was set the stage and then get out of the way and allow the power of private actors to advance the material interests and values of the United States. It was this privatized approach to grand strategy that allowed President Harding to declare that an America that would "be a party to no permanent military alliance, . . . enter into no political commitments, nor assume any economic obligations" would still be "not only an inspiration and example, but the highest agency of strengthening good will and promoting accord."[53]

For an example of privatization in practice, perhaps the central economic problem of the post–World War I period centered on the linked issues of reparations and war debts. The victorious allies had all incurred huge debts to the United States during the war. Where were they going to get the money to pay off those debts? One hoped-for source of funds was war reparations that were to be levied on the defeated Germans. Where was Germany going to get the money to pay these reparations? Private banks in the United States or U.S. businesses looking to invest abroad were likely to be the central source of capital that would allow Germany to rebuild and pay these reparations. This system thus relied on a circular flow of money. U.S. banks loaned money to Germany or to businesses willing to invest in Germany, the Germans used this money to rebuild and to pay reparations to the allies, and then the allies would use the money to pay off their war loans to U.S. banks. This circle was calibrated such that by the early 1930s U.S. loans to Germany had totaled about $2.5 billion, Germany had paid the allies $2.5 billion in reparations, and the allies had paid U.S. banks about $2.6 billion on its war debts.[54] As long as this circular flow of money continued, an international financial crisis could be avoided, but only some level of self-sustaining economic growth in Europe would solve the underlying issue.

Because U.S. banks were at the center of the loan and reparation issues, the United States played a major role in the negotiations involving these issues, epitomized in the formation of the Dawes Plan and the Young Plan to avoid an international financial crisis. One of the most striking parts of the Dawes and Young plans is the identity of the men these plans were named after. Dawes and Young were not State Department or Treasury officials but were instead private bankers. Here was the business civilization in action. Rather than have government officials conduct the most important international economic negotiations of the postwar era, private citizens acting in their capacities as businessmen would do so. The Dawes Plan, for example, did not need to be approved by Congress or require any appropriation of government funds. Indeed, the secretary of state, Charles Evan Hughes, declined any governmental review of foreign loan or investment decisions, despite the central role such decisions played in international politics.[55]

Rather than turn to a pessimistic isolationism after World War I, the United States instead turned to an optimistic global crusade. Globalization did not first become a buzzword in U.S. foreign policy in the 1990s but was a core part of U.S. foreign policy much earlier in the century. Over one hundred years before Thomas Friedman declared that *The World Is Flat*[56] and approximately forty years before Henry Luce declared the onset of "The American Century," as early as 1902, English journalist W. T. Stead was talking about *The Americanisation of the World*. In 1928, for example, Hollywood films captured 25 percent of Japan's cinema market, about 50 percent of Germany's, 66 percent of France's and Italy's, and over 80 percent of the markets in Britain, Canada, Mexico, and Brazil.[57] Like the globalization optimists of today, many at this time similarly expected the spread of American business, American culture, and American ideals to usher in not a return to normalcy, as Harding's campaign slogan would have it but instead, as the rhetoric of his inaugural address phrased it, "the birth of a new order."[58] It is still a crusade, but it is a privatized one.

The essence of the Republican grand strategy of the 1920s is well captured in Warren Cohen's apt phrase of an "Empire without Tears."[59] The United States, it was believed, could advance its interests and values by making the world more peaceful and prosperous as U.S. business culture spread. Even more appealingly, the costs of creating and maintaining this empire would be low. The United States had to keep a strong military, primarily a dominant navy that could secure the sea-lines of communication and commerce, but otherwise the military would have to be used only in limited policing operations. The United States had to keep a more professional diplomatic corps, but its primary role would be to advance the cause of private U.S. business abroad. Commitments to international organizations would also be unnecessary. Instead, an independent internationalism led by the private sector would do the job better and more cheaply. In short, the belief was that time was on the side of America's global crusade, and not only were multilateral commitments superfluous to that crusade, so were most governmental actions. As Calvin Coolidge put it in a concise summary of this governing philosophy, "four-fifths of all our troubles in this life would disappear if we would only sit down and keep still."[60]

The Depression and the End of the Empire without Tears

Unexpected external shocks often serve as a driver of change in grand strategy. For the Republican foreign policy of the 1920s, it was the Great Depression that provided that shock. The Great Depression undermined many of the key tenets of that strategy because it shattered the optimism that lay at the heart of America's empire without tears. It was not World War I and its messy aftermath that undermined the conviction of U.S. policymakers that time was on America's side and that history was moving in America's direction, it was the Great Depression that played this sobering role.[61] In the midst of the depression private banks virtually ceased making loans overseas, foreign investment by private business abroad dried up, and imports to the United States plummeted. "Business civilization" was not only failing, it was collapsing.

One way the United States responded to the depression was with retrenchment toward a shrinking security perimeter. Despite growing conflicts, an increase in loan defaults, and the history of the Monroe Doctrine, President Herbert Hoover largely declined to use U.S. military forces in Latin America. Similarly, when the Japanese invaded Manchuria, Hoover argued to his cabinet that "he would fight for [the] Continental United States as far as anybody, but he would not fight for Asia."[62]

It was in the realm of values, however, that the Great Depression had the potential for its most far-reaching influence. Ideologically, many Americans feared that the very future of democracy and liberal capitalism as the best way of organizing society was threatened as a result of the economic collapse caused by the depression. To avoid further economic calamity, many Americans feared that the United States would have to develop a far more interventionist state and invest far more power in the hands of a single leader. Although he would not gain prominence in American foreign policy until the 1940s, George Kennan, writing in the 1930s, argued that the only way America's political decline could be reversed was "through constitutional change to the authoritarian state."[63] The increasing power of fascist and communist movements in Europe was seen as a potential omen of what might lay in store for the future of the United States.

Americans at this time looked at these movements with a mixture of horror and sympathy. Although increased state control over the economy and centralizing power was not the direction in which many Americans wanted to go, the fear was that the demands of modernity might not offer any other attractive choices. This is why there was a lot of praise in the United States for leaders like Mussolini and Hitler in their early days. This was combined with a suspicion that the United States as well would have "to substitute the doctrine of the right man for the doctrine of the rights of man."[64] The verdict of history, many Americans feared, no longer seemed to be on the side of liberal democracy and laissez-faire capitalism.

The challenge of responding to this situation in the United States would lie largely in the hands of Franklin Delano Roosevelt (FDR), who would be elected to the presidency an unmatched four times. At home, Roosevelt's policies did lead to the expansion of the role of the state in the economy and an increase in the powers of the presidency. Although in hindsight it is now clear that the United States never moved as far toward communism or fascism as many feared it would, that does not diminish the effect of such fears at the time. As a grand strategist, FDR came to the presidency, in some senses, as the partial heir of both Theodore Roosevelt and Woodrow Wilson. Wilson appointed FDR to his first major national political office, as assistant secretary of the navy, a position his cousin Theodore had previously occupied. Theodore Roosevelt and Woodrow Wilson dominated America's entrance onto the world stage as a significant global power, but it was FDR who dominated U.S. foreign policy as the young great power faced perhaps its most serious crisis, with a depression at home and the rise of aggressive totalitarian movements abroad.

The Grand Strategy of Franklin Delano Roosevelt

At a press conference in 1942, responding to questions about the goals of the United States in World War II and the postwar settlement Washington was seeking, Franklin Roosevelt responded, "Don't you think we might win the war before we start determining all the details of geography and of forms of government, and boundaries and things like that? Wouldn't it be just as well to win the war first, as long as you have principles?"[65] This statement offers an excellent microcosm of FDR's approach to grand strategy.

A reluctance to discuss or to think deeply about crucial issues such as boundaries and forms of government before the war is over can be seen as an inherently antistrategic position. Indeed, if the purpose of war is to construct a better peace, such items should not be afterthoughts, but central to the strategic enterprise. Some have accused FDR of lacking a clear sense of strategy and instead relying on pragmatism and improvisation, but the last phrase in FDR's answer suggests a different possibility.[66] "[A]s long as you have principles," pragmatism over details could coexist with strategic thought. This mixture of pragmatism in the service of a small number of core principles would help make this "chameleon on plaid," in Herbert Hoover's evocative description of FDR,[67] an effective grand strategist for the United States.

One of FDR's key strategic principles was that time was on America's side. Rejecting the pessimism of many of his countrymen that arose out of the Great Depression, FDR radiated optimism. This was not only a public pose but also a core part of his political agenda. The New Deal, for instance, did not end the depression, but it did buy enough social stability to give the U.S. economy time to recover without having to adopt some of the more extreme solutions attempted by the communists or the fascists.[68] In foreign policy as well, procrastination need not indicate a lack of strategy but instead the conviction that time favored the United States and that current problems would work out in America's favor if left alone. As FDR advised Winston Churchill with regard to policy toward the Soviet Union, "I would minimize the general Soviet problem as much as possible because these problems, in one form or another, seem to arise everyday and most of them straighten out."[69]

Another core principle in FDR's grand strategy was that the United States possessed global interests. As the president explained to his ambassador to Japan, "the problems which we face are so vast and so interrelated that any attempts even to state them compels one to think in terms of five continents and seven seas."[70] Indeed, one of the key challenges FDR faced was to try to change the preference of the American people and the U.S. Congress for a more narrowly defined security perimeter, and to get them to accept the global responsibilities that came with global interests. In 1941, for example, Senator Robert Taft (R-OH) called for the United States to keep to a hemispheric security perimeter: "I believe that the peace and happiness of the people of this country can best be secured by refusing to intervene in war outside the Americas and by establishing our defense line based on the Atlantic and Pacific Oceans. I believe that the difficulty of attacking America across the oceans will forever prevent such an attack even being considered, if we maintain an adequate defense on the sea and in the air."[71]

Attempting to explain to reluctant members of the Senate Committee on Military Affairs why events in Europe were of interest to the United States, Roosevelt shocked one senator into worrying that the president's logic implied that the U.S. frontier was on the Rhine. FDR distanced himself from such a bald statement but he also insisted that "practically speaking, if the Rhine frontiers are threatened the rest of the world is too." Following the attack on Pearl Harbor, free to be more explicit about his view of America's universal security perimeter, Roosevelt stressed that, "We have learned that our ocean-girt hemisphere is not immune from severe attack—that we cannot measure our safety in terms of miles on any map any more."[72] In a message to Stalin during the war Roosevelt argued that, "There is in this global war literally no question, either military or political, in which the United States is not interested."[73]

Inevitably, the reality of limited resources challenged the ability of the United States to execute a grand strategy based on a universal security perimeter. As Walter Lippmann characterized the problem during World War II, "it is just as important to define the limit beyond which we will not intervene as it is to convince our people that we cannot find security in an isolationist policy."[74] Rather than shrink America's security perimeter as Lippmann suggested, Roosevelt preferred to deal with limited resources and continued domestic restraints on the use of those resources in another way: through multilateral cooperation with the other great powers.

The core of Roosevelt's plans for postwar order was for a concert of great powers to share the burdens of leadership, each taking on special responsibilities in the regions most important to them.[75] In Roosevelt's conception, the United States, the Soviet Union, Great Britain, and China would cooperate as "four policemen," all with their own local duties and privileges similar to those of the United States in Latin America under the Monroe Doctrine. As is fitting for a political heir of both Theodore Roosevelt and Woodrow Wilson, FDR's vision of the four policemen represented a compromise between recognizing the importance of the balance of power and the particular interests of the great powers while simultaneously recognizing the need for some level of multilateral cooperation among states. This compromise is best represented in the veto power given to the great powers in the United Nations Security Council, accepting that the unequal balance of power among states means that some states are more equal than others when it comes to determining global order.

With Britain decimated by the two world wars and China still emerging from colonialism, the key relationship among the four policemen was going to be between the United States and the Soviet Union. On this front, Roosevelt's policy was to build a cooperative relationship with the Soviets by reassuring them that the world order he envisioned protected core Soviet interests. This need to reassure the Soviets meant the limiting of any crusading tendencies in U.S. foreign policy because attempting to actively spread American values into the Soviet sphere would destroy FDR's hope for a cooperative relationship between Washington and Moscow. FDR's concert meant accepting the ideological differences between the two nascent superpowers.

This part of FDR's grand strategy faced its greatest challenge in Eastern Europe. The logic of the four-policemen strategy not only recognized Soviet interests in Eastern Europe but also put the region squarely within the Soviet sphere of influence. For Roosevelt, however, influence did not mean domination and exclusion. Even if Eastern Europe was to be the "beat" of the Soviet Union, to extend the policing metaphor, this did not imply, for Roosevelt, that the Soviets had the unrestricted right to dictate the internal organization of those states or to exclude the other great powers from pursuing their interests in that region. The spheres of influence Roosevelt envisioned would be open ones where the regional great power would exercise leadership, not domination. Heavy-handed Soviet actions in Eastern Europe cut against FDR's vision, but he had to balance that distaste with an appreciation for the local balance of power and with the need to protect the possibility of cooperation with the Soviet Union. Facing these trade-offs, Roosevelt reluctantly concluded that the United States had limited influence on events in Eastern Europe, so why risk postwar global cooperation over an issue that put the United States at a disadvantage?[76] Given the domestic sensitivities involved for Roosevelt, the best tack was to keep U.S. policy vague and avoid a rupture with Stalin.[77]

In the early years of his presidency, when the looming Cold War with the Soviet Union was still in the distance, Roosevelt's severest policy challenges originated at home rather than abroad. In his first two terms, Roosevelt paid only passing and reluctant attention to foreign policy.[78] The overriding need to deal with the domestic effects of the depression pushed foreign policy concerns to the back of Roosevelt's agenda.

Indeed, if there is any period in American history that could be accurately characterized as isolationist, it is the two years starting with the passage of the Neutrality Act of 1935 and ending with Roosevelt's quarantine speech on October 5, 1937. The Neutrality Act of 1935 forbade Americans to sell arms to any states that were at war and allowed for no distinctions between aggressors and defenders or allies and enemies. The act also warned Americans traveling on the ships of belligerent powers that they did so at their own risk. The Neutrality Act of 1937 forbade loans to states at war, made U.S. travel on belligerent ships unlawful, and required that certain strategically important commodities be sold only on a cash-and-carry basis. These acts merit the label of isolationism because they concede American rights to engage in much foreign commerce and signal that the United States would not fight to maintain the freedom of the seas. The neutrality acts were difficult to enforce and were often ignored by American business, but the laws did represent a major shift in what had been traditional U.S. policy with regard to commerce during wartime.[79]

Even during this high-water mark of isolationism, however, Roosevelt did not abandon his belief in America's mission to spread its values overseas by serving as an example to others. During the 1936 campaign, remarking on other states that had responded to the depression by turning away from democracy, FDR argued that, "Only our success can stir their ancient hope. They begin to know that here in America we are waging a great and successful war . . . for the survival of democracy. We are fighting to save a great and precious form of government for ourselves and for the world." At the end of 1936, the newly reelected president told a meeting of American states, "Democracy is still the hope of the world," and "If we in our generation can continue its successful application in the Americas, it will spread and supersede other methods by which men are governed."[80] As a pragmatist, however, Roosevelt remained cautious about translating such rhetoric into practice. Whereas the Atlantic Charter of 1941, for example, called for the universal right of self-determination, Roosevelt compromised with European colonialism throughout World War II. As Brad Simpson aptly characterizes it, FDR could have his "Atlantic Charter and retreat from it too."[81]

Roosevelt's Quarantine Speech of October 5, 1937, represented the president's first major public challenge to the neutrality acts, and argued that the failure to make distinctions between aggressors and defenders and potential allies and potential enemies was foolish. It would be wiser, Roosevelt suggested, to target these laws in a way more consistent with the national interest of the United States. The Quarantine Speech started the process of shedding isolationism and putting the United States on the side of the allies in the coming world war. For instance, the Neutrality Act of 1939 allowed allies to buy U.S. munitions, provided they did so on a cash-and-carry basis. Roosevelt was not alone in his call for the United States to take a more active role in foreign affairs. It would take World War II and the Cold War to lead to the full flowering of a new security studies establishment in the United States that combined academic and government work, was concerned about issues of grand strategy, and saw the United States has having worldwide interests, but that community got its start in thinking about how to respond to the economic and political crises of the 1930s.[82]

The Continuing Relevance of the Interwar Years

The foreign policy experience of the United States in the 1920s and 1930s raises some enduring issues for U.S. grand strategy. One aspect of U.S. foreign policy in the interwar years that is particularly worth pondering is how U.S. grand strategy in the 1920s helped set the stage for the U.S. reaction, or lack of reaction, to the more troubling events of the 1930s. Washington was not unique in how it responded to the Great Depression. Virtually all of the existing democracies reacted to the depression by turning inward to focus on domestic problems. The dictatorships, in contrast, tended to pursue outward expansion as the key to improving their state's situation. Appeasement is much more than the story of Adolf Hitler and Neville Chamberlain— it stemmed from these different reactions to the Great Depression.

For the United States in particular, this era demonstrates the danger that unilateralism can become the high road to isolationism.[83] How does a state with as long a history of international involvement, especially toward issues like freedom of the seas, turn isolationist, if only for a brief period? A significant part of the answer lies within the policies pursued by the United States during the 1920s, when the United States was committed to internationalism, but a unilateral internationalism. None of the major policymakers of the era intended to push the United States toward isolationism but this became an unintended consequence of attempts to pursue an empire without tears.

Isolationism versus internationalism was not a central part of the foreign policy debate in the United States in the 1920s. Instead, the core of the debate focused more on unilateralism versus multilateralism. This was a key dividing line on a series of major issues like the League of Nations, mutual tariff discussions, and the issues of debt forgiveness and war reparations. In these struggles, the unilateralists tended to come out on top. The United States remained engaged on these issues, but with a minimum of formal governmental commitments.

American unilateralism, however, proved to be a thin basis for internationalism when times turned difficult and the unilateralism of the Roaring Twenties morphed into the isolationism of the Great Depression. Growing difficulties at home led Washington to consistently raise the threshold of what it would take for the United States to accept an active role in warding off global problems. By not being members of any strong international organizations, not having any formal alliance commitments, not having a significant military presence overseas, and not having to consistently coordinate U.S. policy with others, it was possible to ignore growing global dilemmas in the short term. If the United States had been a part of the League of Nations, if Washington had had a formal alliance with any of the major states of Europe, or if the American military had had a significant presence on the continent, the United States would have been forced to take a far more direct and earlier stand on the growing axis threat. Without those multilateral ties, however, it was easier for the United States to attempt to evade and to defer the confrontation of those challenges.

Thus, one grand strategic lesson to learn from this era in U.S. foreign policy is about the dangers of unilateralism leading to isolationism and about the related benefits of multilateralism in seeing internationalism through difficult times. U.S. policymakers are properly concerned about mission creep or the dangers of alliances and international institutions "chain-ganging" the United States into a war. The interwar years suggest that U.S. policymakers should also be concerned about the opposite; that unilateralism can undermine internationalism, especially during difficult times, which ironically may be the periods when internationalism is most needed.

These concerns remain relevant for U.S. grand strategy. After the collapse of the Soviet Union and later after the terrorist attacks of September 11, 2001, the United States was strong enough and enraged enough to sustain its international commitments unilaterally. America's interwar experience raises the question of how sustainable this unilateral internationalism is. Whereas comparisons between current economic conditions and the Great Depression are overwrought, the continuing ill effects of the global financial crisis, combined with America's growing entitlement obligations as the baby-boom generation hits retirement age is putting a significant strain on government resources. Can unilateral internationalism survive in such an environment? Although the United States may not have needed allies to evict the sitting regimes in Afghanistan or Iraq, allied assistance proved far more consequential in seeing these states through a protracted period of reconstruction. If the United States lets its links with its allies and its connections to international organizations wither in order to protect American freedom of action when the United States is strong enough and willing to act on its own, what will happen to U.S. internationalism if the United States finds itself in a position where it may not be strong enough or willing to act on its own?

Rousseau once wrote: "The strongest is never strong enough to be master all the time, unless he transforms force into right and obedience into duty."[84] The United States is the strongest state in the world today and is likely to maintain that status for some time. As a result, the United States can be master of much, even unilaterally. U.S. internationalism could be more sustainable, even at the cost of short-term freedom of action, if U.S. foreign policy focused instead on building international relationships and international institutions that can create a sense of duty to deal with common problems both for Washington's potential allies and for the United States itself.

The interwar years in U.S. foreign policy also offer a cautionary tale to those who hope that maintaining an acceptable world order need not inflict significant costs on the United States. Just as the spread of America's "business civilization" in the 1920s did not herald the start of a new peaceful era in world politics in which private business could replace state power, the same is likely to be true for globalization today. Are foreign aid programs still necessary in a world where international trade and investment flows dwarf government assets? Trade, not aid, is the mantra of supporters of a more privatized approach to international development. Are international organizations and alliances necessary when the United States can construct rolling coalitions of those willing to handle any problems that arise in the future? Now that the United States has moved on from its costly state-building efforts in Iraq and Afghanistan, could the defense budget not be substantially cut?

As will be discussed in subsequent chapters, the appeal of an empire without tears repeatedly tempts American policymakers. In pursuit of the post–Cold War "peace dividend" the United States slashed its already small foreign aid budget and spending on diplomacy, and its military budget declined in real terms. Even if military interventions were still necessary, those missions could be kept at low cost or abandoned because discussions of exit strategy often put more emphasis on exit than strategy. Even what critics derided as "cruise missile hegemony" and the promise of "immaculate coercion" proved politically controversial as exemplified by George W. Bush's condemnation of even the limited military missions undertaken by the Clinton administration as "missions without end." On the congressional side, payment of America's dues to the United Nations were held up by the domestic agenda of a few well-placed members, the Comprehensive Nuclear Test-Ban Treaty was defeated, and fast-track negotiating authority for trade agreements was regularly withheld.

The terrorist attacks of September 11, 2001, only partially undermined the notion of an empire without tears. A huge increase in defense spending quickly followed those attacks, as did major operations in Afghanistan and Iraq. Beyond the military instrument of power, however, changes have been less evident. There have been many calls for revitalizing America's diplomatic and intelligence services, but budgetary increases for the former have been small and reform in the latter has focused on organizational reshuffling. Moreover, despite high-profile initiations such as the Millennium Challenge Account, the president's AIDS initiative, and the U.S.-Middle East Partnership Initiative, the funding levels for these and other foreign aid programs have remained low. Even on the military side, troop levels for the invasion of Iraq were kept far lower than prewar plans had estimated would be necessary and the human costs of the war fell on a small and relatively isolated segment of American society. As the United States prosecuted three wars

(Iraq, Afghanistan, and the War on Terror), Americans were encouraged to take their tax cuts and go shopping, rather than to share in the sacrifices of the wars. The surge of troops in Iraq helped enable a steady drawdown of U.S. forces there; similarly, President Obama initially increased the troop level in Afghanistan, but did so only as a temporary measure as part of an overall plan to reduce the U.S. presence in Afghanistan. In 2012 and 2013 Congress preferred to make automatic cuts in the defense budget rather than to directly tackle the difficult fiscal situation in the United States with a broader measure of tax increases and entitlement reductions. The allure of an empire without tears remains strong. Although the depression and World War II temporarily shattered the myth that America could enjoy an empire without tears, Franklin Roosevelt's more ambitious plans for a post–World War II order based on a concert of great powers would also not long survive his death. What would replace it in American grand strategy is the subject of the next chapter.

The Debates Raised by Containment in the Truman Administration

At the end of World War II, the United States faced a set of questions similar to those it had faced following the end of World War I. Having emerged as one of the victors in a great power war, indeed having emerged as by far the most powerful state in the world, the United States had to grapple with the question of how to advance its national interests in the postwar era. One critical difference between these two eras, however, is that the post–World War II policymakers had the experience of the post–World War I period to reflect upon, which spurred a determination to do better this time. This chapter will explore the origins of containment and early debates regarding the best way to pursue that grand strategy, contrasting the diverging views of George Kennan, who is justifiably credited as being the father of containment, with the policy views of Paul Nitze as embodied in the National Security Council Report 68 (NSC-68). Although containment is often considered to be the gold standard in U.S. grand strategy in terms of coherence and longevity, as the title of John Lewis Gaddis's indispensable book argues, there were multiple strategies of containment.[1]

The Domestic and Global Scenes

The person leading the United States into the postwar world was not Franklin Delano Roosevelt (FDR), the man who led the nation through the war and who sought to build a concert of great powers to keep the peace, but his vice president, Harry S. Truman. A failed businessman from Missouri, virtually appointed to the Senate by a local political boss, Truman gained the vice-presidential nomination in 1944 largely because his limited political résumé meant that he had not offended any of the competing wings within the Democratic Party. Truman was never close to FDR, was only vice president for eighty-three days, and during that time had only spoken to the president a handful of times. Roosevelt's preference for tailoring his moves to developing events, moreover, meant that any discussions the two had on future strategic issues were likely vague.[2]

As Truman recorded in his diary on the day he assumed the presidency, "the weight of the Government had fallen on my shoulders. . . . I knew the President had a great many meetings with Churchill and Stalin. I was not familiar with any of these things and it was really something to think about." As Truman later admitted, he "was plenty scared."[3] In a surprising success story, however, Truman's handling of the foreign policy responsibilities that were thrust upon him has consistently placed him on the list of "near great" presidents and his example has been a regular source of inspiration for presidents and presidential aspirants who lack foreign policy experience.

The problems confronting the United States abroad were daunting. As a result of its defeat, Germany had fallen from the ranks of the great powers. The allied air campaign and subsequent invasions had destroyed much of the nation's infrastructure; Germany no longer exercised sovereignty over its territory and was instead occupied by the victorious powers, Britain, the Soviet Union, the United States, and eventually France. Japan was similarly destroyed and occupied, but in a key difference had only one occupying power because, except for a few islands claimed by the Soviets, the United States shouldered sole responsibility for the future of Japan.

Even significant victorious countries could no longer be considered powers of the first rank. France's initial defeat and occupation by the Nazis and its subsequent liberation by the allies left the country crippled. During the war, Japan had evicted France from most of its possessions in Asia and, after the war, Paris faced revolts in virtually all of its colonial possessions. Although spared occupation, Britain was in only marginally better shape as it ended the war deeply in debt, having suffered from a sustained bombing campaign and facing similar colonial uprisings. Even during the war U.S. policy toward European colonialism had created strains in the alliance, which were to accelerate as decolonization moved forward in the postwar period.[4]

For the Soviet Union, the price of its victory was enormous. The United States lost about 300,000 men in the war, but the Soviet Union lost over 25 million, which as Gaddis calculates, means that for every American who died, 90 Soviets died.[5] As Melvyn Leffler enumerates the destruction:

> The German invaders had destroyed over 1,700 cities and towns and more than 70,000 villages and hamlets. They demolished more than six million buildings and over 31,000 industrial enterprises. They wrecked 61 of the largest power stations, 1,100 coal pits, and more than 3,000 oil wells. They dismantled 40,000 miles of railroad track, blew up 56,000 miles of main road, and ruined 90,000 bridges. The Germans ransacked the countryside, destroying tens of thousands of collective farms and machine and tractor stations. They stole and slaughtered 17 million head of cattle, 20 million hogs, 27 million sheep and goats, 110 million poultry and 7 million horses.[6]

Although the Soviet military had marched far into Europe by the end of the war, as Kennan recognized, the Red Army was more in need of rebuilding than ready for future conquests.[7] To give one example, even as late as 1950, the United States estimated that half of the Soviet Union's military transport was still horse-drawn.[8] The massive damage Moscow endured at the hands of and inflicted on the Nazi war machine did, however, show the great power potential of the Soviet Union. Whereas it is hard to recapture today given the subsequent failures of the Soviet state, in the immediate postwar years the communist model was an attractive one for many because it had triumphed over German arms and initially achieved impressive postconflict economic growth. After World War I, many in the United States hoped to see the spread of U.S. values overseas. After World War II, the United States had an ideological competitor and many Americans feared that the Soviet model would spread throughout the world, starting in wardestroyed Europe.

By most physical measures of power, the United States emerged from World War II as the strongest power on the globe, perhaps the greatest power the world had ever seen. By the end of the war, the United States possessed two-thirds of the world's gold reserves, three-quarters of its investment capital, half the world's manufacturing capability, and it produced a third of the world's goods. Militarily, in 1943 the United States produced $37.5 billion worth of arms, whereas the Soviets produced only $13.9 billion, the Germans $13.8 billion, the British $11.1 billion, and the Japanese $4.5 billion. When the war was over the U.S. Navy was larger than all the navies of the world combined, and America's air and naval supremacy meant that Washington alone possessed the ability to project power to anywhere on the globe. Moreover, in the immediate postwar years, the United States possessed a monopoly on the most devastating weapon mankind had ever produced, the atomic bomb.[9]

Even given these substantial material advantages over potential competitors, U.S. policymakers were remarkably anxious about America's strategic position. First, there were strong doubts about the extent to which the United States could maintain its wartime pace and for how long. After overt hostilities ended, the United States quickly demobilized its armed forces. In 1939 the United States Army consisted of 170,000 men and its budget was less than $500 million. At its World War II height, the armed forces reached about 12 million and the defense budget totaled over $80 billion. By July 1947, however, the armed forces were down to 1.6 million and the budget was down to $12.8 billion.[10] Whereas this was a significant increase over prewar levels, it was far below the wartime peak. Moreover, most of those remaining forces were tied down with occupation duties in Germany and Japan. The secretary of state, George Marshall, expressed frustration about the constraints this placed on U.S. foreign policy: "I was being pressed constantly . . . to give the Russians hell. . . . At that time, my facilities for giving them hell—and I am a soldier and know something about the ability to give hell—was one and a third divisions over the entire United States. That is quite a proposition when you deal with somebody with over 260."[11]

America's atomic monopoly also offered U.S. policymakers little comfort. It was proving difficult to acquire and develop the nuclear material, and the United States was initially able to produce only a handful of weapons. It was more worrisome that the atomic monopoly of the United States would not last forever because it was only a matter of time before other states also unlocked the secrets of the atom. Once that happened, what would America's security situation look like when its enemies possessed the atomic bomb?

On the economic front, U.S. policymakers were also operating in the shadow of the Great Depression. World War II had ended the depression but would economic troubles return once the war ended? Would the economy create enough jobs to employ all the returning soldiers, especially because military production was significantly curtailed? Even if production were to quickly shift from military to consumer goods, who would be able to buy these goods in a war-ravaged world? As Kennan pessimistically assessed it, trying to sustain the current position of the United States in the world "will, in the long run, be beyond our resources."[12]

This directly influenced the U.S. perception of the threat it faced. Rather than seeing the Soviet Union as an immediate military threat, it was seen more as a long-term political one. As Kennan bluntly phrased it in 1947, "The Kremlin does not wish to have another war and does not expect to have one."[13] Instead, the danger was that the Soviet Union could take "advantage of the power vacuums left by the collapse of Germany and Japan and by the natural wave of radicalism following on the heels of any great military-political upheaval."[14] U.S. policymakers feared that the Soviets could dangerously increase their influence in Europe and throughout the world without firing a shot because populations living in war-created misery would turn of their own accord to the radical solution of communism. If that happened, the United States and its liberal democratic experiment would find itself increasingly isolated—could the United States survive as the United States in an ideologically inhospitable world?[15]

Kennan and the X-Article

The first person to offer an influential, coherent, and novel answer to many of the strategic questions then confronting U.S. foreign policymakers was George Kennan. Kennan was a career State Department employee, then working at the U.S. Embassy in Moscow. From that vantage point, he became frustrated by what he saw as Roosevelt's (and initially Truman's) misplaced strategy of trying to appease the Kremlin and encourage its cooperation with the United States in forging a postwar order along the lines of FDR's four policemen. He poured these frustrations into a long cable sent back to Washington on February 26, 1946. This message, which would become known as the "long telegram" found a receptive audience in Washington, and Kennan was recalled from Moscow to head up the State Department's new Policy Planning Staff, after serving a short stint as a professor at the National War College. Kennan's analysis got a public airing in a *Foreign Affairs* article published anonymously in 1947 under the pseudonym "X,"[16] although Kennan's cover was quickly blown by Arthur Krock, a columnist for the *New York Times*, who had been shown an earlier version of some of Kennan's writings and quickly recognized Kennan's authorship of the X-Article.

Kennan's analysis started from his understanding of the internal nature of the Soviet Union. This emphasis can be seen in the title of the X-Article, "The Sources of Soviet Conduct." As Kennan read the situation, communism played only a subsidiary role in determining Moscow's foreign policy. Ideology was simply too malleable a tool to serve as a guide for Soviet foreign policy because communism was whatever the Kremlin said it was. Reading the *Communist Manifesto* or *Das Kapital* was going to be of limited help in understanding Soviet foreign policy. Instead, for Kennan, the key to unlocking the "Sources of Soviet Conduct" was the Kremlin's deep-seated sense of insecurity both abroad and at home. Historically, Kennan stresses, Russia had always felt exposed and vulnerable to invasion, and the Soviet regime had just barely survived an incredibly destructive attack. The brutality of the Soviet regime domestically also influenced its foreign policy behavior insofar as having enemies abroad helped to justify the communist dictatorship at home. For these reasons, Kennan believed that FDR's attempts to engage the Russians and encourage them to take part in a cooperative postwar order were doomed to failure. The insecurity and distrust of the Soviet Union was simply too great to overcome.[17]

In one of his missives from Moscow, Kennan condemned the idea that the Soviets could be appeased "by personal contacts, rational arguments, or official assurances" as "the most insidious and dangerous single error which Americans can make." Instead, "nothing short of complete disarmament, delivery of our air and naval forces to Russia and resigning [the] powers of government to American Communists would even dent this problem: and even then we believe—and this is not facetious—that Moscow would smell a trap and continue to harbor the most baleful misgivings." In Kennan's estimate, the Soviet Union was "constitutionally incapable of being conciliated."[18] Similarly, when the U.S. ambassador to the Soviet Union, Averell Harriman, had asked the Soviet diplomat Maxim Litvinov what the United States could do to improve relations with the Soviet Union, Litvinov's response was "Nothing."[19] In a later discussion with a reporter, Litvinov argued that even if the West met all of Stalin's present demands, he would just come up with more demands.[20] Kennan interpreted any Soviet actions in favor of negotiation or agreements as short-term tactical deceptions. As he warned his colleagues about such seemingly cooperative moves, "there will always be Americans who will leap forward with gleeful announcements that 'the Russians have changed' and some will even try to take credit for having brought about such 'changes.' But we should not be misled by tactical manœuvres."[21] Ironically then, Kennan is just as suspicious of the Soviets as he accuses the Soviets of being of the United States.

These mutual suspicions need not lead to war in Kennan's estimation because he also stresses that the Soviets have no timetable for the communist conquest of the world and that if the United States confronts any aggressive moves with superior force, the Soviets will back away and simply wait for a more favorable moment. The metaphors Kennan uses to describe the Soviet Union emphasize constant pressure and patience. He likens Soviet foreign policy to a stream that will fill up any available beds or to a wind-up car that will head inexorably in one direction until a barrier is put up.[22] U.S. policy, therefore, needs to be equally constant and patient. In another metaphor, Kennan likens the Soviet Union to a tree that could be shaped by "steady pressure over a period of years" but "not by any sudden or violent application of force."[23] This meant rejecting any crusading impulses on the part of the United States to force an immediate change in Soviet politics. In discussing American strategy in the Cold War, Kennan was fond of quoting John Quincy Adams's famous advice that America "goes not abroad in search of monsters to destroy."[24]

Kennan's approach to the Soviet Union was also based on his conviction that time was on America's side. Kennan was not impressed by the long-term economic prospects of the communist experiment: "Russia will remain economically a vulnerable and in a certain sense an impotent, nation, capable of exporting its enthusiasms and of radiating the strange charms of its primitive political vitality but unable to back up those articles of export by real evidences of material power and prosperity."[25] Politically, Kennan also did not consider the post–World War II empire the Soviets had acquired as built to last: "It is unlikely that approximately one hundred million Russians will succeed in holding down permanently, in addition to their own minorities, some ninety millions of Europeans with a higher cultural level and with long experiences in resistance to foreign rule."[26] Although Kennan also harbored strong doubts about certain aspects of American society and the U.S. political system,[27] he ended the X-Article with a pep talk encouraging his countrymen to live up to the standards of the Promised Land that would make America a model for the rest of the world:

> The issue of Soviet-American relations is in essence a test of the over-all worth of the United States as a nation among nations. To avoid destruction the United States need only measure up to its own best traditions and prove itself worthy of preservation as a great nation.

> Surely, there was never a fairer test of national quality than this. . . . [T]he thoughtful observer of Russian-American relations will find no cause of complaint in the Kremlin's challenge to American society. He will rather experience a certain gratitude to a Providence which, by providing the American people with this implacable challenge, has made their entire security as a nation dependent on their pulling themselves together and accepting the responsibilities of moral and political leadership that history plainly intended them to bear.[28]

Kennan's rough estimate in the X-Article that the United States might need to "contain Soviet power over a period of ten to fifteen years"[29] turned out to be well short of the mark, but he accurately predicted that the Soviet Union could "be changed overnight from one of the strongest to one of the weakest and pitiable of national societies."[30] Kennan was not alone in his conviction that time was on America's side in the Cold War. For example, fellow Soviet expert Chip Bohlen similarly warned that the United States had to be prepared for a struggle "reaching into the indefinite future," but instead of pessimism called for a U.S. policy rooted in "an 'element of rational hope' based on confidence in the intrinsic superiority of our system over the Soviet system."[31]

This assessment of "The Sources of Soviet Conduct" led Kennan to recommend a policy of "long-term, patient, but firm and vigilant containment of Russian expansive tendencies." Further describing the central concept of containment, Kennan called for "the adroit and vigilant application of counter-force at a series of constantly shifting geographical and political points, corresponding to the shifts and manœuvres of Soviet policy" and for confronting the Russians "with unalterable counter-force at every point where they show signs of encroaching upon the interests of a peaceful and stable world."[32] When Stalin was provided a copy of the X-Article, the word "containment" was translated with the far more threatening Russian word for "strangulation."[33] Similarly, when Nikita Khrushchev declared in 1956, "Whether you like it or not, history is on our side. We will bury you!"[34] the United States interpreted it as a threat rather than a statement of historical confidence on Khrushchev's part that the Soviet model would outperform and outlast the American one.[35] Despite these cases of worst-case translating and interpreting, however, one of the key factors that helped to stabilize the Cold War was that neither side saw an urgent need for a crusade because both believed time was on their side.

No crusade needed to be launched at once against the Soviet Union, but Kennan did immediately regret publishing the X-Article. His attempt at anonymity failed and he worried that having been written for a general audience, the X-Article offered an incomplete and potentially misleading reflection of his thinking. After writing the X-Article, Kennan described his situation as that of a man "who has inadvertently loosened a large boulder from the top of a cliff and now helplessly witnesses its path of destruction in the valley below, shuddering and wincing at each successive glimpse of disaster."[36]

Containment as a grand strategy begged two important questions. First, how should the United States contain the Soviets; what mix of the instruments of national power would work most effectively? Second, where should the United States contain the Soviets? This second question goes to the fundamental question of defining the security perimeter of the United States. Were all Soviet attempts at advancement equally threatening or was it more important to contain the Soviet Union in some regions or issue areas as opposed to others?[37]

The X-Article was ambiguous in addressing the question of how to contain the Soviet Union, whether the United States should emphasize its military power, its economic power, or what Joseph Nye would later term its "soft power," which lies in "the attractiveness of a country's culture, political ideas and policies."[38] The repeated use of the term "counter-force" in Kennan's definitions of containment could suggest a military focus for containment. On the other hand, Kennan's characterization of the Cold War as a psychological and political struggle and his concluding emphasis on the importance of the United States "coping successfully with the problems of its internal life" and maintaining its "spiritual vitality" suggest the opposite. Throughout the Cold War, Kennan himself would remain a constant critic of those who put too much emphasis on the "counter-force" part of his definition of containment and not enough emphasis on the more societal and ideational aspects of the Cold War that he stressed in his conclusion to the X-article. The issue of how to properly mix the instruments of national power, especially the tension represented in the X-article between "counter-force" and "spiritual vitality," would run throughout the entire containment era.

In defining the security perimeter of the United States, it is easy to read the X-Article as offering an expansive definition, but part of Kennan's regret surrounding the article is that this was not his intent. Does the United States need to contain the Soviet Union everywhere or should U.S. policymakers be more selective in determining the regions and issues that require a U.S. response? The definitions of containment offered in the X-Article offer no clear geographical or functional limits and instead imply a universal approach to containment. The article talks of containing the Soviets "at a series of constantly shifting geographical and political points, corresponding to the shifts and manœuvres of Soviet policy" and "at every point where they show signs of encroaching upon the interests of a peaceful and stable world." As Gaddis does an excellent job of relating, however, Kennan did not see the security perimeter of the United States as unlimited.[39] Kennan saw U.S. resources as limited and strongly believed that the United States had to prioritize what it would attempt to defend.

Although the X-Article does limit containment to areas where the Soviets encroach "upon the interests of a peaceful and stable world," the article does not discuss how those interests should be operationalized. Looking beyond the X-Article, the key factor for Kennan in defining the security perimeter of the United States was industrial capacity. The United States had to keep access open to key lines of communication and protect its supplies of critical raw materials, but it was the ability of states to produce military equipment on a large industrial scale that was central to Kennan because in his assessment only a state capable of such production could pose a serious threat to the United States. Furthermore, Kennan saw only five places on earth capable of producing military-industrial power on a significant scale: the United States, the Soviet Union, Great Britain, Western Europe, and Japan. To prevent a dangerous shift in power against the United States, Kennan reasoned, Washington had to keep the latter three members of this list outside of the Soviet Union's orbit. In contrast, if the Soviets expanded into the mainland of Asia or into Africa there was no reason for the United States to be particularly worried or to expend its scarce resources in containing the Soviets in those places because the United States lacked vital interests there. As Kennan phrased it, the aim of the United States should not be "to hold equally everywhere," instead Washington should seek to "hold in enough places, and in strategic places, to accomplish our general purpose."[40] For Kennan, U.S. interests had to determine threats, and in places where the United States possessed few interests, it could not be threatened.

Moreover, Kennan believed that for the United States to be secure it did not need to dominate these key areas, it just had to make sure no one else could. This also positioned Kennan in opposition to any crusading impulses in U.S. foreign policy. The United States did not have to remake the world in its image, it just had to ensure that the Soviet Union could not remake the world in its image. In contrast to the punitive peace imposed on the defeated powers after World War I, Kennan's analysis supported the conclusion that the United States would be better off helping Germany and Japan to rebuild rather than leaving them weak and bitter and thus more susceptible to potential Soviet influence. Given Kennan's concerns about limited U.S. resources, the quicker the United States could build up independent centers of power in Europe and Asia that could help share the burden of balancing against the Soviets, the better.[41]

These debates over how and where to contain the Soviet Union ran throughout the containment era. On the how question, keeping in mind the tension in the X-Article between the "counter-force" definitions of containment and the conclusions that stress the political nature of the conflict, policymakers were forced to balance immediate military responses with more long-term political ones. On the where question, proponents of a perimeter approach to containment (who insisted that the Soviets had to be contained everywhere) regularly squared off against those who favored a strong-point approach that focused on avoiding conflicts in the periphery to concentrate on certain key areas. Such disputes involved not only disagreements over the relative importance of competing issues to U.S. interests but also differences over how interdependent U.S. commitments were: would reduced commitments in one area put all of America's commitments in doubt? All sides in these debates found support for their positions within the X-Article. Indeed, when Walter Lippmann published a string of critiques of the X-Article for overemphasizing military force and potentially squandering America's limited resources in peripheral areas, Kennan agreed and regretted how susceptible the X-Article was to misinterpretation.[42]

In the initial years of the Cold War the Truman administration's approach to containment favored nonmilitary instruments of power and focused on Kennan's strongpoints. Viewing the Soviet threat principally as a political and psychological one, the administration primarily used economic measures to inoculate Europe and Japan against the Soviet threat. The war-induced economic boom in the United States paired with the war-destroyed economy in Europe meant that the United States was exporting far more than it was importing. In 1946 the United States ran an $8 billion trade gap and by 1947 the gap was $12 billion. This trade imbalance created a dollar gap in the world economy, similar to the one following World War I, when the world needed to come up with dollars to pay for these goods if such trade flows were to continue. Without dollars to buy U.S. goods, trade would collapse and the European economies would continue to falter, which would open the door to increased Soviet influence. The collapse of international trade would also do significant damage to the U.S. economy, as the specter of the potential return of the depression continued to lurk in the background.[43]

Seeking to avoid a repeat of the failed policies that had helped lead to the collapse of the world economy a decade after the end of World War I, U.S. policymakers took several steps to deal with the dollar gap. Even before World War II was over, U.S. policymakers were working on a set of rules to help regulate the international economy. The rules and institutions they developed became known as the Bretton Woods system, named after the resort in New Hampshire where the key meetings took place. Rather than pursue the unilateral and more market-based approach that the United States pursued after World War I, U.S. policymakers after World War II explicitly constructed a network of multilateral organizations in an attempt to prevent a repeat of the 1930s. Central to the Bretton Woods system was a commitment to fixed exchange rates and a dollar that was tied to gold ($35 an ounce). The gold standard was seen as central to maintaining confidence in the dollar, and fixed exchange rates were designed to promote trade by easing currency convertibility. The United States also pushed and helped to fund the International Monetary Fund (IMF) to assist states in dealing with short-term balance-of-payments problems stemming from an excess of imports over exports. The International Bank for Reconstruction and Development, better known as the World Bank, was also created as part of the Bretton

Woods system to provide a source of long-term loans to fund economic rebuilding efforts. Also central to the international economic system that the United States helped to create after World War II was the General Agreement on Tariffs and Trade (GATT), which was designed to be a forum for trade negotiations leading to tariff reductions.[44]

A second way that the United States dealt with the dollar gap was to pick up some of the costly responsibilities that its allies were shouldering. In February 1947, Great Britain informed Washington that it could no longer afford to aid the governments of Greece and Turkey. If the United States did not step in to replace this aid, policymakers feared, these countries would be more vulnerable to Soviet influence. In asking Congress for a $400 million aid package for Greece and Turkey, encouraged by congressional leaders to "scare the hell out of the American people," Truman phrased his request in sweeping terms. "Unless we are willing," the president argued, "to help free peoples to maintain their free institutions and their national integrity against aggressive movements that seek to impose upon them totalitarian regimes . . . the foundations of international peace and hence the security of the United States" would be undermined. "[I]t must be the policy of the United States," Truman concluded, "to support free peoples who are resisting attempted subjugation by armed minorities or by outside pressures."[45]

The expansive rhetoric of what would be called the "Truman Doctrine" offers an early indication of the challenges that a strong-point approach to containment would face throughout the Cold War. For Kennan, the pledge to help "free peoples" anywhere was beyond U.S. interests and capacities. Whereas Kennan supported the aid package to Greece and Turkey as a way of alleviating Britain's financial problems and demonstrating the reliability of the United States as an ally, the indiscriminate rhetoric of speech was anathema to him. Even if only adopted as a domestic expedient to secure congressional approval, such universalizing rhetoric undermined the ability of the United States to keep its Cold War commitments limited. Once such statements are uttered, pressure to live up to them increases. Such rhetoric also increases the risk of ideological blowback as policymakers come to believe their own propaganda, forgetting its instrumental origin.[46]

The epitome of the strong-point and nonmilitary approach to containment practiced by the early Truman administration was the Marshall Plan, under which the United States sent about $13 billion to Europe, mostly in the form of U.S. goods, to help ease the dollar gap, restore faith in the capitalist economies of Europe, and sustain domestic demand to inoculate the U.S. economy against the return of the depression. Like the Dawes and Young plans of the interwar years, the Marshall plan enabled trade by providing money to the Europeans that would allow them access to U.S. goods, but unlike the post–World War I plans, this time the plan was named after the U.S. secretary of state, used governmental funds, required congressional approval, and mandated European multilateral cooperation as a requirement for the allotment of the funds. Whereas Europe got the Marshall Plan, Latin America, being further down on the U.S. list of priorities, had to content itself with Truman's Point Four program, which focused on private assistance, not governmental aid.[47]

Even when military force was used by the Truman administration, it was used more for psychological than military effects. The best example is the Berlin Airlift, which may have been the most effective strategic use of air power in history. The United States responded to the closing of the road and rail links to Berlin not with a direct effort to reopen those conduits, but with an airlift that proved a propaganda coup for the United States. Similarly, although it was a military alliance, the creation of the North Atlantic Treaty Organization (NATO) was at its outset primarily an economic and psychological rather than a military instrument. The security guarantee provided by the United States through NATO was designed to afford the political space to allow for economic recovery in Europe, and the alliance also proved to be a domestically acceptable way in the United States to continue to send money overseas to deal with the dollar gap after the conclusion of the Marshall Plan.

The Twin Shocks of 1949

In U.S. grand strategy, external shocks have often provoked a greater impulse for change than internal shifts in personnel. The year 1949 would prove to be one of those times. Throughout 1947 and 1948 U.S. grand strategy in the Cold War seemed to be on track. Both the Truman Doctrine and the Marshall Plan had cleared the necessary congressional hurdles, the Bretton Woods system for the international economy was beginning to operate, the Berlin Airlift was successful, and NATO was in its formative stages. In 1949, however, the United States was hit with two massive external shocks that persuaded the Truman administration of the need to rethink the basic tenets underlying U.S. foreign policy, a process that resulted in the writing of NSC-68, which represented a significant evolution in the U.S. approach to containment.[48]

The first shock was the victory in the Chinese Civil War of Mao Tse-Tung's communists who defeated Chiang Kai-shek's Nationalists and forced them to flee to Taiwan. In June 1949 Mao announced that China would "lean" toward the Soviet Union, and by February of 1950, China and the Soviet Union had signed a formal alliance. Franklin Roosevelt had hoped that a China allied to the United States could play the role of regional policeman in Asia, but in the Cold War context, the victory of Mao's forces meant that the territory controlled by communist powers had doubled and the population under communist control had increased fourfold.[49]

The communist victory in China led to a bitter (and self-centered) domestic debate in the United States over "who lost China?" assuming that China was America's to win or lose and that if Mao's forces had won, it must be because someone in the United States had failed. One person who became famous, and eventually notorious, for answering the question of who "lost" China was the junior senator from Wisconsin, Joseph McCarthy, who claimed that the State Department was riddled with communists bent on betraying the United States and that the Democratic party, which had held the White House for the past twenty years, had either acquiesced or even assisted in those efforts. Although McCarthy's accusations and methods were eventually discredited, fears of the domestic ramifications of "losing" other countries to communism continued to haunt U.S. policymakers, especially those in the Democratic Party, throughout the Cold War.

The second strategic shock of 1949 was the successful Soviet test of an atomic bomb, years ahead of U.S. predictions. Lacking any reliable delivery methods, the challenge presented by Soviet atomic capability at this time was not direct attack, it was what Melvyn Leffler calls "the diplomatic shadows cast by strategic power."[50] Would the possession of nuclear weapons make the Soviets more aggressive? Would U.S. foreign policy have to become more restrained now that it faced a nuclear-capable foe? Could America's more exposed allies still resist pressure from a nuclear-armed Soviet Union? How credible were U.S. promises to defend its allies from Soviet attack if doing so risked a nuclear attack on the United States?

For Kennan, neither of these events directly undermined his approach to containment. The Soviets were eventually going to develop nuclear weapons, and in the long term it meant little whether they did so in 1949 or the mid-1950s. Similarly, in his conception of the key centers of military-industrial power, Japan was the strongpoint to defend in Asia, not China. For others, however, the twin blows of 1949 challenged a core underlying assumption of Kennan's strategy—the conviction that time was on America's side. Although the Truman administration tried to publicly play down its concerns, as the secretary of state, Dean Acheson, saw it, the Soviet nuclear test "changed everything."[51] For Paul Nitze, who replaced Kennan as the head of the State Department's Policy Planning Staff, the developments led to "a feeling that the United States was losing the peace."[52]

NSC-68 and U.S. Grand Strategy

Doubts over whether time was on the side of the United States had important implications for U.S. grand strategy. If the Soviet Union was not going to collapse of its own weight, was containment as practiced in the opening years of the Cold War going to be enough? In 1949, the Soviet system did not appear to be in its death throes, but was instead expanding in China, generating impressive economic growth rates, and had just quickly matched the American defense establishment's greatest technological achievement. NSC-68's reevaluation of U.S. grand strategy was a result of these doubts.

Although NSC-68 took U.S. grand strategy in new directions, some elements of continuity remained. First, NSC-68 largely accepted Kennan's analysis of the Soviet threat, seeing tension as inevitable and discounting the potential of negotiations to significantly improve relations. Viewing the Soviets as "animated by a new fanatic faith, antithetical to our own" seeking "to impose its absolute authority over the rest of the world," NSC-68 asserted that "conflict has therefore become endemic."[53] NSC-68 also accepted Kennan's definition of the Cold War as fundamentally a struggle between different ways of organizing society and having a strong ideological and economic component.[54] Consistent with earlier efforts like the Marshall Plan, NSC-68 also saw key linkage between economic problems abroad and the potential spread of communism. In regard to Asia, NSC-68 worried that communism could elicit "favorable responses in vulnerable segments of society" who "have been impressed by what has been plausibly portrayed to them as the rapid advance of the USSR from a backward society to a position of a great world power."[55] Finally, NSC-68 also accepted the argument that to secure the United States and its way of life, a potentially hostile power could not be allowed to dominate significant parts of Eurasia.

The departures from Kennan's strategy were also significant. Perhaps the central difference was that NSC-68 offered a far more alarmist reading of the world situation and denied the idea that time was currently on the side of the United States. In place of the long-term optimism of the X-Article, NSC-68 asserted that a "continuation of present trends would result in a serious decline in the strength of the free world relative to the Soviet Union."[56] Instead of playing for time as Kennan had recommended, NSC-68 declared that "time is short."[57] This fear that time was short and was now working against the United States underpinned NSC-68's call for "a rapid build-up of political, economic, and military strength."[58] Less sure that war with the Soviets was an unlikely prospect, NSC-68 characterized a military buildup as a "precondition" for everything else the United States wanted to do in the Cold War. The writers of NSC-68 feared that without significant military exertions, containment would be "no more than a policy of bluff."[59]

In both world wars, U.S. policymakers had been able to use time to America's advantage. After being relatively unprepared for the military challenges that awaited it, the United States prevailed in both conflicts by launching massive military mobilization efforts, confronting U.S. enemies with what German Field Marshal Paul von Hindenburg called America's "pitiless industry."[60] With its homeland protected by weak neighbors and large oceans from direct attack, the United States did not need to keep its military forces in a constant state of readiness. If a military challenge arose, the United States had time to mobilize its resources. Soviet nuclear capabilities called into question whether the United States could continue to rely on its mobilization potential rather than its forces in being.[61] A nuclear first strike that destroyed America's industrial potential meant that the United States might have to fight the next world war with the forces it had at the outset rather than relying on wartime mobilization. "In the light of Soviet military capabilities," NSC-68 asked, "a question which may be of decisive importance in the event of war is the question whether there will be time to mobilize our superior human and material resources for a war effort."[62] The implication of this question for U.S. strategy was revolutionary because if answered negatively, it necessitated a large peacetime military establishment.

NSC-68 also significantly expanded the security perimeter of the United States. Rather than focus on strongpoints, it offered a universal definition of American interests captured dramatically in its argument that "a defeat of free institutions anywhere is a defeat everywhere."[63] NSC-68 rejected distinctions between vital and peripheral interests and worried instead that any "gradual withdrawal under the direct or indirect pressure of the Soviet Union" would result in America's belated discovery that it had in fact "sacrificed positions of vital interest."[64] Rather than focus on military-industrial power potential, as Kennan had, NSC-68 focused more on questions of American credibility. Throughout the Cold War, arguments about credibility came in various forms. Questions of reputation, concerns about face, references to the lessons of the 1930s, and worries about falling dominoes all centered on credibility. Do other states believe that the United States will do what it pledges to do? Will Washington defend the interests it has promised to defend? Will the United States come to the assistance of its allies if they are attacked?

One part of the credibility equation is material. A state must have the resources to carry out its threats if these threats are to be believable. It is the psychological aspects of credibility, however, that substantially expanded America's security perimeter.[65] If all the United States had to worry about were the material aspects of credibility, there would be no need to expand U.S. security commitments beyond the five areas identified by Kennan as capable of producing military power on an industrial scale. Soviet gains outside those areas would make only marginal differences in the overall balance of power, so they could be safely dismissed as peripheral. If, however, psychology was central to credibility, then any material definition of the security perimeter of the United States was insufficient.[66] In NSC-68 it is the psychological aspect of credibility that takes center stage and makes a defeat anywhere a defeat everywhere. The danger of Soviet expansion lay less in the loss of tangible resources and more in the damage those losses would inflict on perceptions of U.S. credibility. Consider what NSC-68 had to say about the Soviet crackdown on Czechoslovakia: "The shock we sustained in the destruction of Czechoslovakia was not in the measure of Czechoslovakia's material importance to us. In a material sense, her capabilities were already at Soviet disposal. But when the integrity of Czechoslovak institutions was destroyed, it was in the intangible scale of values that we registered a loss more damaging than the material loss we had already suffered."[67]

Credibility must be maintained with several audiences. The most obvious one is a state's enemies. If potential foes do not believe you can or will fight to defend your interests, attacks on those interests are far more likely. This is part of the reason why NSC-68 called for a significant military buildup, to convince the Soviets that containment was more than a bluff. This was also the reason that the United States could not ignore Soviet encroachments even in materially peripheral areas, because if the United States failed to respond to those challenges, the Soviets could conclude that the Americans might not respond to more serious challenges later.

Maintaining credibility with one's allies is also vital. If partners doubt the credibility of your pledges to protect them, they have less reason to remain allies and could be encouraged to cut a deal with your enemies. This was another area in which NSC-68 worried about the psychological component of credibility. "As we ourselves demonstrate power, confidence and a sense of moral and political direction," it argued, "so those same qualities will be evoked in Western Europe." If the United States fails to demonstrate such qualities, U.S. allies will become "demoralized."[68] NSC-68 explicitly commends the "psychological impact—the revival of confidence and hope in the future" that its proposed buildup would have on America's allies.[69]

In addition, a state has to retain credibility with its own population. If the American people began to doubt the ability or the willingness of the United States to stand up to the Soviet challenge, NSC-68 worried, they too might become demoralized. This worry posed a challenge to any particularized approach to containment that focused on strongpoints because as Secretary of State Acheson saw it, the "public mind was not delicate enough"[70] to make the distinctions Kennan had made between core and peripheral interests. What the American people would see instead were Soviet advances going unchallenged. This led the writers of NSC-68 to warn against the "imponderable, but nevertheless drastic, effect on our belief in ourselves and in our way of life," that would creep in if the United States did not respond to Soviet challenges. "Americans would feel a deep sense of responsibility and guilt for having abandoned their former friends and allies," and as a result, "our national morale would be corrupted and the integrity and vitality of our system subverted."[71] Although Kennan's more nuanced approach to containment was strategically attractive in the abstract, Acheson criticized this approach for relying on "noncommunicable" wisdom.[72]

Concern about domestic support for containment helps to explain the strident tone of NSC-68. For a top-secret government document that would not be declassified for decades, its analysis reads surprisingly like an advocacy piece. The reason for this is that NSC-68 was constructed, in part, explicitly for bureaucratic purposes. Concerns about domestic buy-in to U.S. grand strategy were limited not only to worries about public opinion but also to winning over the large and growing national security bureaucracy. One of the objectives of NSC-68, according to Acheson, was to "bludgeon" the national security bureaucracy into going along with this policy.[73]

Concerns over the psychological aspects of credibility were at the center of the Truman administration's decision to get deeply involved in the Korean War. After World War II, Kennan had privately argued that because Korea "is not of decisive strategic importance to us, our main task is to extricate ourselves without too great a loss of prestige."[74] More publicly, Acheson had indelicately placed Korea outside of the U.S. security perimeter in the Pacific by drawing that line as running along the offshore island chains from the Aleutians through Japan and into the Philippines. U.S. war plans at the time similarly maintained that if a large-scale war broke out in Asia, the United States would abandon its position in Korea. Given all this, why did the Truman administration immediately decide to come to the aid of South Korea after it was invaded by forces from the North? The answer lies in the nonmaterial aspects of credibility. Even if Korea was not particularly important to U.S. security at a physical level, it became important to U.S. security because it was attacked.

In this way, as Gaddis has concisely phrased it, NSC-68 allowed threats to define interests, rather than letting interests define threats.[75] Worries about credibility meant that the United States did not have the luxury of mapping out its areas of interest and then responding to direct threats only in those areas. Instead, the logic of NSC-68 implied that any challenge the Soviets offer represented a threat to U.S. interests. What would the Soviets conclude if the United States failed to come to the assistance of the South Koreans? What would the allies of the United States think of Washington's security guarantees if the United States failed to come to the defense of South Korea? Would the American people conclude that the United States was losing the Cold War? If communism was allowed to spread in Korea, how long would it take before areas included in the defense perimeter of the United States came under increasing threat?

Acheson likened aggression in Korea to a rotten apple in a barrel that, if left alone, would eventually spread to infect the entire barrel. More famously, President Eisenhower later captured this argument with the metaphor of falling dominoes, in which he stated that if one falls, even if that one was unimportant in itself, it had to be propped up lest all the other dominoes fall in a chain reaction. In a perhaps more telling, but less-often noted metaphor, Acheson likened this aspect of American strategy to writing blank checks to one's enemies: "In Korea the Russians presented a check which was drawn on the bank account of collective security. The Russians thought the check would bounce. . . . But to their great surprise, the teller paid it. The important thing was that the check was paid. The importance will be nothing if the next check is not paid and the bank account is not kept strong and sufficient to cover all checks which will be drawn upon it."[76]

The implication of these metaphors was that the United States had to think of its security perimeter as universal. Defending a universal security perimeter, however, was going to require a lot of resources because providing blank checks to one's opponents is likely to be an expensive proposition. NSC-68, in another departure from Kennan's analysis, emphasized the potential of the United States to generate vastly greater resources rather than the limits of those resources. Accepting the Keynesian argument that deficit spending could benefit the economy under certain circumstances, NSC-68 saw less need to make strategic choices, as the United States could easily triple or quadruple its defense spending without damaging the U.S. economy.[77]

As concerns about the psychological aspects of credibility pressured U.S. foreign policymakers to extend the security perimeter of the United States, concerns about limited resources constantly exerted a counterpressure to shrink that perimeter. This dynamic can also be seen in U.S. policy toward the Korean War. Whereas upholding U.S. security commitments by coming to the aid of South Korea made sense to Kennan, he was virtually alone in the Truman administration in dissenting from the decision to attempt to unify Korea by force of arms. Kennan calculated that this attempt was likely to be quite expensive and not worth the limited stakes the United States had in the Korean peninsula. Chinese intervention and the protracted war that followed eventually forced the United States to accept the wisdom of limiting its goals in Korea. This, however, remained controversial in U.S. politics, and General Douglas MacArthur, after being relieved of command in Korea for continuing to publicly disagree with President Truman about taking the fight into China, spoke for proponents of a universal security perimeter when he argued: "What I advocate is that we defend every place, and I say we have the capacity to do it. If you say we haven't, you admit defeat."[78]

The decision to go to war in Korea, in addition to flowing from the strategy embodied in NSC-68, also had a significant influence on the further implementation of that strategy.[79] Although Truman liked what he read in NSC-68, he saw no way of implementing it and after its initial drafting the document largely sat on the shelf collecting dust. Then, as Dean Acheson (or Paul Nitze) famously put it, "Korea came along and saved us."[80] The invasion of South Korea confirmed arguments that communism was on the march, that the dominoes were starting to fall, and that the United States was not ready, especially militarily, to respond.[81] Before the Korean War, the defense budget was only about $13–14 billion, which was a third of the federal budget and 5 percent of gross national product (GNP). During the Korean War, the defense budget grew to $40–60 billion, which was two-thirds of the federal budget and over 10 percent of GNP.[82]

Interestingly, most of this military buildup funding was spent outside of Korea, especially in Europe. This buildup in Europe was premised on the fear that the decision to invade South Korea might merely be a feint to draw U.S. attention away from Europe and thus ease Soviet advances there. For those, like Kennan, who were concerned about limited U.S. resources, this was an argument for keeping U.S. commitments in Korea as limited as possible. For those less concerned with the costs involved in a universal approach to containment, this was an argument for making the buildup so massive that the United States could handle both a large war in Korea and whatever the Soviets threw at America in Europe. The tension between focusing on core areas of concern to the material interests of the United States and defending a universal periphery would run throughout the entire Cold War era.

The Continuing Relevance of the Early Cold War

The debates that the Truman administration grappled with in the early days of the Cold War not only reverberated throughout the containment era, but are still relevant to foreign policy debates today. Is time on America's side in the War on Terror, with the rise of China, and in dealing with rogue states? Does America need to launch a crusade against its enemies or can Washington simply wait out its enemies, relying on what Bohlen called an "element of rational hope" that ultimately the United States would offer a more attractive and promising political model than that offered by its opponents? Or is the United States falling behind? As Secretary of Defense Donald Rumsfeld worried with regard to terrorism, "we lack metrics to know if we are winning or losing the global war on terror. Are we capturing, killing or deterring and dissuading more terrorists every day than the madrassas and the radical clerics are recruiting, training and deploying against us?"[83] Similarly, does time make the clerical regime in Iran or Kim Jong-Un's regime in North Korea stronger and more dangerous opponents or does it allow the opportunity for domestic reformers in both countries to change their governments from within in a way that will decrease the level of conflict with the United States? Indeed, the entire issue of preemptive or preventive war is a question of whether time is on the side of the United States or its enemies.

How should the United States define its security perimeter in a war on terror? Can the United States point to key areas of the world to focus the country's limited resources or do concerns about credibility require the United States to defend everywhere? Adopting a strong-point approach to the War on Terror would certainly be more affordable and require fewer interventions than a universal approach, but does it risk strengthening unappeasable enemies and demoralizing potential allies abroad and at home? Speaking of allies, how important are they for the United States? How much does Washington need the support of its allies in implementing its grand strategy or is the United States capable of executing its grand strategy on a mostly unilateral basis? Should potential rising powers be kept weak so they represent less of a threat or should their growth be encouraged as a way of strengthening support for a U.S.-backed multilateral order?

America's attempts to implement containment throughout the Cold War, the story of which will be continued in subsequent chapters, will help provide an additional historical perspective for grappling with these recurring questions in U.S. foreign policy.

Debating the Implementation of Containment

Eisenhower, Kennedy, and Johnson

The election of Dwight Eisenhower returned the Republican Party to the White House for the first time in twenty years. Although the rhetoric surrounding Eisenhower's campaign suggested that a major readjustment in U.S. foreign policy was in the offing, once Eisenhower was in power, containment remained at the heart of U.S. grand strategy. This pattern repeated itself eight years later when John F. Kennedy returned the White House to Democratic control in 1960 and also retained containment as the organizing principle for U.S. foreign policy. The continuity of containment did not mean that debates over U.S. foreign policy ceased. As was the case under the Truman administration, important debates remained about the best way of implementing containment, and U.S. foreign policy needed to be constantly updated to deal with new developments. This chapter explores how the Eisenhower and Kennedy administrations accepted and revised containment.

Rejecting Rollback

One of the most important decisions the Eisenhower administration made when it came to power was to accept containment rather than a more ambitious strategy aimed at rollback as the centerpiece of U.S. foreign policy. Well before he was a presidential candidate Eisenhower argued that U.S. security did not require any crusade to topple the Soviet government. In speeches given in 1946, using Lincoln's house-divided metaphor, Eisenhower stressed that the former president had not argued that "two houses constructed differently, of different materials, of different appearance could not stand in peace within the same block" and that "good neighbors do not pry into the domestic life of each other's families."[1] Even in the heat of the presidential campaign, Eisenhower and his soon-to-be secretary of state, John Foster Dulles, limited their rhetoric about rollback as an alternative to containment. When he discussed the possibilities of actively pushing the Soviets backward, Dulles tended to limit the means of rollback to nonmilitary instruments of power and stressed how long it would take to produce significant internal changes within the Soviet bloc. Similarly, when candidate Eisenhower talked about liberation he too stressed long-term peaceful means with the United States in the role of a model rather than a crusading state.[2] One problem the United States faced in presenting itself as a democratic model for the world, however, stemmed from the continuing presence of racial discrimination at home. Eisenhower recognized the damage this was doing to the image of the United States abroad but his dispositional caution and limited view of the proper role of the federal government led him to a generally passive and reactive response to the issue. As a Promised Lander, he preferred slow evolution over more ambitious attempts at revolution.[3]

If Eisenhower's rhetoric during the campaign was kept limited, the realities of government also dampened his administration's enthusiasm for rollback as a successor organizing principle for American foreign policy. Whereas Dulles expressed "some sympathy . . . in favor of greater dynamism in the American attitude toward the Soviet Union," seeing it as consistent with what he had called for during the presidential campaign, he also stressed: "experience indicated that it was not easy to go very much beyond the point that this Administration had reached in translating a dynamic policy into courses of action." Directly addressing calls for "strong and forceful measures to change the basic character of the Soviet system," Dulles concluded "that this kind of aggressive policy was not in the best interest of the United States."[4]

Early in his tenure in the White House, Eisenhower directed a large-scale study of U.S. foreign policy options in an effort that became known as the Solarium Project. The methodology of the Solarium Project was to appoint different teams to assess various foreign policy options and to make the best case they could for a selected path forward. One of these teams, Team A led by George Kennan, was to argue for a continuation of containment. Another group, Team C, was selected to make the case for rollback. (There was also a Team B that advocated for a more assertive form of containment according to which the United States would draw a line around the Soviet Union and threaten the Soviets with general war if they crossed that line at any point.)

The principal and ultimately unbridgeable gap between the reports of Team A and Team C centered on the question of whether time was working for the United States or against it. Team A argued that time was on America's side so rollback was too costly, provocative, and ultimately unnecessary. Team C, conversely, asserted that time was working against the United States, which meant that containing the Soviets would simply lead to a slow defeat of the United States and that a bolder policy of rollback was there-fore required. Team C spoke for the critics of containment in the Republican Party, such as Arizona Senator Barry Goldwater, who saw the Soviet Union as more determined than the United States to win the Cold War and the defen-sive nature of containment as leading to slow defeat rather than eventual victory.[5] Eisenhower's conviction that time was on America's side ensured the victory of Team A and the continuation of containment.[6] Containment, however, as it would be throughout the Cold War, was the starting point for debates about U.S. grand strategy, not the ending point.

Eisenhower's New Look

One question containment begged was how to delineate the security perim-eter of the United States. Where do the Soviets have to be contained and what areas of the world, if any, were outside of U.S. strategic concerns? On this debate, Eisenhower sided with the universalism of National Security Council Report 68 (NSC-68), rather than with Kennan's military-industrial strongpoints. In his inaugural address, the new president explicitly dis-missed any attempt to rank different parts of the world as more or less im-portant to U.S. interests. Echoing NSC-68 claims that a defeat anywhere is a defeat everywhere, Eisenhower argued that he held "the defense of free-dom, like freedom itself to be one and indivisible" and that the United States "hold[s] all continents and peoples in equal regard and honor. We reject any insinuation that one race or another, one people or another, is in any sense inferior or expendable."[7]

As with NSC-68 it was concerns about credibility that drove the adminis-tration to accept such an expansive security perimeter. Indeed, it was Eisen-hower who popularized the most enduring image of credibility worries in U.S. foreign policy by introducing the falling domino metaphor to a na-tional audience. At a press conference on April 7, 1954, when asked about the importance of Indochina to the United States, Eisenhower, after initially talking about the material value of the area, concluded: "you have broader considerations that might follow what you would call the 'falling domino' principle. You have a row of dominoes set up, you knock over the first one, and what will happen to the last one is the certainty that it will go over very quickly. So you could have a beginning of a disintegration that would have the most profound influences."[8] If Vietnam were allowed to fall to com-munism, then Burma, Thailand, Indonesia, and eventually Japan would be threatened. The logic of the domino theory undermines any attempt to focus on strongpoints in U.S. foreign policy because the survival of those strong-points is seen as dependent on the protection of their peripheries.

Strategy requires matching means to ends. If the United States were going to defend a universal security perimeter, what means did it have available to do this? Here, Eisenhower found himself more aligned with Kennan's analysis than with the more optimistic economic assumptions of NSC-68. Instead of believing that U.S. foreign policy means could be easily expanded as NSC-68 had asserted, Eisenhower was determined to keep down the costs of the Cold War. As a fiscal conservative, Eisenhower doubted the Keynesian notion that deficit spending could be good for the economy and instead saw balanced budgets as a key measure of fiscal responsibility. According to Andrew Goodpaster, his White House staff secretary, Eisenhower was convinced that spending on the level recommended by NSC-68 "would not be sustainable on a long term basis."[9] If the Cold War was likely to be a protracted struggle, Eisenhower wanted to do more than assert that time was on America's side, he wanted to ensure that time did work to the advantage of the United States by keeping the U.S. economy and society strong, and this mandated keeping defense costs in check. What was the point of amassing foreign policy resources to deal with the Soviets in the short term, when those expenditures crowded out other spending that would be more important for the long-term health of the United States. As Eisenhower put it in what is perhaps his most eloquent speech as president:

> Every gun that is made, every warship launched, every rocket fired signifies, in the final sense, a theft from those who hunger and are not fed, those who are cold and are not clothed. This world in arms is not spending money alone. It is spending the sweat of its laborers, the genius of its scientists, the hopes of its children. The cost of one modern heavy bomber is this: a modern brick school in more than 30 cities. It is two electric power plants, each serving a town of 60,000 population. It is two fine, fully equipped hospitals. It is some 50 miles of concrete highway. We pay for a single fighter plane with a half a million bushels of wheat. We pay for a single destroyer with new homes that could have housed more than 8,000 people. . . . This is not a way of life at all, in any true sense. Under the cloud of threatening war, it is humanity hanging from a cross of iron.[10]

Beyond worrying about squandering money that could be better invested in the American economy and society, Eisenhower also worried that large defense expenditures could undermine the very way of life that it was meant to protect.[11] Eisenhower's farewell address is perhaps best known today for its political warning about the "acquisition of unwanted influence" in U.S. government "by the military-industrial complex." Eisenhower's fears also had a strong economic component. Because the Cold War was likely "to be of indefinite duration," Eisenhower worried that Americans would fall victim to the "temptation that some spectacular and costly action could become the miraculous solution to all current difficulties." Instead of succumbing to that temptation, Eisenhower implored the country not to overreact to any crises that arose in a way that undermined long-term U.S. strength: "Another factor in maintaining balance involves the element of time. As we peer into society's future, we—you and I, and our government must avoid the impulse to live only for today, plundering, for our own ease and convenience, the precious resources of tomorrow. We cannot mortgage the material assets of our grandchildren without risking the loss also of their political and spiritual heritage. We want democracy to survive for all generations to come, not to become the insolvent phantom of tomorrow."[12]

Pursuing containment universally, while simultaneously trying to limit costs, presented a strategic puzzle. How does one defend an unlimited perimeter with limited resources? Kennan avoided this problem by constricting the areas he wanted the United States to defend. NSC-68 avoided this problem by assuming that the United States had virtually unlimited means at its disposal. Unwilling to limit ends or increase means, Eisenhower opted to vary the ways in which the United States used its resources. There is no free lunch in grand strategy, however, and in order to implement his strategy, Eisenhower had to accept greater risk.[13]

Eisenhower called his reevaluation of U.S. ways of implementing containment, the "New Look." At the heart of Eisenhower's approach was a disinclination to compete with the Soviets based on the means Moscow chose, but instead an attempt to pit U.S. strengths against Soviet weaknesses. The goal of the New Look was to stave off Soviet challenges at a vastly cheaper price than that entailed by the more symmetrical approach of NSC-68. One U.S. strength, in the president's view, was its allies.[14] From his service in World War II and as the first supreme allied commander of NATO, Eisenhower had extensive experience in dealing with the European allies of the United States. A recovered Great Britain, France, and Germany, Eisenhower calculated, could pick up many of the costs that the United States was currently bearing in confronting the Soviet Union. As the administration concluded in National Security Council Report 162/2 (NSC-162/2), the United States could not "meet its defense needs, even at exorbitant costs, without the support of allies."[15] Minimizing the U.S. cost of the Cold War thus made multilateralism an important part of the New Look. By using what Eisenhower saw as the "great industrial complex of Western Europe," the United States could prosecute the Cold War at a lower cost.[16]

Although it reduced costs, relying on allies to bear more of the burdens of the Cold War introduced certain risks into U.S. foreign policy. The United States could be dragged into a conflict by the actions of its allies. The weakness of allies could force the United States to expend resources in their defense. Needed allies could threaten to defect and disagreement among allies could prevent concerted action. For example, during the Eisenhower years it was the weakness of France's position that first pulled the United States more deeply into Vietnam and it was the continuing weakness of America's Vietnamese allies that kept the United States involved in Vietnam long after the French had left. Similarly, when the French and the British collaborated with the Israelis to try to remove Nasser's regime in Egypt, the United

States was inevitably pulled into the resulting Suez Crisis. For Eisenhower, as for Truman, such risks were worth running if it meant that America's allies could shoulder a larger share of the burden of the Cold War.

Another way of prosecuting the Cold War at lower cost was to rely more heavily on relatively inexpensive "psychological operations." Such operations go under many names, including propaganda, information operations, public diplomacy, and public relations. At their root these operations entail using rhetoric, ideas, and argument to advance a state's cause or to undermine an enemy's. Since talk is cheap, exploiting ideas, rhetoric, and argument was not going to push the federal budget into the red. Publicly denouncing the evils of communism and hinting at American support for the rollback of the Soviet empire through the liberation of captive states did not cost the United States anything materially as long as that support remained rhetorical. Such statements, however, could increase the challenges the Soviets faced within their sphere of influence and force Moscow to expend its own material resources to counter U.S. claims or the internal threats that can result from them. If the U.S. system was superior to the Soviet one, moving the Cold War competition into the realm of ideas was a cheap and potentially effective way of prosecuting that war.

The administration's approach to negotiations with the Soviets can also be seen in part as a form of psychological operations. Eisenhower and Dulles shared the doubts of Kennan and the writers of NSC-68 about what concrete achievements could result from negotiations with Moscow. Even given such doubts, however, a willingness to negotiate was still an important part of U.S. foreign policy as it was a low-cost way of bolstering Washington's image and building alliance relationships.

Psychological operations were materially inexpensive but they also introduced risks into U.S. grand strategy. If a country within the Soviet orbit responded to U.S. calls for liberation, was the United States then willing to move from moral to material support? Psychological operations can also set up the U.S. public and its allies for disillusionment if physical actions do not follow rhetoric. How long can the United States talk about rollback and support for liberation without offering tangible resources to further those causes? Could the United States remain a Crusader State in rhetoric, but not in action? If credibility was central to the Cold War struggle, was it only a matter of time before the United States had to back up its claims with physical resources?

Covert operations were also seen as a potentially promising Cold War tool. Attempting to prop up challenged governments across the globe with large conventional military forces would require far more resources than Eisenhower thought it prudent to spend. Smaller amounts of money, used in the right way by covert operators might be a more cost-effective approach for fending off potential Soviet challenges and supporting governments allied to the United States. U.S. covert operations scored initial successes in Iran (1953) and Guatemala (1954), but failed to get the desired results in Indonesia (1958) and Cuba (1960–61). These failures demonstrate the risks inherent in such an approach, and moreover, even when initially successful, as in Iran in 1953, the long-term costs to U.S. foreign policy of associating the United States with unpopular leaders would also prove to be one of the risks inherent in this part of Eisenhower's strategy.

Nuclear weapons and the doctrine of massive retaliation also played a central role in the New Look. As John Foster Dulles defined massive retaliation, it meant that the United States would "be willing and able to respond vigorously at places and with means of its own choosing" with a "deterrent of massive retaliatory power."[17] Stripped to its essentials, massive retaliation meant that the United States would threaten to go to a nuclear war to deter conventional Soviet challenges to U.S. interests. Trying to defend Western Europe, for example, with conventional forces would be an expensive undertaking and would shift the competition in the Cold War into an arena where the Soviets had a relative advantage, both in size and location. In the phrase of the day, however, nuclear weapons provided far "more bang for the buck." If conventional forces were to be used in distant theaters, Eisenhower preferred that these forces be supplied by local allies rather than the United States, as Washington would concentrate on providing cheaper nuclear forces. As a result, whereas Eisenhower attempted to limit the growth of the defense budget, nuclear weapons and their means of delivery were a growth area in that budget.

Nuclear weapons were still a relatively new technology and the Eisenhower administration had to figure out what these weapons could and could not do in U.S. grand strategy. As a foreign policy tool, nuclear weapons also brought the issue of credibility to the forefront of U.S. concerns. Could the U.S. threat to respond massively to Soviet challenges be believed? If the threat was seen as a bluff, it would not be an effective deterrent. Credibility concerns were particularly problematic for Eisenhower because his administration was seeking to use nuclear weapons to defend a global security perimeter. It might be relatively easy to convince Moscow that Washington would use nuclear weapons if the Soviets invaded California, but what if the Soviet challenge entailed a proxy force challenging a U.S. ally at a distant point on the Asian mainland? How important and direct did the Soviet challenge have to be before others would see America's threat of massive retaliation as credible? Could massive retaliation be undermined by "salami tactics," according to which the Soviet Union made each individual challenge small enough to avoid provoking a massive U.S. response, but over time the individual slices added up to significant gains?[18] Such questions were more than theoretical. For example, in 1953–54 when Mainland China threatened to take two small islands (Quemoy and Matsu) from the nationalist government on Taiwan both the secretary of state and the president publicly commented that the United States would consider using nuclear weapons to defend the islands.

The Eisenhower administration was aware of the difficulties of making such threats credible and took steps to ameliorate them. Deliberately creating uncertainty was one way of dealing with the credibility problem. If the Soviets (or any potential enemy) were never sure about what actions would provoke a massive nuclear response, this uncertainty could induce caution. Even if the probability of a nuclear escalation was low, the mere possibility of it might be enough to deter challenges. As for salami tactics, why would an aggressor risk a nuclear war, even if that risk were small, for a minor gain?

Another way of decreasing the credibility problem is to make the jump from conventional to nuclear forces less stark. By pursuing lower-yield nuclear weapons that created a new category of tactical nuclear weapons, the line between conventional and nuclear forces could become blurred. If lower-yield, tactical nuclear weapons were just other weapons in the arsenal, threatening their use in response to lower-level conventional attacks would be seen as inherently more credible.[19] Under Eisenhower the army reorganized itself into "pentomic divisions" that were designed to give U.S. troops the dispersion and mobility they would need to fight effectively on a nuclear battlefield where tactical nuclear weapons served mainly as more destructive artillery rather than as a qualitatively different type of weapon.[20]

Another way of making the deterrent threats of the United States more credible was to bolster U.S. stakes in threatened areas through tough talk, alliances, or tripwire forces. Even if a particular region or conflict was of little material interest to the United States, once the president went on record as saying that it was important and that any hostile actions would provoke a serious U.S. response, that issue would become more important to the United States because reputational costs would now be added to the physical costs of inaction. Alliance commitments are a more formalized version of this tactic. Once the United States made an official commitment to defend a certain place, that commitment increased the interests the United States had at stake because now any conflict there involved not just that region alone, but the value of all U.S. foreign policy commitments. This helps explain the Eisenhower administration's penchant for formal alliance commitments, as they served a credibility purpose. Putting small numbers of U.S. troops into contested areas as tripwire forces is also a way of increasing credibility because it ensures that even limited attacks would result in U.S. casualties, which makes U.S. retaliation more likely. Thomas Schelling looked at the isolated U.S. garrison in Berlin and asked what this small group of soldiers could do against a determined Soviet attack. "Bluntly," he answered, "they can die. They can die heroically, dramatically, in a way that guarantees that action cannot stop there."[21]

Credibility could also be manufactured by combining these methods. One example would be putting the newly developed tactical nuclear weapons in the hands of forward-based U.S. military commanders. A decision maker who is safe in Washington might be more hesitant to initiate the first use of nuclear weapons in response to a conventional attack than would a commander in the field who finds his position in danger of being overrun. Similarly, supporting allied development of nuclear weapons or giving allies some control over the use of U.S. nuclear weapons could also bolster credibility because in this case the allies' homeland would be under immediate threat.

As with the New Look as a whole, the cost savings from a greater reliance on nuclear deterrence came at the expense of introducing greater risk in U.S. foreign policy. What if a specific nuclear threat was defied? This would leave the Eisenhower administration with the unpalatable choice of either initiating a nuclear war or backing down. U.S. efforts to build credibility also increased the danger of putting the United States in the position of having its commitments in a particular area far outweigh its material interests in that area. Credibility concerns feed on themselves because the more America stresses its commitments, the more committed it is. As Frank Ninkovich aptly observed of the entire U.S. Cold War strategy, "Diplomatic commerce in the coin of credibility was inherently inflationary."[22] Furthermore, any steps taken to make nuclear threats more credible by decentralizing command and control over nuclear weapons increased the risk of accidental or unauthorized launches.

The key reason that these risks were acceptable to Eisenhower is that Washington possessed an overwhelming nuclear advantage. The United States had a large air defense system under construction, its intercontinental jet bombers were coming into production in large numbers, its atomic stockpile was growing, and it possessed a string of air bases around the Soviet Union. Conversely, the Soviets possessed only a small number of atomic weapons and had no reliable way of delivering them. None of their aircraft could make the round trip to the United States and back (although a one-way trip was possible) and they had no bases close to the United States. As a result, mutually assured destruction was not guaranteed and any nuclear exchange was likely to hurt the Soviet Union far more than the United States.

The U.S. nuclear advantage suffered a serious psychological blow on October 4, 1957, when the Soviets succeeded in putting a satellite into orbit. If the Soviets could put Sputnik into space atop a missile, they were well on the way to creating a missile that could reach the United States. Since the United States had no effective defense against missiles, the capability demonstrated by Sputnik meant that the United States was now far more vulnerable to a Soviet nuclear attack. Sputnik presented a clear challenge to the credibility of U.S. commitments to its allies. Now that the Soviets had a demonstrated retaliatory capability against the American homeland, were U.S. pledges to defend its overseas allies with nuclear weapons still credible?

Could America's nuclear deterrent still be extended so easily to its allies now that the United States was no longer immune from Soviet nuclear retaliation? Would the United States be willing to trade New York to defend Paris?

Sputnik was also a blow to U.S. confidence that time was on its side in the Cold War. The launching of a man-made satellite was a major technological achievement and the Soviets had accomplished it first. In ways that are hard to imagine now given the eventual failures of the Soviet economic model, at the time, many in the United States feared that this model was succeeding. In the immediate postwar years the Soviets were racking up impressive rates of economic growth. Whereas much of this growth was the result of starting from a small and war-devastated base, if these trends continued, maybe time was working to the Soviets' advantage and not to America's. More ominously, technology was supposed to be an area of particular U.S. strength, but here were the Soviets beating the United States to the technological punch.

If time was not on America's side, a grand strategy of patience like containment was a losing one. In response to Sputnik, *Life* magazine ran articles "Arguing the Case for Being Panicky." Lyndon Johnson, a potential Democratic presidential aspirant, characterized Eisenhower's patience as dithering and causing Washington to fall behind Moscow. In the presidential campaign of 1960, John F. Kennedy would make the supposed missile gap between the United States and the Soviet Union a major issue. Despite these criticisms, Eisenhower stuck with the patience that was at the core of his New Look approach to containment.[23] Rather than pour money into more missiles or missile defense, Eisenhower believed that "this alarm could be turned to a constructive result" and opted to focus America's post-Sputnik energies on educational and civilian technological efforts that he maintained would better prepare the United States for the long-term struggle with the Soviet Union.[24] One informational advantage Eisenhower had over his critics was his access to intelligence gathered by the U-2 spy plane, which demonstrated that even after the shock of Sputnik, the Soviet Union was still far behind the United States in its nuclear delivery capability. There was a missile gap, but it was in America's favor.

The Sputnik episode does, however, demonstrate one of the problems of the New Look as an approach to containment. Although Eisenhower's strategy was explicitly designed for the long term, the credibility of its nuclear pillar depended to a large extent on America's massive post–World War II nuclear advantage. This advantage, though, was unlikely to hold for the long term. In the years immediately after Sputnik, Eisenhower could still be confident in the U.S. nuclear advantage but for how long could his successors depend on this as a lasting advantage? As the Eisenhower administration itself recognized, "increasing Soviet atomic capability may tend to diminish the deterrent effect of U.S. atomic power against peripheral Soviet aggression" and "as general war becomes more devastating for both sides the threat to resort to it becomes less available as a sanction against local aggression."[25] This became on object of intense internal debate in the later years of the Eisenhower administration as key advisers like John Foster Dulles responded to the Soviets' growing nuclear capability by calling for a conventional buildup similar to what, under Kennedy and Johnson, would be called "Flexible Response" to give Washington more options than just the threat of massive nuclear retaliation. President Eisenhower continued to hold the line against a large conventional buildup but he nevertheless became far more conciliatory and open to negotiation in crises that risked a nuclear exchange, such as those over Berlin or Quemoy and Matsu.[26]

Even with its nuclear pillar intact, the New Look failed to square the circle of defending a universal security perimeter at a low cost. When the French faced defeat in Vietnam, the United States had no inexpensive and effective means of helping them. Eisenhower's assertion, "If we have the weapons to win a big war, we can certainly win a small one," turned out to be wrong.[27] Although it provided a great deal of material support to the French, more direct U.S. intervention in Vietnam was ruled out once the administration failed to generate greater allied or congressional support.[28] With France reaching the limits of its ability to hold on and Britain averse to greater intervention, the allies of the United States could do little to help prevent a communist victory in North Vietnam. Psychological operations and covert actions were ineffective and nuclear weapons were largely irrelevant. Closer to home, the Eisenhower administration also proved unable to prevent Fidel Castro's victory in Cuba.

When faced with the trade-off between maintaining a universal security perimeter and the costs that more direct intervention would have required, Eisenhower accepted losses on the perimeter, which pushed him closer to Kennan's more limited conception of the geographical scope of containment. Eisenhower was averse to Ho Chi Minh's victory in North Vietnam or Fidel Castro's in Cuba but he could not defend a universal security perimeter at a tolerable cost. Just as credibility concerns expanded the security perimeter of the United States, cost concerns constricted it. As a Republican and a war hero, Eisenhower was in a relatively strong position domestically to accept these foreign policy defeats. Because it was the Democratic Party that had been blamed for "losing China" and because Eisenhower's impressive military record made him immune to charges that he was weak against U.S. enemies, Eisenhower faced fewer constraints at home than his immediate successors would.[29]

Kennedy, Johnson, and Flexible Response

Upon taking the oath of office, John F. Kennedy affirmed that "the torch has been passed to a new generation of Americans," an image that symbolized both continuity and change. Focusing on the continuities, the Kennedy administration not only accepted containment as the overarching concept for U.S. grand strategy but also accepted many of the specifics of that strategy as pursued by both the Truman and Eisenhower administrations. The Kennedy team was squarely in the Cold War consensus with regard to the importance of multilateralism in the Cold War. Speaking of U.S. allies in his inaugural address, the new president argued that, "United there is little we cannot do in a host of cooperative ventures. Divided there is little we can do."[30]

As had the authors of NSC-68 and Eisenhower as well, the new team also embraced a global security perimeter for the United States. In support of his first defense budget, Kennedy argued that U.S. security "can be endangered not only by a nuclear attack, but also by being slowly nibbled away at the periphery, regardless of our strategic power."[31] Rejecting the distinctions Kennan had stressed between core and peripheral interests, Kennedy's secretary of state, Dean Rusk, maintained that, "If you don't pay attention to the periphery, the periphery changes. And the first thing you know the periphery is the center."[32] The rhetoric of the young president celebrated the unlimited nature of U.S. interests and responsibilities. The United States, Kennedy averred, was willing to "pay any price, bear any burden, meet any hardship, support any friend, oppose any foe to assure the survival and the success of liberty."[33]

This expansive vision of U.S. interests did not mean that the Kennedy administration embraced rollback over containment. The Cold War remained a challenge to be overcome not a battle to be won. As the president explained, "the trumpet summons us again—not as a call to bear arms, though arms we need—not as a call to battle, though embattled we are—but a call to bear the burden of a long twilight struggle, year in and year out, 'rejoicing in hope, patient in tribulation.'" Using the image of the United States as the Promised Land rather than as a Crusader State, Kennedy argued that U.S. efforts "will light our country . . . and the glow from that fire can truly light the world."[34]

If the Kennedy administration was going to play the role of exemplar, however, it was going to be an active one. Here is an area in which the new administration differed from its predecessor. As long as the costs of containment were kept manageable, Eisenhower believed that time was on the side of the United States. Kennedy was far less sanguine and, as a presidential candidate, he warned against assuming that the world was "bright and promising and moving in our direction." Instead, he saw a world in flux and worried that "Africa, Latin America, and Asia will all change. The question is, will they move with us or will they move with Mr. Khrushchev? Will they decide that the future belongs to him or to us?" To ensure that history moved in America's direction, Kennedy insisted that the next president had to "give an impression around the world of force and vitality."[35] This preference for

activism also made Kennedy, and especially Lyndon Johnson, more energetic than Eisenhower had been in advancing the civil rights movement in
America.[36]

This fear that time was working against the United States was not limited
to Kennedy. Writing in 1960, Henry Kissinger worried that, "Throughout a
decade of almost continuous decline the notion that time was on our side
has been the basis of much of our policy." Such mistaken convictions, in Kissinger's assessment, led to "passive" policies that "doomed us to sterility."
Like Kennedy he called for a new dynamism in U.S. foreign policy and for
embracing a universal security perimeter. After listing a series of tasks facing the United States, Kissinger concluded, "If we cannot do all these things,
we will not be able to do any of them."[37]

The Kennedy team, in its self-conception, represented the youthful men of
action and vigor who were replacing the elder statesmen of the Eisenhower
years. Whereas Eisenhower stressed the importance of not overreacting to
events like the launch of Sputnik, Ho Chi Minh's victories in Vietnam, and
the revolution in Cuba, Kennedy emphasized the importance of boldness
and decisive actions. As one State Department official, quoting Winston
Churchill, characterized the spirit of the Kennedy administration, "It is a
pushing age, and we must shove with the best."[38] As always, separating boldness and confidence from arrogance would prove difficult.[39]

The United States cannot simply be a status quo power and trust that it
will win in the end, Kennedy argued in his speech in acceptance of the Democratic nomination for president, because "today there can be no status quo."
"The world is changing. The old era is ending. The old ways will not do."[40]
Kennedy feared that time was working against the United States. Just days
after taking office he warned Congress that, "Each day the crises multiply.
Each day their solution grows more difficult. Each day we draw nearer the
hour of maximum danger, . . . in each of the principal areas of crisis—the tide
of events has been running out and time has not been our friend."[41] For Kennedy the United States could not resist change, nor could it blithely assume
that it was on the right side of change, instead it had to more actively work
to make sure that time operated in its favor.

One of the difficulties the New Look had encountered was in dealing with
nationalist revolutions in former colonial areas. Rather than resisting such
movements, Kennedy reasoned that the United States was better off embracing them. In what was perhaps his most noteworthy foreign policy speech
as a senator, discussing U.S. and French policy in Algeria, Kennedy argued
that "Instead of abandoning African nationalism to the anti-Western agita-
tors and Soviet agents who hope to capture its leadership, the United States,
a product of political revolution, must redouble its efforts to earn the respect
and friendship of nationalist leaders."[42] Later in his presidency, rather than
talk about Woodrow Wilson's goal of making the world safe for democracy,
Kennedy instead talked about making "the world safe for diversity."[43]

Accepting diversity in practice, however, proved more difficult than accepting it in rhetoric. Nationalist revolutions, even if not clearly communist, could still threaten America's credibility in the Cold War. Because the United States feared the perception of weakness or humiliation, its grand strategy entailed, aside from geographic universalism, a certain amount of ideological universalism as well. Fears of falling dominoes undermined any attempt to accept diversity if that diversity was seen as a blow to America's global standing. The United States may not have needed to dominate the world to be secure, but it did have to be sure that no one else could. If all commitments are interdependent, however, the most effective means of ensuring that no one else could dominate the world was to avoid any losses, material or perceived.

Another area in which the Kennedy and Johnson administrations differentiated their policy from their predecessor was in the attempt to minimize the reliance of the United States on its nuclear weapons. As the Soviets increased their nuclear arsenal and improved their delivery systems, the risks of relying on nuclear deterrence and the threat of massive retaliation increased enormously. Even if they had not yet reached nuclear parity, once the Soviets had the capability to make the assured destruction of a nuclear conflict mutual, Kennedy and Johnson believed that U.S. policy had to change. Kennedy feared that relying too much on the nation's nuclear arsenal could force U.S. foreign policy into a corner, where its only options would be to do nothing or to start a devastating nuclear war. Pushing the Soviets into a correspondingly uncomfortable position with nuclear threats and brinkmanship was similarly dangerous. As Kennedy saw it, "nuclear powers must avert those confrontations which bring an adversary to a choice of either a humiliating retreat or a nuclear war."[44] There had to be options in between, and Kennedy wanted a military policy that would provide those options.

The development of capabilities to give the president more flexibility, however, required a conventional buildup that Eisenhower had been unwilling to pay for. Kennedy's decision to pursue this buildup came, not coincidentally, at a time when the United States was downgrading its estimate of Soviet conventional capabilities. As long as Moscow's conventional advantage in Europe was seen as unassailable, the incentive for any American conventional buildup was small. Once Soviet capabilities were seen as more limited, however, a nonnuclear balance became a possibility worth pursuing.

Flexible Response did not mean that the United States would take nuclear weapons or the threat of massive retaliation off the table. Even after it increased conventional forces in Europe, the United States remained unwilling to declare a "no first use" policy with regard to its nuclear weapons. Still seeing itself as the weaker side conventionally, Washington wanted to retain the option of using nuclear weapons to hold off a conventional Soviet assault, even if that option would not be America's first choice. Indeed, part of

Flexible Response entailed creating more limited and adaptable nuclear options, instead of just using the bulk of U.S. nuclear forces in a spasm of massive retaliation. Continued doubts in military circles about whether a nuclear exchange could be kept limited, however, meant that Kennedy faced much bureaucratic resistance to translating this part of Flexible Response into operational plans.[45]

Fundamentally, the basic idea of Flexible Response was to tailor America's actions to fit the situation as closely as possible. If credibility was a central concern of the New Look, calibration was a central concern of Flexible Response. The goal was to have an array of options that would allow the United States to avoid doing too much or too little in response to any Soviet challenge. Precise calibration is laudable in intent but it is difficult in a field as complex as foreign policy. Calibration requires an ability to measure, whereas some of the most important variables in any foreign policy crisis, such as the commitment of an enemy to a particular outcome, may resist precise quantification. Another difficulty lies in determining toward whom your response should be calibrated. Should your response be calibrated to assure your allies, calculated to deter your enemies, measured to persuade neutrals, or designed to maintain domestic support? If the answer is all of the above, how tailored can any response be, given these multiple audiences? Calibration also requires that the receivers of your policies read the same messages that you intended to send. Calibration is attractive in theory but problematic in practice.

Another potential difficulty with Flexible Response was its affordability. As Andrew Bacevich observes, "an enthusiasm for limited war served chiefly to open the door to unlimited military expenditures."[46] Eisenhower had purposively limited the ways in which he implemented U.S. foreign policy because of his concerns about limited means. This strategic choice, as discussed above, introduced greater risk into U.S. grand strategy. Kennedy and Johnson were unwilling to accept that increased risk. They could have decreased the risk by scaling back America's goals, but their conviction that America's security perimeter was global foreclosed that option. Instead, Kennedy and Johnson attempted to keep the ends, ways, means, and risk equation in balance for U.S. grand strategy by expanding the means available to implement that strategy. Rejecting the fiscal conservatism of Eisenhower for a more Keynesian approach where government deficits could spur future growth, Kennedy and Johnson believed that the United States could indeed afford to pay any price and bear any burden.

To understand the advantages and disadvantages of Flexible Response, it is instructive to consider two cases from the Kennedy and Johnson era, one often pointed to as statesmanship at its best in Kennedy's handling of the Cuban Missile Crisis, and the other often pointed to as statesmanship at its worst—the way that Kennedy and Johnson handled the conflict in Vietnam. Both were examples of Flexible Response in action, but their outcomes differed significantly.

The U.S. discovery that the Soviets were installing intermediate range nuclear missiles in Cuba provoked perhaps the most dangerous crisis of the Cold War. In Robert Kennedy's dramatic retelling of the crisis he notes that although "a small minority" argued that "the missiles did not alter the balance of power and therefore necessitated no action," "the general feeling in the beginning was that some form of action was required" and that the president himself "was convinced from the beginning that he would have to do something." Although it made little material difference whether a missile delivering a nuclear warhead on a U.S. city originated in Cuba or elsewhere, credibility concerns convinced Kennedy that the United States had to resist the Soviet move. "If we did nothing," Kennedy worried, "the Russians would move on Berlin and in other areas of the world, feeling the U.S. was completely impotent."[47]

Trying to minimize the risks of brinkmanship in a nuclear crisis, Kennedy preferred policies that kept his options open rather than limited them. Instead of threatening a nuclear war, invading Cuba, or bombing the missile sites, Kennedy ordered a blockade of Cuba until the missiles were removed. The quarantine of Cuba, as the Kennedy team euphemistically referred to it, demonstrated U.S. concerns without escalating to nuclear threats or to the offensive use of force. To further avoid pushing the Soviets into a corner, Kennedy also privately promised to remove U.S. missiles in Turkey and even made plans for making that trade public if it were necessary in order to resolve the crisis, as long as the proposal was seen as coming from the secretary general of the United Nations, rather than as a Soviet demand. No public exchange was needed, however, because the Soviets agreed to pull the missiles out of Cuba in return for the private pledge regarding the U.S. missiles in Turkey and a promise from the United States that it would not invade Cuba.[48] Kennedy's preference for a private pledge to remove the missiles in Turkey rather than a public one underscores the idea that credibility concerns were not limited to maintaining credibility with the Soviets, but with U.S. allies as well as the people of the United States. Whether the trade was public or private, the Soviets would know of the U.S. concession, but a private deal meant that America's allies and its people would not know of the exchange for many years.

The successful resolution of the Cuban missile crisis was a triumph for Flexible Response. Not limiting his options to doing nothing or carrying out a risky escalation, Kennedy had found a more measured response that defused the crisis. Flexible Response, however, would fare far worse in Vietnam. Rather than make nuclear threats or invade North Vietnam and risk a wider war in the same way that the invasion of North Korea had expanded the Korean War,[49] Kennedy and Johnson opted for more limited military measures, epitomized in an air campaign named "Rolling Thunder." The idea behind Rolling Thunder and the U.S. approach to the war as a whole was to use a slow squeeze rather than overwhelming force. The concept was to gradually ratchet up the pressure until the North Vietnamese concluded that the costs of continuing were not worth it. Unfortunately for the U.S. plan, the North Vietnamese never reached that point.[50]

Why Flexible Response worked far better in one context than in the other says something about the broader applicability of Flexible Response as an approach to strategy. One pivotal difference between the cases is that the Soviet commitment to keeping missiles in Cuba was quite limited, whereas the commitment of the government of North Vietnam toward unification was far deeper. The more committed the foe, the less likely flexible (and therefore limited) responses are to succeed.

Furthermore, a state's strategy can only be as flexible as its instruments of implementation. Any strategy requires competence at a tactical level to succeed and Flexible Response requires tactical skills in multiple areas. If a state's foreign policy tools lack such skills in the arena in which has to operate, success is unlikely. In Cuba the U.S. Navy was acting close to home in an area where it had overwhelming conventional superiority and it was conducting a mission it had long held to be part of its core skill set. In contrast, U.S. forces in Vietnam were operating far afield, often lacked the tactical initiative, and were asked to conduct a counterinsurgency campaign that was outside the skill sets they had been emphasizing since World War II. The flexibility of one's strategies must not outpace the flexibility of one's instruments.

Finally, for the calibration at the heart of Flexible Response to work, policymakers must be able to accurately see the conflict through the eyes of their enemies. Without empathy, Flexible Response is blind. The Kennedy and Johnson teams did a far better job of understanding the Soviets in Cuba than of understanding the enemy in Hanoi. Even decades after the Vietnam War, Robert McNamara, the secretary of defense, expressed mystification regarding the North Vietnamese unwillingness to come to terms, given the costs the United States inflicted upon them.[51] Thomas Schelling, one of the driving intellectual forces behind Flexible Response, came face to face with the limits of calibration in Vietnam when, upon being consulted by the administration, he failed to come up with any implementable ideas for how to effectively use air strikes to send messages to Hanoi.[52] Given the differences between how the United States, the North Vietnamese, the Chinese, and the Soviets looked at the situation and given the many intervening steps between an order from Washington to carry out a certain action and that action's interpretation by the other side, any closely calculated messages were likely to be jumbled. Flexible Response is unlikely to work when messages get lost in translation.

As the costs of implementing Flexible Response in Vietnam spiraled upward, credibility concerns prevented the United States from simply cutting its losses and withdrawing. Perversely, the longer the United States stayed in Vietnam to protect its credibility, the more its credibility was on the line.

Far less so than Eisenhower, Kennedy and Johnson also had to contend with the potential domestic costs of admitting defeat. After taking a hit for the "loss of China" early in the Cold War, could the Democratic Party survive another such loss?[53] Moreover, the idea that the country that had just won World War II could be beaten by what Johnson characterized as a "raggedy-ass little fourth-rate country" was, in some ways, unthinkable.[54] At each step along the way into Vietnam, it seemed more prudent to simply raise the stakes a bit further in the hope that the next escalation would do the trick, rather than admit defeat.

Conclusion

The ultimate U.S. defeat in Vietnam raised important questions about Flexible Response as a grand strategy and led John Lewis Gaddis to question whether it was even a strategy at all.[55] To simply react to what the other side does and progressively increase the amount of resources directed at a problem until a solution is found is, at best, an expensive approach to strategy. The desire to avoid such expenses had led Eisenhower to accept greater risk in U.S. grand strategy with the New Look. If Soviet growth, especially its attainment of nuclear parity, made such risks unacceptable, would the costs of Flexible Response be any more acceptable in the long term? In Vietnam, the answer was no.

Debates about the New Look and Flexible Response recapitulated earlier arguments about containment as a grand strategy from Kennan's "long telegram" through NSC-68. Where was the security perimeter of the United States? How important were allies, given the costs of defending them? How active did the United States have to be in exporting its values? How should the United States ensure that time worked for it rather than against it? Answers to these questions were interrelated. If concerns about credibility and falling dominoes constantly pressured the security perimeter of the United States to expand and called for greater activism in U.S. foreign policy, the costs of defending allies in places like Korea and Vietnam constantly pressured the U.S. security perimeter to shrink and called for more restraint in its execution of containment. The next chapter will explore how the successors of Eisenhower, Kennedy, and Johnson continued to grapple with these questions: first, by significantly adapting containment for what was seen as a new era of détente, and second, by attempting to dispense with containment entirely.

Beyond Containment?

Nixon, Ford, and Carter

When President Richard Nixon and national security adviser and later secretary of state Henry Kissinger assumed office, both were convinced that much had changed since the start of the Cold War and that U.S. grand strategy had to change accordingly. Eight years later, when Jimmy Carter ascended to the White House, he sought even more far-reaching changes in U.S. grand strategy. For Nixon, containment needed to be updated. For Carter, in contrast, containment needed to be transcended. Nixon attempted to adapt containment to a new era and Carter made a more radical attempt to downgrade the centrality of containment. Both encountered difficulties in their efforts to reshape America's approach to the world.

Détente

Having served in the navy during World War II, as a congressman and senator during the early years of the Cold War, and as vice president for eight years under Eisenhower, Richard Nixon was a product of the Cold War and had been a participant in many of the previous debates about containment. Having returned to a position of power, however, Nixon sought not to restore earlier policies but to update containment, which he believed had to evolve as the world had evolved.[1]

For realists like Nixon and Kissinger, the most significant change that U.S. foreign policy had to adapt to was the rise of multipolarity. No longer could world politics be usefully conceptualized as a simple bipolar distribution of power between the United States and the Soviet Union. The economic growth of Japan and Western Europe meant that both needed to be treated as significant powers and not simply as clients of the United States. In 1973, for example, the economic output of Western Europe exceeded that of the United States.[2] Although the reconstruction of these states had been a goal of U.S.

foreign policy from the start of the Cold War, the achievement of that goal created challenges as well as opportunities for the United States. Japan and Western Europe were now capable of carrying more of the burden of the Cold War, but this also meant that they were more capable of acting independently of the United States. A similar, although less intended, dynamic had also occurred within the Soviet bloc as Moscow and Beijing moved further apart. In 1968 China condemned the Soviet intervention in Czechoslovakia, in March 1969 the Soviets and the Chinese fought along their disputed border, Moscow shared Washington's worries about Beijing's nuclear program, and China and Russia supported opposing sides in the India–Pakistan War in 1971, the Angolan Civil War (1975), and the Chinese–Vietnamese War of 1979. For Nixon and his administration, the United States needed to start thinking about world politics in terms of five great powers rather than as a bipolar struggle.

Washington also had to adapt the way it thought about its bilateral relationship with Moscow as a result of another important change in the global context since the early Cold War—the overall recovery and reconstruction of the Soviet Union itself from the destruction of World War II. Between 1950 and 1973, gross domestic product (GDP) in the Soviet Union and Eastern Europe had grown about 5 percent a year and per capita GDP had doubled.[3] Although this postwar economic boom for the Soviet bloc in Europe would come to an end in the early 1970s and be succeeded by an era of economic stagnation, Nixon and Kissinger did not know this at the time. One particularly important facet of Moscow's growth was its achievement of nuclear parity. Attributing their defeat in the Cuban missile crisis in part to the U.S. nuclear advantage, the Soviets had embarked on a crash nuclear buildup, which meant that by the time Nixon returned to power, the days of U.S. nuclear dominance were at an end. Nixon and Kissinger thus believed they had to formulate and implement a grand strategy against a far more capable opponent.

The domestic environment in the United States had also changed significantly. Nixon and Kissinger worried that support for containment was weakening due to the unpopularity of the Vietnam War. Whereas Kennedy could call upon the American people to pay any price or bear any burden, after the years of conflict in Vietnam, the Nixon administration feared that it did not have this luxury. Not only could the new administration not embrace new burdens, it saw itself as hard-pressed just to prevent Vietnam from destroying the popular consensus needed to sustain containment. Like Kennan and Eisenhower before them, the Nixon team also needed to find a way to limit the costs of containment.

One way of cutting the costs of containment would be to shrink America's security perimeter by reducing the number of issues or places the United States had to expend its resources to defend. Whereas the Eisenhower administration had earlier rejected this path for bringing America's resources in line with its commitments, Nixon embraced it. When a young Donald Rumsfeld volunteered to become the White House's special envoy to Southeast Asia, Nixon declined his offer, advising Rumsfeld not to waste his efforts on a peripheral issue because Europe, Russia, China, and Japan were the only regions "that matter in the world."[4] The president offered a similar prioritization in an interview with *Time* magazine, where he argued, "I think it will be a safer world and a better world if we have a strong, healthy United States, Europe, Soviet Union, China, [and] Japan."[5] This list is strikingly similar to that of Kennan when he noted the five places of military and industrial power that the United States needed to concern itself with in the Cold War. In Nixon's formulation Great Britain and Central Europe were collapsed into a single European category and China was added, but the underlying concept and its purpose were parallel.[6] Kennan recognized the similarity and estimated that Kissinger "understands my views better than anyone at State ever has."[7] Ironically, in coming up with a way to adapt containment to the new circumstances the United States faced, Nixon and Kissinger ended up rediscovering a central part of Kennan's original model of containment.

Just as the United States found it hard to concentrate only on Kennan's strongpoints in the early years of the Cold War, Nixon and Kissinger encountered similar forces pressing them to the periphery. Nixon attempted to extricate the United States from Vietnam by expanding the war into Laos and Cambodia. Although Africa did not occupy a critical position in world politics in Nixon's calculation of U.S. interests, his administration got pulled into the Angolan civil war and the rivalry between Ethiopia and Somalia. Credibility concerns were again the source of this drive toward the periphery. In defending the expansion of the Vietnam War into Cambodia, Nixon insisted that if the United States "acts like a pitiful, helpless giant, the forces of totalitarianism and anarchy will threaten free nations and free institutions throughout the world." Directly pointing to the importance he placed on the psychological aspects of credibility, the president elaborated that, "It is not our power but our will and character that is being tested."[8] Concerns about credibility again forced U.S. foreign policy into a situation where threats defined interests rather than the other way around. As Raymond Garthoff explains, "The American stake in the Angolan situation was not threatened by the Soviet involvement on the other side, it was *created* by it."[9] The defense of credibility did not demand rollback. The United States could accept communism where it was, but worries over credibility meant that potential Soviet victories anywhere in the world, no matter how peripheral, still could not be ignored.

Kennedy and Johnson had tried to deal with peripheral conflicts by expanding the means of the United States as their strategy of Flexible Response sought to match the Soviets tank by tank and war by war if necessary. Eisenhower tried to keep the costs of his universal approach to containment low by relying, in part, on America's nuclear superiority in the New Look. The debilitating costs of Flexible Response and Soviet strategic nuclear parity closed both of those options for Nixon. One way that was open to Nixon for keeping the costs of containment manageable was to exploit the developing multipolar distribution of power using a Bismarckian hub-and-spoke approach. The aim was to put the United States at the center of international politics by maintaining closer relations with the other great powers in the system than those other powers had with each other. If the other poles valued their relations with the United States more than they valued their ties to each other, the United States would have more leverage than any of the other great powers, especially the Soviet Union. Because the United States already had better relations with the Europeans and the Japanese than either of the latter had with the Soviets or with each other, Nixon's efforts focused on China. By far the most dramatic initiative in U.S. foreign policy under Nixon came in its successful efforts to improve Sino-American relations. Taking advantage of the now clear Sino-Soviet split, the Nixon administration attempted to play these two communist powers against each other. If the United States maintained better relations with both the Chinese and the Soviets than the latter maintained with each other, the United States would find itself in a privileged position in this particular triangle and could use the threat of better relations with one to get concessions from the other. Nixon and Kissinger attempted to use this leverage, for example, to persuade both Moscow and Beijing to put pressure on Hanoi to end the war in Vietnam.[10]

Another way that the diffusion of power in world politics away from the twin superpowers could be used to keep the costs of containment low was to rely on America's now stronger allies to do more. Under the Nixon Doctrine the United States insisted that although it would honor its commitments, including the continued provision of its nuclear shield to allies, when it came to countering lower-level conventional threats, the United States preferred a division of labor under which Washington sold the needed weapons but the allies supplied the needed manpower. In essence, the Nixon Doctrine attempted to subcontract the costliest parts of containment out to regional allies, assisted by American arms sales. The Nixon Doctrine included but went beyond the great powers, encompassing regional powers as well. In the Middle East the United States would rely on Israel, Saudi Arabia, and especially Iran to contain communist advances and in Africa, South Africa could play a similar role.[11] Nixon's plan for ending U.S. involvement in the war in Vietnam, called Vietnamization, was a variant of the Nixon Doctrine. Under Vietnamization the United States continued to provide arms and airpower to U.S. allies in Saigon, but the burden of the fight on the ground was shifted to the South Vietnamese. Whereas alliances had played a key role in Eisenhower's approach to containment, at that time these alliances were used more as a way of communicating and increasing U.S. commitment to certain areas than as a means of burden sharing. Now that the allies of the United States were strong enough to do more on their own, Nixon wanted to preserve U.S. resources by asking these allies to do more.

The growth of Soviet power and the Soviet economy also meant, Nixon and Kissinger reasoned, that negotiations could play a greater role in America's Cold War strategy than they had in the past. In a 1970 report on U.S. foreign policy the administration talked about moving from an "era of confrontation to an era of negotiation."[12] Whereas earlier administrations had considered the role negotiations could play in containment, that role had typically been limited to portraying a willingness to negotiate with the Soviets as a useful public relations tool. The growth of Soviet power meant that Moscow now had more to offer as a negotiating partner and had more to lose from a serious deterioration of U.S.–Soviet relations. In John Lewis Gaddis's apt description, the logic behind this part of Nixon's strategy was to offer "a new combination of pressures and inducements" designed to "convince Kremlin leaders that it was in their country's interest to be 'contained.' "[13] "Linkage" was the preferred term for this, which at its heart represented basic carrot-and-stick diplomacy. As Kissinger later described it, "The idea was to emphasize those areas in which cooperation was possible, and to use that cooperation as leverage to modify Soviet behavior in areas in which the two countries were at loggerheads."[14]

One particular area in which the Nixon administration believed cooperation was possible was in slowing the growth of nuclear weapons. Now that the days of clear U.S. nuclear superiority were over, how many nuclear weapons did the United States need and what did it need them to do? Just as nuclear weapons required a rethinking of the U.S. approach to war, they also required a rethinking of arms control. If the goal of arms control is to reduce the chances of war while saving money, what sort of weapons does it make sense to limit? In a conventionally armed world, the answer is to limit weapons that give the advantage to the offense, but not to limit those that give a relative advantage to the defense. A world in which the existing array of weaponry favored the defense of territory and people over the seizure of territory and people was likely to be more peaceful than one in which offensive weapons dominated.[15] Although clear in theory, in practice it was difficult to differentiate offensive from defensive arms because most weapons could be used in both roles. Even something as seemingly defensive as the Maginot Line could be seen as increasing France's offensive capabilities because if this elaborate system of fortifications allowed France to defend its borders with fewer soldiers, the manpower saved could be shifted to offensive operations. In a conventional world, the psychological barrier that arms control negotiations had to overcome was the tendency for each state to see its weapons as defensive and the weapons of other states as offensive.

With nuclear weapons, however, the concepts of offense and defense in arms control got turned on their heads. Nuclear weapons are not war-fighting weapons, they are primarily weapons of deterrence; more specifically, they are weapons of deterrence by punishment. That is, nuclear weapons do not deter war by guaranteeing that any attack will be repelled (deterrence by denial), they deter war by threatening to inflict unacceptable damage on an opponent. The central purpose of nuclear weapons is not to fight other nuclear weapons, the way tanks fight other tanks, but to deter war from starting and escalating. As Robert Jervis cogently notes, in a nuclear world, "it is the prospect of fighting the war, rather than the prospect of losing it that induces restraint."[16] To work as weapons of deterrence by punishment, nuclear weapons must maintain their offensive capabilities because their effectiveness comes not in their ability to defend against the attacks of an opponent, but in their ability to destroy whatever an opponent values. In regard to nuclear weapons, therefore, reducing the chances of war requires protecting their offensive capabilities, not limiting them.

The important distinction for nuclear arms control is not between offensive and defensive weapons, but between weapons that encourage a first strike and those that bolster a state's second strike capability. To reduce the possibility of a nuclear war it is necessary to reduce as far as possible the advantage any state would see in using its nuclear weapons first and to protect the ability of states to absorb a first strike and to still have enough offensive capability left to impose intolerable costs on the other side. In a nuclear world, defensive weapons can be dangerously destabilizing. No defensive system, no matter how sophisticated, was likely to be capable of fully repelling an all-out attack by a well-armed nuclear power. Such defenses, however, might be far more effective if the opposing side were first weakened by a surprise first strike. In that case, a state's defensive countermeasures would need to cope only with a disorganized and weakened counterattack (a second strike). If both sides had unlimited, but still porous defenses, the side that struck first could gain an enormous advantage. Thus, defensive systems, in a nuclear world, might encourage war by giving both sides an incentive to shoot first.

To stabilize a nuclear world, arms control aims not to weaken the offense or strengthen the defense, but to protect a state's second strike capability. Although both sides in the Cold War had a tendency to define stabilizing and destabilizing nuclear weapons in self-serving ways,[17] the mutual interest both sides had in avoiding a nuclear war gave them an incentive to limit weapons that encouraged a first strike. As part of the Strategic Arms Limitation Talks (SALT), the United States and the Soviet Union agreed to limit antiballistic missile (ABM) efforts to two sites, presumably one to protect each side's capital and the other to protect an intercontinental ballistic missile (ICBM) site. This agreement was later amended to allow only one site for each side. The logic of this agreement was that unlimited ballistic missile defenses could dangerously destabilize the U.S–Soviet nuclear standoff by encouraging both sides to strike first in a crisis. More limited defenses that protected each side's command-and-control systems and nuclear-tipped missiles, conversely, would strengthen the ability of both sides to launch a devastating second strike if attacked, and thus would discourage any first strikes.

The United States never seriously pursued the option of building a ballistic missile defense system to protect Washington, DC. Spending huge sums of money to protect the city in which most politicians lived and worked while telling other cities that they were on their own was a losing proposition domestically. The United States did, however, field an ABM system to protect an ICBM complex in North Dakota, but that program too was soon disbanded as being too expensive. The Soviets, less encumbered by the domestic need to sell such a program, did build a system to protect Moscow.

The first strike/second strike distinction also helped to answer the question of how many weapons the United States needed. To deter a Soviet attack, the United States did not need nuclear superiority. Instead, all the United States needed was the ability to absorb a Soviet first strike and still have enough nuclear weapons to inflict unacceptable damage on the Soviets. This move from nuclear superiority to nuclear sufficiency also opened up the door for arms control and allowed the United States to limit the resources it put into the defense budget. These nuclear arms control deals were consistent with the entire approach of détente (French for "relaxation"), which sought to keep the Soviets contained, but do so at reduced costs and reduced tensions.[18]

The Failures of Détente

As a grand strategy, détente ran into severe difficulties. One fundamental problem was that détente's success required some level of acceptance and cooperation from the Soviets, but Washington and Moscow had different views of what détente meant and what type of behavior it required. For the United States, the purpose of détente was to stabilize the status quo and protect America's international position. The Kremlin, however, had little interest in a détente that froze the status quo, only in one that allowed its power to continue to grow in a way that minimized the risk of a catastrophic war. The United States saw détente as a way to protect its hegemony; the Soviet Union saw it as a way of peacefully managing the decline of U.S. hegemony.[19]

These competing views undermined the possibility of meaningful cooperation between the two sides throughout much of the developing world. One of the perpetual challenges that any strong-point definition of America's security perimeter faces involves how to avoid being dragged into peripheral conflicts. Nixon hoped that détente could minimize this danger by persuading the Soviets to avoid challenging the United States throughout the developing world. In return for the benefits of cooperation that Moscow sought in certain areas, the United States expected the Soviet Union to exercise restraint in others. For Washington, any Soviet-backed change to the status quo was contrary to détente, but for Moscow, détente allowed continued challenges to the status quo; it only mandated that those challenges and the responses to those challenges be kept within bounds so as to avoid risking a world war. As a result, competition for allies and influence continued outside the five regions Nixon had identified as most important for the United States. Between 1975 and 1979, pro-Soviet revolutionary groups succeeded in gaining power in diverse locales such as Angola, Mozambique, Ethiopia, Afghanistan, South Yemen, Nicaragua, and Grenada.[20] Most dramatically, linkage failed to get the Soviets to restrain North Vietnam from invading and overrunning the south in 1975.

A second area where détente ran into trouble was that it failed to generate sufficient domestic support. Indeed, criticism of détente had become so widespread that in the 1976 election, Gerald Ford, who succeeded to the presidency following Nixon's resignation due to the Watergate scandal, banned the word in his campaign. As the Soviets and the Americans continued to vie with each other in a series of regional conflicts, many concluded that détente had failed and that its reality did not match its rhetoric. In the end, détente pleased neither the hawks nor the doves.[21] To critics on the hawkish end of the spectrum, the cooperative aspects of détente smacked of appeasement. Although Kissinger would later insist that détente was designed to buy time until the ultimate collapse of the Soviet Union,[22] with history still on the U.S. side even if the short-term trends were less favorable, for the hawks, détente seemed designed as a way to live with and accept Soviet power, not defeat it. As realists, Nixon and Kissinger were also more comfortable encouraging the independence of East European governments than promoting democratic revolutions in those states as some of their more hawkish critics would have preferred.[23] The dovish end of the spectrum, on the other hand, criticized the competitive aspects of détente as being too confrontational in areas where U.S. interests were limited. Moreover, critics on both the left and the right agreed that détente was an immoral foreign policy. The right criticized the administration for trying to cooperate with an evil empire and the left criticized the administration for tying the United States to unsavory allies such as the Shah in Iran or the apartheid regime in South Africa. A grand strategy that relies on a mix of cooperation and conflict must have its domestic flanks carefully protected. The collapse of the Nixon administration in the Watergate affair made this difficult in the case of détente.

Détente was also undermined by the decentralized nature of the American political system. Linkage required centralized control to ensure that rewards and punishments were doled out in the right measure to respond to Soviet actions. For the United States, who would get to allocate the carrots and the sticks? Nixon and Kissinger sought to centralize this power in the White House,[24] but the divided nature of the U.S. government made this unworkable. In the aftermath of the Vietnam War and in the midst of the Watergate scandal, Congress was unwilling to cede this amount of foreign policy control to the president. When the administration wanted to send military aid to Angola or to use American air power to help the South Vietnamese government defend itself from the North Vietnamese invasion in 1975, Congress said no. At other times, Congress added sticks that the administration did not want. Kissinger, for example, ardently resisted congressional efforts to tie U.S. security assistance to the human rights policies of recipient countries.[25] Congress also attempted some linkage of its own with the Jackson–Vanik amendment, which threatened to withdraw Moscow's most-favored-nation trading status if the Kremlin failed to loosen its restrictions on Jewish emigration. In Kissinger's assessment, seeking a far-reaching change in the internal nature of the Soviet political system was a link too far and he worried that this type of embarrassing public criticism would cause the Soviets to be less cooperative here and in other areas. The point is not to determine whether the Congress or the president had a better approach to linkage, but too stress that in the U.S. system of government, centralized control over a policy mix of rewards and punishment is going to be difficult. If the legislative and executive branches do not agree on the precise nature of this mix, then confusion rather than calibration is likely to be the result.

Instead of accepting the limits that the decentralized nature of U.S. politics imposes on U.S. grand strategy, the Nixon administration tried to overcome them, but in a way that ended up exacerbating them. Nixon and Kissinger were quite open about what their overall approach to U.S. foreign policy was, but the implementation of their strategy was frequently done secretly and at times deceptively. This secrecy often applied not only to the people of the United States and to Congress but also to large parts of the executive bureaucracy itself, which although nominally headed by the president was distrusted by both Nixon and Kissinger.[26] Instead of trying to build public, congressional, and bureaucratic support for détente, Nixon and Kissinger preferred to circumvent the need for such support with secret tactics.[27] This may have made things easier in the short term, but in the long term it furthered the domestic criticism that undercut détente. The failures of détente led not only to questions about it as an approach to containment but also to more far-reaching questions about the continued relevance of containment as an organizing principle for American foreign policy.

Carter and U.S. Grand Strategy

In every presidential election after 1948, polls indicated that voters ranked foreign policy as the most important issue facing the country. That streak came to an end in 1976 when 78 percent of voters ranked economic problems as the most important issue and foreign policy scored a relatively meager 6 percent.[28] The declining salience of foreign policy in U.S politics, combined with the disillusionment caused by the failed Vietnam War and Watergate, not only helped elect a relative outsider to the presidency—a former governor of Georgia with little foreign policy experience—but also allowed that new president, Jimmy Carter, to attempt a significant reshaping of U.S. foreign policy. What Carter chose to do is what all U.S. post–Cold War presidents have been forced to do—to try to devise and implement a grand strategy for the United States to replace containment.

Trained as an engineer and possessing a tendency toward micromanagement, the new president demonstrated some aversion to the entire idea of grand strategy.[29] Viewing policy issues as discrete problems to be solved, Carter spent relatively little time thinking about an overarching framework to tie these problems and their solutions together into a broader whole. Further complicating the development of a coherent grand strategy for the Carter administration, the new president's two key foreign policy advisers, his secretary of state, Cyrus Vance, and his national security adviser, Zbigniew Brzezinski, were far apart in temperament and their preferred approaches to international affairs. The Warsaw-born Brzezinski, more aggressive and more of a risk taker, preferred to work through informal channels, and as one of his colleagues at the White House joked, liked being "the first Pole in 300 years in a position to really stick it to the Russians."[30] The more dovish Vance, in contrast, was the archetype of the cautious, professional diplomat who tended to take a far less Soviet-centric view of the world. Whereas Carter welcomed these divergent perspectives in his advisory circle, his refusal to clearly choose between the two made it problematic to implement a coherent grand strategy. Leslie Gelb, then a State Department official, summarized the Carter administration's approach to grand strategy by arguing: "The environment we are looking at is far too complex to be reduced to a doctrine in the tradition of post–World War II American foreign policy. Indeed the Carter approach rests on a belief that not only is the world far too complex to be reduced to a doctrine, but that there is something inherently wrong with having a doctrine at all."[31]

These factors have led some to conclude that the Carter administration had no grand strategy. Gaddis, for example, argues that Carter's team had "difficulty aligning itself with . . . any coherent conception of American interests in the world, potential threats to them, or feasible responses."[32] It is not surprising that a book titled *Strategies of Containment* would find little to say about Carter, because his strategy was not one of containment. Just because Carter did not have a strategy of containment, however, does not mean that his administration did not have a strategy. If one compares Carter not with what came before him in the Cold War, but with what would come after him in the post–Cold War era, his approach to U.S. grand strategy is less anomalous. In this context, Carter's foreign policy looks more like a harbinger of things to come, than a confused interlude in the Cold War.[33] The lack of clarity in Carter's approach may tell us less about the administration itself and more about the challenges of formulating a grand strategy in a context not dominated by on overarching, yet relatively static, threat.

The key starting point for Carter's approach to U.S. foreign policy was a conviction that containment had outlived its utility and that it was no longer sensible to put the Soviet Union at the center of America's international attention. U.S. foreign policy, Carter asserted, should be "free of that inordinate fear of communism" and should no longer be built around the "belief that Soviet expansion was almost inevitable but that it must be contained." Although he conceded that U.S. competition with the Soviet Union had become more geographically extensive, he also maintained that "the unifying threat of conflict with the Soviet Union has become less intensive."[34] In the place of the Cold War, Carter described a world characterized by what would later become commonly referred to as globalization. "In less than a lifetime, world population has more than doubled, colonial empires have disappeared, and a hundred new nations have been born. Mass communications, literacy, and migration to the world's cities have all awakened new yearnings for economic justice and human rights among people everywhere." For Carter, in this new world, containing the Soviet Union was somewhat beside the point because, "In such a world, the choice is not which super power will dominate the world. None can and none will."[35]

Although it attempted to move beyond containment, the Carter team still had to answer many of the same questions grappled with by the implementers of containment. The fundamental questions of U.S. foreign policy had not changed. In this new world, for example, where did the strategic perimeter of the United States lie? If the Soviet Union was no longer at the center of U.S. security concerns, what parts of the world and what issues did the United States have to be deeply concerned with and what parts of the world and what issues, if any, could the United States safely ignore? Carter's attempt to decentralize the Cold War in U.S. foreign policy implied a geographic shift in Washington's attention away from East–West issues that pitted the United States against the Soviet Union and toward North–South issues that divided developed and developing countries. Explicitly rejecting Nixon's Kennanesque focus on the five most economically advanced parts of the globe, Carter argued: "We can no longer have a policy solely for the industrial nations as the foundation of global stability, but we must respond to the new reality of a politically awakening world." This wider aperture was vital for U.S. security, Carter asserted, because "more than 100 years ago, Abraham Lincoln said that our nation could not exist half slave and half free. We know a peaceful world cannot long exist one-third rich and two-thirds hungry."[36] Rather than signal just a shift to different strongpoints, Carter's emphasis on issues arising from globalization led him to a reuniversalization of the U.S. security perimeter. In rhetoric reminiscent of National Security Council Report 68, although this time outside of the Cold War framework, Carter argued that "each of us is threatened when peace is not secured everywhere."[37]

As always, the attempt to protect a universal security perimeter with finite resources presents a strategic challenge. Carter certainly recognized the limits of U.S. power, especially in the aftermath of the war in Vietnam. "We have learned," he explained in his inaugural address, "that even our great Nation has its recognized limits, and that we can neither answer all questions nor solve all problems. We cannot afford to do everything."[38] One way Carter wanted to close the gap between aims and resources in U.S. foreign policy was to use the resources of other countries through multilateralism. Rather than rely solely on U.S. resources, the intent was "to create a wider framework of international cooperation suited to the new and rapidly changing historical circumstances" and to conduct U.S. foreign policy through a "new, worldwide mosaic of global, regional and bilateral relations." Democratic countries, in particular, would play an important role in this new mosaic of international institutions. Seeking to increase the "bonds among our democracies" Carter called on like-minded countries to play a leading role "to help shape the wider architecture of global cooperation."[39]

Limited resources and ambitions following failure in Vietnam also minimized any crusading impulses in U.S. foreign policy in favor of an emphasis on spreading American values through the force of its example rather than through the direct use of military or economic power. Speaking as a proponent of the United States as the Promised Land, Carter averred that "the best way to enhance freedom in other lands is to demonstrate here that our democratic system is worthy of emulation."[40] Arguing that "there is a preoccupation with the subject of human freedom [and] human liberty" in the world, Carter maintained "No other country is as well-qualified as we to set an example."[41]

One conviction that survived the U.S. defeat in Vietnam and that Carter held in common with his more containment-focused predecessors was that time remained on America's side, particularly on the side of the values the United States represented: "I have a quiet confidence in our own political system. Because we know democracy works, we can reject the arguments of those rulers who deny human rights to their people. We are confident that democracy's example will be compelling, and so we seek to bring that example closer to those from whom in the past few years we have been separated and who are not yet convinced about the advantages of our kind of life. We are confident that the democratic methods are the most effective, so we are not tempted to employ improper tactics at home or abroad."[42] This historical confidence was as central to Carter's approach to U.S. grand strategy as it was to containment. On this point, Carter was probably closer to the containment consensus than Nixon and Kissinger were. The latter's emphasis on stability and adapting to the realities of Soviet power pushed into the background the argument Kennan made from the start, which was that the Soviet experiment was doomed to failure. Carter, like Kennedy before him, did not want to get the United States forced into an untenable and counterproductive defense of the status quo, but instead sought to embrace and shape change rather than resist it.

One advantage Carter had in taking this position was that for the first thirty years of the Cold War, for the most part, the dominoes had not fallen. Whereas previous administrations had also called for shaping rather than resisting change, those intentions often ran afoul of worries related to the domino theory, which included the idea that accepting change that seemed to favor the Soviets would make the United States look weak and, as a result, increase the challenges the United States would face in the future. Instead of the dominoes falling in favor of the Soviets, however, Moscow's gains often proved to be transitory. They had ended up at war with China, for example, were running into trouble in their relations with India, and had been expelled from Egypt. As one State Department official explained, the Carter administration rejected the argument "that specific places around the world were turning points and that if the Soviets gained influence in, for example, Ethiopia or South Yemen, or in any other place, that this (a) was irreversible and (b) would transform fundamentally the strategic balance." Instead, the administration believed "that the world is a place that is in constant flux . . . and, on balance, Soviet influence has been diminishing in recent years in a whole series of countries that seemed to be firmly in the Soviet camp."[43]

These factors capture the core of U.S. grand strategy under the Carter administration. Diminishing the centrality of the Cold War, Carter wanted an approach to U.S. foreign policy that focused more on North–South economic issues, increased multilateralism, and emphasized U.S. values and the conviction that time was on the side of those values. As Carter summarized, "It is a new world, but American should not fear it. It is a new world, and we should help to shape it. It is a new world that calls for a new American foreign policy—a policy based on constant decency in its values and on optimism in our historical vision."[44]

Carter's attempt to move U.S. grand strategy beyond containment achieved some successes. One of the administration's earliest foreign policy achievements was the successful ratification of a treaty to turn over control of the Panama Canal to Panama, negotiations that had languished since the Johnson administration. From Carter's perspective, U.S. possession of the canal was a relic of imperialism and by negotiating its transfer to the Panamanians, Washington demonstrated its willingness to treat the interests of the developing countries with respect. Trying to maintain U.S. control over the canal, Carter worried, would only spur animosity and violence against the United States throughout Latin America. Getting the treaty approved by the Senate was a struggle. To critics, the giveaway of the canal was a demonstration of weakness, not restraint. As one senatorial opponent of the treaty viewed the canal, "It's ours, we stole it fair and square."[45] Whereas the Senate eventually gave its consent to the treaty, this victory left the administration bruised and on the defensive to critics who wanted to remilitarize the U.S. approach to the Cold War, not move beyond it.[46]

Perhaps Carter's greatest foreign policy accomplishment was his successful mediation of the Camp David Accords, which resulted in a peace treaty between Egypt and Israel. Besides providing a location for talks, ideas for negotiation, and constant prodding, the United States also greased the way for the peace treaty by offering both countries large amounts of foreign aid. The Egyptian–Israeli peace treaty remains the most significant achievement in the history of the Arab–Israeli peace process and this peace has now held for over thirty-five years in the face of multiple challenges. The agreement also significantly strengthened the U.S. position in the Middle East, albeit at the cost of worsening relations with Moscow. In 1977 Carter and his Soviet counterpart, Leonid Brezhnev, issued a joint statement on the Middle East that the Soviets interpreted as a U.S. promise to allow Moscow to play a significant role in any subsequent negotiations. Kept out of the Camp David negotiations, the Soviets watched from the sidelines as Egypt, which had been their most important ally in the region, completed its realignment toward the United States.[47]

Carter's championing of human rights in U.S. foreign policy also had some benefit for the United States. Although it increased hostility with the Soviets and with some of America's traditional allies, Carter's emphasis on values represented an attempt to reclaim the moral high ground for U.S. foreign policy, territory that had seemed under threat in the aftermath of the Vietnam War and the Watergate scandal. The successful implementation of grand strategy requires a certain level of domestic and international support, which was in danger of waning in the face of increased questions about the moral basis of America's global role.

Carter was also able to further the work that had been started by Nixon and Kissinger by, on New Year's Day in 1979, completing the normalization of U.S. diplomatic relations with China in a way that did not cause a rupture over or with Taiwan. Despite this auspicious beginning for the year, 1979 proved a difficult one for Carter. Similar to the twin blows that had undermined Kennan's approach to containment in 1949 (the Soviet atomic bomb test and the victory of the communists in the Chinese Civil War), thirty years later another series of blows hit U.S. foreign policy, this time undermining Carter's attempt to move U.S. grand strategy away from containment.

The first blow came from Iran, where the Shah, who was a close U.S. ally throughout the Cold War and was supposed to play an especially important role in the Middle East under the Nixon Doctrine, was overthrown and replaced by a vehemently anti-American clerical regime. To add insult to the injury of the loss of a key ally, in November 1979, when the U.S. embassy in Tehran was overrun and scores of Americans were taken hostage, the revolutionary government in Iran supported their seizure rather than reversing it. For the next 444 days, the Iran hostage crisis dominated U.S. foreign policy, being resolved only on the day Carter left office. The second major jolt came quickly on the heels of the hostage crisis when, in December 1979, the Soviets launched a massive invasion of Afghanistan, sending in 85,000 troops to shore up the pro-Moscow government in Kabul, fearing the contagion of Islamic-based political movements that might eventually spread to the Muslim populations of the Soviet Republics in Central Asia and the Caucasus. This was the first time during the Cold War that the Soviets had sent large numbers of combat troops outside the areas they had conquered by the end of World War II. Carter contended that the Soviet invasion of Afghanistan "made a more dramatic change in my own opinion of what the Soviets' ultimate goals are than anything they've done in the previous time I've been in office," and later characterized the invasion as "the most serious threat to the peace since the Second World War."[48]

The hostage crisis and the war in Afghanistan were the two major blows to Carter's grand strategy, but they were not the only ones. In Nicaragua the Somoza regime, which had been put in power in the 1930s by the United States, was overthrown by the Cuban-supported Sandinistas. Russian aid and Cuban troops also continued to play an active role in Africa, with large numbers of Cuban troops fighting in Angola and Ethiopia. In the late 1970s the Soviets were also in the process of deploying new intermediate range ballistic missiles in Europe. The newly deployed SS-20s represented a significant upgrade, improving the mobility of the Soviet missiles, decreasing launch times, and offering the capability of placing multiple warheads on a single missile.

Domestically, things were also going poorly for the administration because the United States was suffering from a nasty combination of a stagnant economy, high inflation, elevated interest rates, and increasing energy prices. Besides the domestic troubles stemming from the dismal economic climate, the Carter administration was also damaged by the embarrassing false discovery of a "new" Soviet combat brigade in Cuba, which had actually been there since the conclusion of the missile crisis in 1962, and an unwanted public relations fiasco related to an alleged attack on the president by a rabbit.[49]

Just as the twin blows of 1949 led the Truman administration to question whether time was on the side of the United States in the Cold War, the many blows of 1979 led to similar doubts for Carter. In the X-Article, Kennan had argued that at heart the Cold War was "a question of the degree to which the United States can create among the peoples of the world generally the impression of a country which knows what it wants, which is coping successfully with the problems of its internal life, and with the responsibilities of a World Power, and which has a spiritual vitality capable of holding its own among the major ideological currents of the time."[50] Economic stagnation at home led Carter to abandon his earlier optimism and to worry that the United States was falling short in Kennan's test.

In what would become known as the "malaise" speech, even though that word was not used, Carter warned about "a fundamental threat to American democracy" stemming from "a crisis of confidence" that can be seen "in the growing doubt about the meaning of our own lives and in the loss of a unity of purpose for our nation." "We've always believed," Carter continued, "in something called progress. We've always had a faith that the days of our children would be better than our own. Our people are losing that faith." Carter feared that the United States, instead of being a self-confident great power that knew what it wanted, was becoming increasingly anxious and directionless. "Too many of us tend to worship self-indulgence and consumption. Human identity is no longer defined by what one does, but by what one owns. But we've discovered that owning things and consuming things does not satisfy our longing for meaning. We've learned that piling up material goods cannot fill the emptiness of lives which have no confidence or purpose." Reversing this negative trend had to become central to U.S. grand strategy: "Restoring that faith and confidence to America is now the most important task we face." Carter chose the energy crisis as the opening front in this campaign, arguing that "Energy will be the immediate test of our ability to unite this Nation, and it can also be the standard around which we rally. On the battlefield of energy we can win for our nation a new confidence, as we can seize control again of our common destiny." Carter called for conservation efforts and greater investment in alternative energy sources, stressing that there "is simply no way to avoid sacrifice."[51]

Soon after this call for economic sacrifice was issued, however, the twin foreign policy blows of 1979 hit, with the taking of the American hostages in Iran in November and the Soviet invasion of Afghanistan in December. When these foreign policy crises hit on top of the domestic economic crisis, rather than respond by embracing sacrifice, the Carter administration responded by embracing containment. Carter shelved his earlier criticism that U.S. Cold War strategy was based on an "inordinate fear of communism," and instead argued that "Now, as during the last 3½ decades, the relationship between our country . . . and the Soviet Union is the most critical factor in determining whether the world will live at peace or be engulfed in global conflict." Consciously linking his responses with the legacy of containment, the president offered the Carter Doctrine to stand alongside the doctrines of Truman, Eisenhower, and Nixon, averring that "an attempt by any outside force to gain control of the Persian Gulf region will be regarded as an assault on the vital interests of the United States of America, and such an assault will be repelled by any means necessary, including military force."[52]

To further this return to containment, Carter called for a vastly increased military budget, he expanded arms sales abroad, pulled SALT II from Senate consideration, restarted the registration system for a potential military draft, implemented new sanctions against the Soviet Union, boycotted the 1980 Olympics being held in Moscow, increased aid to the Afghan resistance, and put an end to efforts to woo pro-Soviet groups like the Sandinistas in Nicaragua with U.S. aid. So ended the first attempt of the United States to build a post–Cold War grand strategy.

Many of the elements of Carter's postcontainment approach to U.S. foreign policy would return over a decade later when U.S. policymakers again grappled with the issue of defining a grand strategy outside of the Cold War. Carter was, in this sense, ahead of his time. Being ahead of one's time might be a great compliment for an artist or a scientist, but it is not necessarily a great compliment for a grand strategist. Although grand strategy should focus on the long term, the job of the grand strategist is to make the right decisions for today. As George Kennan recognized, "in political matters a truth prematurely uttered is of scarcely greater value than error."[53]

Carter's return to containment offered him few rewards at home. In the 1980 elections, Carter was soundly defeated by Ronald Reagan, a candidate who had built his national reputation by criticizing the attempts of both Nixon and Carter to move U.S. foreign policy beyond containment. Carter's return to containment would, however, help set the stage for his successor's policies. The Reagan defense buildup, in this sense, started under Carter. Robert Gates, who served in both the Carter and the Reagan administrations, argued that it was Carter who "took the first steps to strip away the mask of Soviet ascendancy and exploit the reality of Soviet vulnerability."[54] Reagan's continuation of that policy and the role it played in bringing about the end of the Cold War are addressed in the next chapter.

The Culmination of Containment

Reagan's Grand Strategy and the End of the Cold War

Unlike his predecessor, Ronald Reagan entered the White House with a well-established foreign policy profile. As an anti-Soviet hawk of longstanding, Reagan had not only rejected Carter's attempts to move U.S. grand strategy beyond containment but also had run for president in 1976 as a critic of détente. Whereas Reagan's ascension to the Oval Office therefore promised a return to a more antagonistic Cold War, by the end of his eight years as president, U.S.–Soviet relations were unexpectedly cooperative. In Carter's last year in office he had pivoted U.S. foreign policy back toward containment. Reagan's pivot in his final years was equally dramatic, but in the opposite direction. Reagan entered office as a committed anti-Soviet hawk but at the end of his tenure in the White House he was presiding over a sudden and far-reaching warming of U.S.–Soviet relations. The transformation in U.S. foreign policy brought about not a return to containment in U.S. grand strategy but to its culmination.

Containment on the Offensive

Soon after Reagan's victory in the 1980 presidential election, a group of his foreign policy advisers wrote a "Strategic Guidance" report to flesh out the new administration's thinking on foreign policy. Rejecting détente's focus on accommodating the United States to Soviet power, the report argued that the "United States does not accept as a permanent historical fact the occupation or control by a power hostile to the United States of any territory beyond the borders of that power."[1] Such language could be seen not only as a rejection of détente but also as a wider rejection of containment as a whole in favor of a more offensive-oriented strategy of rollback. That, however, is not the way the Reagan administration saw it. They saw their approach to U.S. grand strategy as a complement to containment, not a rejection of it.

For one thing, no time frame was offered for scaling back Soviet imperial power. Indeed, the Strategic Guidance's emphasis on Moscow's external empire as not being a "permanent historical fact" recalls the initial optimism that drove Kennan to containment in the first place, which was based on his conviction that the Soviet experiment was bound to fail. In addition, the geographic scope for rollback was restricted to areas outside the borders of the Soviet Union. A direct challenge to the Soviets' hold on power at home was still off the table. Reagan's grand strategy embraced containment but also sought to supplement it with a more offensive component; yet this offensive component was kept strictly limited.

Like National Security Council Report 68 (NSC-68), the New Look, and Flexible Response, Reagan's approach to U.S. grand strategy embraced a universal security perimeter. The "Strategic Guidance" report concluded that "no area of the world is beyond the scope of American interest."[2] Disdaining any attempt to differentiate between vital and peripheral interests, Caspar Weinberger, Reagan's secretary of defense, when asked which areas of the world were most important to the United States, simply answered, "All of them."[3] The United States, the Reagan administration believed, had to be ready to "compet[e] effectively on a sustained basis with the Soviet Union in all international arenas."[4] In a worldwide Cold War, local problems inevitably became global problems. As the secretary of state, Alexander Haig, explained these links in one instance, "El Salvador was not merely a local problem. It was also a regional problem that threatened the stability of all of Central America, including the Panama Canal and Mexico and Guatemala with their vast oil reserves. And it was a global issue because it represented the interjection of the war of national liberation into the Western Hemisphere."[5]

Reagan's predecessors offered two distinct models for how the United States could go about attempting to defend a universal security perimeter. One model, offered in NSC-68 and central to Flexible Response, was to strive to match any Soviet challenges not only in the places of their choosing but also with the means that the Soviets chose: placing missile against missile, tank against tank, and insurgent against counterinsurgent. Eisenhower's New Look offered a second potential model. The United States would still strive to counter the Soviets in places of their choosing but would retain freedom of choice regarding the means by which Washington would respond. Both of these approaches had proved problematic. The principal difficulty of a symmetrical approach was its cost. For the United States to sustain forces capable of countering the Soviets at the time, place, and by the method of Moscow's own choosing, was immensely expensive. The central problem presented by a New Look approach is that asymmetrical responses often failed to prevent Soviet gains. Indeed, in implementing the New Look, Eisenhower had been forced to accept setbacks in Cuba and Vietnam, for example, when America's asymmetrical means came up short in meeting the universal aspirations of the administration's strategy.

In choosing between the problems associated with these alternative approaches to containment, Reagan preferred to accept the costs of symmetry rather than risk ceding even small victories to the Soviets. Responding to the Soviet deployment of SS-20 missiles in Europe, Reagan pushed the deployment of the Pershing II missiles to Europe. Responding to Soviet support for revolutionary movements in the third world, Reagan supported their opponents. As were the costs of NSC-68 and Flexible Response, the costs of this approach were substantial. In his final year in office Carter had initiated a vast increase in the defense budget, an increase that Reagan furthered. This buildup included the B-1 bomber, the Trident submarine, the restart of work on the neutron bomb, the deployment of Tomahawk sea-launched cruise missiles, the near attainment of the goal of a six-hundred-ship navy, and the continued buildup of the rapid deployment force, which eventually became the core of the U.S. Central Command for the Middle East. During the 1990s the United States would debate whether it should size its military to be prepared to fight two nearly simultaneous regional conflicts; however, under Reagan the force-planning construct was based on the need to fight three and a half regional wars while prevailing in a nuclear conflict. Carter's final defense budget anticipated spending about $1.3 trillion on defense over five years; Reagan accepted that increase and raised it to $1.5 trillion.[6] When forced to choose between balancing the budget and increasing defense spending, Reagan abandoned any commitment to balanced budgets and turned instead to trickle-down economics, a conservative, but not fiscally conservative, equivalent of Keynesianism.

How long could the United States afford such expenditures? For Reagan, the answer was long enough. Assessing U.S. strengths and Soviet weaknesses, Reagan maintained that time would stay on America's side during the Cold War, even given huge defense expenditures, because the Soviets would be less able than the United States to afford the costs of this competition. Reagan had been arguing since the 1960s "that in an all out race our system is stronger."[7] The economic failings of communism made Moscow vulnerable and Reagan sought to "force the Soviet Union to bear the brunt of its economic shortcomings."[8] As Reagan himself later summarized it, "we could outspend them forever."[9]

Taking this one step further, not only was symmetrical containment affordable, it could also be supplemented with limited experiments aimed at rollback to put even more pressure on the Soviet Union. For Kennan, the fact that time was on America's side meant that there was no need to take the offensive against the Soviet Union because in time it would collapse on its own. Indeed, in the early parts of the Cold War, only those who feared that time was not on the U.S. side found rollback attractive. Reagan, however, took an opposite, optimistic path to rollback. For him, it was that the advantages of the United States made limited rollback possible, not that its weaknesses made rollback necessary. The United States need no longer limit itself to simply containing the Soviet Union, it could also take a limited offensive designed to "reverse the expansion of Soviet control and military presence throughout the world."[10]

One means of furthering this reversal was the Reagan Doctrine, which put an offense-oriented spin on the Nixon Doctrine. The United States would continue to arm, fund, and train local allies, but the goal was not limited only to fending off Soviet-backed challenges, it was also directed at weakening Soviet influence in places where the Soviets had already established themselves. Under the Reagan Doctrine the United States funneled resources to anti-Soviet forces in Nicaragua and Afghanistan, and more quietly into Eastern Europe. As Reagan calculated it, "more encouragement to the dissidents might be worth a lot of armored divisions."[11]

The idea of replacing the costs of armored divisions with the less expensive method of encouraging dissidents points to another noteworthy aspect of Reagan's approach to U.S. grand strategy, his willingness to pair asymmetrical offense with a more symmetrical defense as a way of maximizing pressure on the Soviet Union. Beyond material support for anti-Soviet guerrillas, the Reagan administration, like the Eisenhower administration before it, embraced information operations as a relatively inexpensive way of putting pressure on the Soviet Union.[12] Reagan's sense of U.S. strengths and, just as important, his assessment of Soviet weaknesses encouraged him to take the ideological offensive in the Cold War. "U.S. policy," the administration explained, "must have an ideological thrust which clearly affirms the superiority of the U.S. and Western values of individual dignity and freedom, a free press, free trade unions, free enterprise, and political democracy over the repressive features of Soviet Communism."[13] As an example of the results of this policy, by one estimate, during the mid-1980s the Soviet Union was spending about $3 billion a year to try to keep Radio Free Europe broadcasts from being heard within the Soviet Union, confirming that the "costs of policing an ideological empire are enormous."[14]

The Reagan administration's hope for and commitment to these more offense-oriented additions to containment, it is worth reiterating, were sharply limited. The overriding need to avoid a direct confrontation with a still powerful Soviet Union meant that any ideological and especially military crusades had to be kept within certain boundaries. Rather than seeking the sudden collapse of the Soviet Union, the Reagan foreign policy team talked about even its more offensive measures as "designed to bring about evolutionary change of the Soviet system." Moreover, those offensive measures were to be limited to "ideological/political" means and were not meant to close the door on the possibility of fruitful negotiations with Moscow. Reagan's strategy toward the Soviets attempted to combine symmetrical containment, ideological pressure for change within the Soviet empire, and negotiations with Moscow.[15] When the Soviet-backed regime in Poland declared martial law in response to the growing Solidarity movement, many hawks encouraged Reagan to challenge the Soviets more directly, which Reagan declined to do, instead opting to respond indirectly by quietly funneling money to the Solidarity movement and bolstering the position of Pope John Paul II, a Pole, who was adamantly making the moral case against the Soviet empire. Reagan's use of the military during his tenure in office was similarly restrained, keeping missions narrow and brief. He directed the invasion of the tiny island of Grenada and launched punitive strikes against Libya; and when America's military deployment in Lebanon threatened to expand in scope and time, Reagan quietly pulled out U.S. forces.[16] As Raymond Garthoff summarizes it, although Reagan "inclined naturally toward a confrontational *attitude* toward the Soviet Union . . . He did not necessarily intend a confrontational *policy* aimed at weakening the Soviet system."[17]

The Reagan approach to U.S. grand strategy was based on the conviction that the "West won't contain communism, it will transcend communism,"[18] but that conclusion was based more on what the administration saw as the inherent weaknesses of the Soviet system than on what U.S. policies could do to speed the Soviet Union's demise. In thinking about U.S. leverage over internal developments in the Soviet Union, the Reagan strategy stressed "the narrow limits available to us" to affect the pace of those changes.[19] Even as late as 1987, as it assessed economic reform efforts in the Soviet Union, Reagan's foreign policy team was thinking in terms of asking "what kind of Soviet Union we wish to see in the next twenty or thirty years" and accepting that "we can affect the outcome only at the margin."[20]

By the end of Reagan's second term in office, however, events within the Soviet Union and in U.S.–Soviet relations started changing far more quickly than anyone expected.[21] Whereas Reagan's initial years in office were characterized by a substantial military buildup, no negotiations with the Soviet Union, and increasing Cold War tensions, by the time he left office Soviet–American relations were improving so rapidly that the Cold War was essentially coming to an end. Nuclear arms control represents one arena where rapid turnabout was most evident.

In his run for the presidency in 1980, Reagan had criticized the SALT process and questioned whether the United States should abide by the limits imposed by the SALT II Treaty, which had never been approved by the Senate. Although summit meetings between the United States and the Soviet Union had become a regular part of the Cold War since the Eisenhower administration, Reagan held no meeting with his Soviet counterparts during his first term. Proponents of arms control worried that the Reagan administration was uninterested in arms control and only willing to make offers that the Soviets were sure to reject. Reagan talked about "peace through strength,"[22] but doubts remained over whether the administration would ever feel strong enough to negotiate.

One prominent example of what was seen as the administration's lack of seriousness on arms control was the "zero option" it put forward regarding theater nuclear missiles. At the time that the United States was in the process of deploying the upgraded Pershing II missiles in Europe, Reagan proposed that both the United States and the Soviet Union reduce their intermediate range missiles to zero. Those suspicious of the administration's sincerity on arms control saw this proposal as an empty ploy that the Soviets were sure to reject as one-sided. The zero option would obligate the Soviets to withdraw missiles they had already deployed in return for U.S. missiles that were only starting to be deployed. The proposal also pertained to missiles only, the area in which the Soviets had the bulk of their nuclear capability, but did not include aircraft-carried weapons based in Europe, an area in which the United States had a large capability. Moreover, the proposal only limited U.S. and Soviet weapons, which meant that Moscow would still be facing an intermediate range nuclear missile threat from American allies in Europe. Finally, Soviet worries about China's nuclear capabilities on their eastern border also made them reluctant to go to zero. Some thought of this not as a serious arms control proposal, but instead as a public relations ploy to pacify the antinuclear movement, which would find it hard to oppose a proposal for eliminating an entire class of weapons. As one contemporary analyst argued, "on all counts the proposal was loaded to Western advantage and Soviet disadvantage, and it was clearly not a basis for negotiation aimed at reaching agreement."[23]

This proposal, however, turned out not to be just propaganda because President Reagan proved willing to take yes for an answer when Soviet leader Mikhail Gorbachev accepted the zero option as a basis for negotiations. Confident that the United States had reached a position of strength and that Gorbachev was interested in pursuing better relations, Reagan was willing to negotiate. Whereas many of Reagan's advisers remained distrustful of Moscow and opposed any far-reaching arms control agreements, Reagan himself proved to be a firm supporter of these efforts and pushed them through despite opposition from his own administration. The highlight of Reagan's arms control efforts came on December 7, 1987, with the signing of the Intermediate-Range Nuclear Forces Treaty (INF Treaty). The SALT agreements had placed limits on what could be built, but the INF Treaty entailed getting rid of an entire class of weapons because the Soviets essentially accepted the zero option.[24] Elected as a staunch Cold Warrior, Reagan left office working closely with Gorbachev to initiate the end of the Cold War.

Reagan and the End of the Cold War

At the outset of the Cold War, George Kennan foresaw a day when the Soviet Union might "be changed overnight from one of the strongest to one of the weakest and most pitiable of national societies."[25] By the late 1980s and early 1990s that day had come. In 1989 the Soviet empire in Eastern Europe quickly unraveled; in 1990 Germany reunified but remained part of NATO; and on Christmas Day 1991, a few months after a failed coup attempt, Mikhail Gorbachev signed a decree terminating the Soviet Union as a political entity.[26] Tellingly, when Gorbachev attempted to sign this decree, his pen had no ink and he had to borrow one from a CNN crew member to complete the ceremony.[27] How much credit does Reagan's approach to U.S. grand strategy deserve for this sudden and stunning turn of events? Did Reagan's tougher line toward the Soviet Union bring on its collapse? Was it irrelevant as events were largely determined by internal Soviet developments? Or did it make ending the Cold War more difficult and costly than it otherwise would have been? Asking these questions goes beyond simply apportioning political praise or blame as it speaks to the broader issue of how the U.S. grand strategy of containment should be judged.

Writing in the immediate aftermath of Reagan's tenure, John Lewis Gaddis recommended that "it would be uncharitable—and historically irresponsible—to begrudge the strategic vision of an administration once thought by many of us to have had none at all."[28] Following his own advice, Gaddis later offered a more extensive and positive review of Reagan's grand strategy: "What one can say now is that Reagan saw Soviet weakness sooner than most of his contemporaries; that he understood the extent to which détente was perpetuating the Cold War rather than hastening its end; that his hard line strained the Soviet system at the moment of its maximum weakness; that his shift toward conciliation preceded Gorbachev; that he combined reassurance, persuasion and pressure in dealing with the new Soviet leader; . . . Reagan's role here was critical."[29]

Gaddis is not alone in praising Reagan's strategy. Henry Kissinger, who had been sharply critical of many of Reagan's policies at the time, later concluded: "Reagan's was an astonishing performance" that "put forward a foreign policy doctrine of great coherence and considerable intellectual power. He possessed an extraordinary intuitive rapport with the wellsprings of American motivation. At the same time, he understood the essential brittleness of the Soviet system, a perception which ran contrary to most expert opinion, even in his own conservative camp."[30] Looking back on the Cold War as a whole, George Kennan concluded that "although historical forces were a greater factor in overcoming the Cold War than were the actions of any individuals," he also maintained that Reagan "did what few other people would have been able to do in breaking this log jam."[31]

Reagan's foreign policy also has its critics. Richard Ned Lebow and Janice Gross Stein, for example, reject the argument that "American defense spending bankrupted the Soviet economy and forced an end to the Cold War." Instead, "the critical factor in the Soviet economic decline was the rigid 'command economy' imposed by Stalin in the early 1930s." Indeed, in their analysis, Reagan's policies prolonged the Cold War by making it harder for Gorbachev to convince Soviet hawks that the United States was not a threat.

Throughout most of the 1980s the Soviet defense budget remained roughly constant as a percentage of gross domestic product, challenging the notion that Reagan's buildup forced Moscow to respond with an unaffordable buildup of its own.[32] Kennan himself took little solace in the results of containment, regretting the time and expense of the strategy.[33]

To assess Reagan's role in the end of the Cold War, the later conciliatory aspects of his strategy probably merit more credit than the earlier confrontational aspects. Reagan undoubtedly believed that communism was an inherently flawed system and that the United States could speed the day of the collapse of the Soviet empire by exploiting economic and ideological weaknesses of the Soviets. The conviction that time was on the U.S. side in the Cold War had, however, been part of the argument for containment since Kennan first enunciated the strategy. Moreover, the Reagan administration was as surprised as everyone else by Moscow's sudden collapse. In thinking about potential internal changes in the Soviet Union that could lead to the end of the Cold War, the administration used words like "evolutionary" and stressed the "narrow limits" in which the United States could influence those changes. As National Security Decision Directive 75 (NSDD-75) explicitly argued, "promoting evolutionary change in the Soviet Union cannot be accomplished quickly," and the policy the administration was pursuing was "for the long haul. It is unlikely to yield a rapid breakthrough in bilateral relations with the Soviet Union."[34]

Although Reagan acolytes would later invoke his example to argue for the possibility of bold U.S. actions leading to radical internal changes in foreign states, Reagan's policies and timetables were far more modest.[35] Reagan was cautiously looking to speed up evolution and was not expecting a precipitate revolution. In the article that brought her to the attention of President Reagan, Jeane Kirkpatrick criticized the Carter administration's human rights policy as being based on the "belief that it is possible to democratize governments, anytime, anywhere, under any circumstances," a belief that she argued was "belied by an enormous body of evidence." For these types of far-reaching internal changes, Kirkpatrick countered, "Decades, if not centuries, are normally required."[36]

It is also a stretch to credit the Reagan buildup as the straw that broke the back of the Soviet economy. There is little evidence that Moscow saw any need to directly respond to the U.S. military buildup of the early 1980s by expanding its defense budget. At best, the Reagan buildup only prevented the Soviets from cutting expenditures here.[37] Again, Reagan's goals were more modest than his later enthusiasts admit. In explaining Washington's economic policies toward Moscow, the Reagan team did not pursue the collapse of the Soviet economy but the more limited goal of not "unduly easing the burden of Soviet resource allocation decisions, so as not to dilute the pressures for structural change in the Soviet system."[38] The resources Moscow was devoting to defense spending were certainly not helping the Soviet economy, but the inefficiencies of its command economy, exacerbated by the collapse of the price of oil in 1986,[39] were the root cause of its demise. As one sign at an East German factory expressed it, paraphrasing Marx, "To the workers of the world: I am sorry."[40] In words consistent with Kennan's original conception of how containment would ultimately succeed, Gorbachev concluded that, "We are encircled not by invincible armies but by superior economies."[41] Moreover, any role that Soviet defense spending played in exacerbating its economic problems is more properly credited to the containment policy as a whole than to the Reagan buildup exclusively.

The area where Reagan deserves more individual credit is in his willingness to take yes for an answer—his decisions to attempt to reassure the Soviets and to respond to Soviet concessions not with suspicion but with a willingness to reciprocate. Perhaps the most striking facet of the Soviet collapse is not that an empire fell, but that it fell peacefully. The rise and fall of empires is a recurring theme in international history, but as Josef Joffe aptly notes, the collapse of the Soviet Union was an "absolute first in the annals of statecraft: an empire that died in bed."[42] The Soviet Union resisted the temptation that had seized previous great powers facing economic decline, which was to strike out militarily in hopes of reversing their deteriorating fortunes. Why?

The containment policy, as implemented by the United States throughout the Cold War, certainly deserves its share of the credit. By convincing Moscow that any attempts at expansion would be actively opposed, containment made a more aggressive Soviet policy look like a dead end rather than a path to economic redemption. Nuclear weapons also played an important role, not only by helping to convince the Soviets that an aggressive foreign policy was dangerous but also by convincing them it was unnecessary. One motivation for declining powers to strike out aggressively is the fear that any moves toward retrenchment could invite further and more dangerous challenges in the future. Nuclear weapons helped to alleviate such fears. Even if the Soviet Union let its empire in Eastern Europe crumble, and even if the Soviet Union itself disintegrated, Russia's vast nuclear arsenal still provided it with a good measure of security against future encroachments on Moscow's core national interests.[43]

President Reagan also deserves much of the credit for the peaceful end of the Cold War. After a nuclear war scare associated with NATO's Able Archer exercise in 1983, but well before Gorbachev's coming to power, Reagan sought to reassure the Soviets that the United States did not intend to attack the Soviet Union.[44] More important, against the advice of many in his administration, against the counsel of influential former policymakers like Richard Nixon and Henry Kissinger, and against the warnings of prominent conservative columnists like Charles Krauthammer and George Will, Reagan treated Gorbachev's reforms as an opportunity to end the Cold War and not as a trap designed to better prepare the Soviet Union to fight the Cold

War.[45] Gorbachev's initiatives played an undoubtedly central role in bring-ing about the end of the Cold War, but Reagan's embrace of those initiatives was also critical. As Melvyn Leffler summarized, Reagan's "greatest contri-bution to ending the Cold War was not the fear he engendered but the trust he inspired."[46]

Managing the End of the Cold War

Although Reagan's successor in the White House came from within his administration, presidential transitions are never seamless. Reagan's more conciliatory second-term policies toward the Soviet Union had been contro-versial within his party and within his administration, and as George H. W. Bush moved from the vice presidency to the presidency, he initiated a re-view of U.S. policy toward Moscow. Expressing the still common distrust of Gorbachev and his intentions, Bush's new national security adviser, Brent Scowcroft, cautioned that the "Cold War is not over" and warned against what he characterized as Gorbachev's "peace offensive" intended to "mak[e] trouble within the Western alliance." The thawing U.S.–Soviet relations were put on hold as the new administration carried out its evaluation.[47]

The conclusion of this review, although still cautious in its embrace of Gor-bachev and his reforms, was generally supportive of efforts to improve rela-tions with Moscow. Referring to the architects and implementers of contain-ment, Bush argued: "They believed that the Soviet Union, denied the easy course of expansion would turn inward and address the contradictions of its inefficient, repressive and inhumane system. And they were right—the Soviet Union is now publicly facing this hard reality." In short, "Contain-ment worked." As a result, Bush continued, "it is now time to move beyond containment to a new policy . . . that recognizes the full scope of change taking place around the world and in the Soviet Union itself. In sum, the United States now has as its goals much more than simply containing So-viet expansionism. We seek the integration of the Soviet Union into the com-munity of nations." Although Bush did caution that "The Soviet Union has promised a more cooperative relationship before, only to reverse course and return to militarism," on balance the assessment was optimistic regarding the possibilities for positive change in U.S.–Soviet relations.[48]

The press of significant foreign policy developments confronting the Bush administration greatly accelerated during the second half of 1989. In June of that year China violently suppressed prodemocracy demonstrations in Tian-anmen Square. The Warsaw Pact faced severe internal challenges as free elections were held in Poland, Hungary, Bulgaria, and Romania. Events in Eastern Europe culminated in November 1989 when the Berlin Wall ceased to divide the city. As Michael Mandelbaum notes, the Berlin Wall was not torn down, its guards opened it. The wall was then peacefully demolished and sold to souvenir seekers. In an irony that signified the end of the Cold War, "What was erected as a barrier against capitalism ended as a capitalist product itself."[49] The collapse of the Soviet bloc did not end in Eastern Europe, it also threatened to spread into the Soviet Union itself as some of its component republics sought to follow the lead of the East Europeans in breaking their political ties to Moscow.

Now, instead of fearing that the Soviet Union would reassert itself as a great power rival, the Bush administration began to fear that the Soviet Union could collapse suddenly and violently. The caution that initially made the Bush administration suspicious of Gorbachev's reforms now led to worries that events were moving too quickly for either Washington or Moscow to peacefully manage.[50] In response, the Bush administration reversed the logic of containment and instead tried to bolster the position of both Gorbachev and Moscow. As Scowcroft concluded, "we have an interest in the stability of the Soviet Union. The instability of the USSR would be a threat to us. To peck away at the legitimacy of the regime in power would not be to promote stability."[51] In a statement critics derided as the "Chicken Kiev" speech, President Bush sought to slow down rather than speed up the disintegration of the Soviet Union. Speaking in Ukraine, the president supported democracy but at the same time he warned that "freedom is not the same as independence. Americans will not support those who seek independence in order to replace a far-off tyranny with a local despotism. They will not aid those who promote a suicidal nationalism based upon ethnic hatred." Attempting to persuade Ukraine to stay within the Soviet Union, Bush pledged that "American investors and businessmen look forward to doing business in the Soviet Union, including the Ukraine."[52]

Although Bush's efforts failed to head off the collapse of the Soviet Union, his administration succeeded in ending the Cold War on U.S. terms and also relatively peacefully. The Warsaw Pact disintegrated without any attempt by the Soviet Union to protect its position by force. Germany reunified and remained within NATO. The Soviet Union broke apart, but it did so peacefully and Moscow retained control over all of the Soviet Union's nuclear weapons. Although critical of the Bush administration for lacking a strategic vision and being more reactive than proactive, Zbigniew Brzezinski also recognizes that the Bush administration's management of the end of the Cold War was "a historic accomplishment . . . especially when one contemplates what might have happened if the American president had been less skillful or lucky. There could have been bloody Soviet repression in Eastern Europe, massive violence in the Soviet Union, or even some unintended East-West collision. Instead, the subsequent peaceful emergences of a democratic Europe, tied to NATO and embraced by the nascent European Union, tipped the historical balance in favor of the West."[53]

Containment and U.S. Grand Strategy

It is perhaps worthwhile to close this discussion of the containment era in U.S. foreign policy by highlighting two overarching lessons about U.S. grand strategy that this period has to offer. First, the forty-plus years of containment indicate that the United States is capable of sustaining a coherent grand strategy over time. The separation of powers that is at the core of the U.S. governmental system, and periodic elections that guarantee a new president every four or eight years have led some to worry that America is incapable of implementing any consistent long-term strategy. For example, Niall Ferguson bemoans "the attention deficit that seems to be inherent in the American political system." "The problem is systemic," he continues, because "the political process militates against farsighted leadership."[54] Similarly, during the Cold War, alluding to the electoral pressures inherent in political events like the Iowa presidential caucus and the New Hampshire primary, John Lewis Gaddis worried that "no single deficiency in our approach to strategy and diplomacy causes us more grief than its subordination to the volatile and irresponsible whims of domestic politics. . . . No other great nation in the history of the world has fallen into the curious habit of re-thinking its foreign policy at quadrennial intervals to meet the anticipated desires of a particular small and snowy northern province, or one chiefly noted for its production of corn and pigs."[55]

Looked at with the benefit of hindsight, however, the continuity in U.S. foreign policy during the containment era is striking. Whereas each new administration put its own stamp on containment and reacted to the successes and failures it encountered, the fundamental idea of containment remained at the heart of U.S. grand strategy for over forty years. In his 2005 edition of *Strategies of Containment*, Gaddis offers a far more positive assessment of the effect of U.S. domestic politics on U.S. grand strategy, arguing that "the shifts that took place can be seen as course corrections imposed by the obligation of accountability inherent in democratic procedures. The requirement to hold an election every four years may have made it difficult to maintain consistency, but it was a safeguard against complacency, against the tendency to persist in counterproductive strategies in the face of evidence that they were just that."[56] Rather than being a hindrance to U.S. grand strategy, the U.S. democratic system can be one of its greatest assets. It need not be a bar to long-term strategy and it offers a mechanism for bringing about modifications and improvements.

The second, perhaps chief lesson of the containment era for U.S. foreign policy is what Gaddis calls the strategic wisdom of allowing "enemies to defeat themselves."[57] Rather than exhaust itself by attempting to immediately overthrow the Soviet Union or to risk a war to bring about its demise, the core strategic insight of containment was that time was on America's side. The United States did not need to directly defeat its Cold War enemy; if it exercised sufficient patience, that enemy would defeat itself. The success of containment should stand in U.S. foreign policy as a constant reminder of the potential benefits of strategic patience over hasty and potentially counterproductive overreactions.

It is fitting to end this discussion of containment with the words of George Kennan, who at the outset of the Cold War asserted that it was the job of the United States to "create among the peoples of the world generally the impression of a country which knows what it wants, which is coping successfully with the problems of its internal life and with the responsibilities of a World Power, and which has a spiritual vitality capable of holding its own among the major ideological currents of the time."[58] This would remain sound advice for the successors of Kennan in the post–Cold War world, who now had to come up with a grand strategy to replace containment.

Grand Strategy in the Absence of a Clear Threat

The Foreign Policy Debates of the 1990s

In the opening days of the Clinton administration, Anthony Lake, the new national security adviser, initiated what he called "the Kennan sweepstakes." Each member of the new foreign policy team, Lake suggested, had the opportunity to become the next George Kennan. All they had to do to win was to develop a new grand strategy to replace containment as a guide for U.S. foreign policy in a post–Cold War world. Jeremy Rosner, a speechwriter for Lake was declared the winner of the Kennan sweepstakes, but what Rosner came up with was not a new strategy, it was a name for a new strategy. That name was "enlargement" and it captured a central goal of the new administration's foreign policy, which was to increase the number of market democracies in the world.[1] Soon however, the word "enlargement" was paired with the somewhat more modest term "engagement," and then engagement fully eclipsed enlargement; but eventually engagement too lost its central place in the Clinton administration's foreign policy rhetoric. The brief shelf life of the ostensible winner of the Kennan sweepstakes is indicative of the difficulty the United States would have throughout the 1990s in developing a new grand strategy in the absence of an overarching but relatively static threat, like the one that had been posed by the now-defunct Soviet Union.[2]

Bush and the New World Order

Although much of the administration of George H. W. Bush was dominated by peaceful management of the end of the Cold War, it did take some tentative steps toward a post–Cold War grand strategy. Its first step in that direction was one that fell back on U.S. values. As James Baker, the secretary of state, concisely put it, "Beyond containment lies democracy."[3] Interpreting the collapse of the Soviet Union not simply as the failure of a single empire, in his inaugural address President Bush argued expansively that "the day of the dictator is over. The totalitarian era is passing, its old ideas blown away like leaves from an ancient lifeless tree." Democracy, in this view, was poised to fill the vacuum. "We know what works," Bush continued, "Freedom works. We know what's right: Freedom is right. We know how to secure a more just and prosperous life for man on earth: through free markets, free speech, free elections, and the exercise of free will unhampered by the state."[4] These views carried through President Bush's four years in office as he started and ended his last formal National Security Strategy document with the aspiration of creating an "Age of Democratic Peace" based on the twin arguments that democracies are destined to flourish and are less likely to go to war with one another.[5]

Giving values a prominent place in U.S. post–Cold War foreign policy did not, however, lead the Bush administration into crusading for those values. The dispositional caution of the Bush team combined with the continuing conviction that time was on America's side kept the Bush administration solidly in the Promised Land camp, supporting the spread of U.S. ideals through encouragement and example rather than direct imposition. According to Richard Haass, who served on the National Security Council staff, the Bush administration's exertions toward the spread of U.S. values were limited to hoping "that some of what is best about us—protection of basic freedoms, respect for the rule of law, etc.—will rub off on them."[6] Declining to crusade, the Bush administration was instead quick to mend relations with Beijing after that government's bloody crackdown on a prodemocracy movement. Similarly, in the administration's largest use of force, neither Iraq nor Kuwait was forcibly democratized as a prerequisite for ending the crisis precipitated by Iraq's 1990 invasion of Kuwait. In Somalia, the Bush administration tried to limit its role to humanitarian efforts to distribute food aid and shied away from a more ambitious effort toward building a functioning democratic state there.

As Jeffrey Engel summarized the Bush administration's mindset, "because American style values are inexorably universal, time and liberalization each remain on Washington's side. They need not be pushed, just as they need not be deeply questioned."[7] The 1990 National Security Strategy talked of "fostering" democracy, which, as Bartholomew Sparrow notes, connotes a passive approach of creating a favorable environment for the spread of U.S. values rather than actively seeking to impose them.[8] "Where authoritarianism still dominates," the Bush administration's final National Security Strategy argued, using the language of the Promised Landers, "we should continue to explain ourselves and to provide factual information and hope. Maintaining our own high standard of democratic practice and the rule of law is vital to our ability to lead by example."[9] Brent Scowcroft later characterized the Bush strategy as one of "enlightened realism" based on the conviction "that the world could be a better place . . . but don't get carried away."[10]

Another key component of President Bush's approach to forging a post–Cold War grand strategy was multilateralism, which stressed the importance of international law and international organizations. As the president described it, "We have before us the opportunity to forge for ourselves and for future generations a new world order—a world where the rule of law, not the law of the jungle, governs the conduct of nations . . . an order in which a credible United Nations can use its peacekeeping role to fulfill the promise and vision of the U.N.'s founders."[11] The standard rhetoric regarding the proper place of multilateralism in U.S. foreign policy is to argue that the more international support the United States can get for its policies the better, but if U.S. interests so dictate, the United States has to be prepared to act on its own. This conventional rhetoric is convenient because it evades rather than directly confronting the trade-offs that are often inherent in policymaking. Of course, unilateralism remains an option if it maximizes U.S. interests, but that is not the core question policymakers face. The real question is how much multilateralism is in U.S. interests? Would U.S. interests be better served by making concessions in one area to maximize international support in another? A key determinant of policymakers' answer to this question lies in how valuable they think the support of other nations and international institutions is. Does working with allies bring vital benefits, significant benefits, or few benefits to U.S. interests? How policymakers answer that question determines how many concessions in other areas they are willing to consider to secure that support.

Whereas the Bush administration always kept the opt-out clause that the "United States will reserve the right to act unilaterally," it put a consistently high value on the support of other countries.[12] In both its 1990 and 1991 National Security Strategies it asserted, "Our first priority in foreign policy remains solidarity with our allies and friends."[13] Designating multilateralism as a top priority meant that the Bush administration calculated that it was typically in U.S. interests to make some concessions in order to maintain that solidarity. Thus, in the 1990–91 Gulf War, the administration not only put a great deal of effort into securing a United Nations mandate and a large coalition but also saw itself, within certain limits, as bound by the constraints imposed on it by that coalition. In language that would later become central to President Clinton's National Security Strategy documents, President Bush talked about U.S. grand strategy in terms of "engagement and leadership" and "collective engagement."[14]

Its attempt to define the security perimeter of the United States was the most difficult problem the Bush administration faced in formulating a replacement for containment. Now that the Soviet Union was no more, how should the United States define and prioritize the threats that its grand strategy was to guard against? Unwilling to physically narrow the U.S. security perimeter, the Bush administration maintained that U.S. interests were universal and that "America must possess forces able to respond to threats in whatever corner of the globe they may occur." Identifying specific threats, however, proved difficult. In place of concrete threats, the president talked more broadly about threats that "can arise suddenly, unpredictably, and from unexpected quarters." "In an era when threats may emerge with little or no warning," Bush continued, "our ability to defend our interests will depend on our speed and our agility. And we will need forces that give us global reach." In this formulation, the relatively isolated geography of the United States was not a strategic benefit but a handicap because it required the United States to develop and maintain power capabilities that it could project over vast distances.[15]

The argument that the United States needed fast and agile forces with global reach, however, provided little strategic guidance. What were these forces supposed to be able to do quickly and nimbly? When they reached the ends of the globe, what problems did they need to help solve? Explaining his administration's relative inaction toward the fighting between Serbia and Croatia during Yugoslavia's initial disintegration, Bush argued that the "concept that we have to work out every problem, everywhere in the world, is crazy."[16] In a pattern that would hold throughout the 1990s, however, the Bush administration could offer only the vaguest description of the threats that the United States did have to be concerned about. "Today's challenges are more complex, ambiguous and diffuse than ever before. They are political, economic, and military; unilateral and multilateral; short- and long-term."[17] This vague threat picture left a gaping hole at the center of U.S. attempts to develop a successor to containment. How do you implement a coherent national strategy if you are looking at such a wide array of diverse threats?

The most controversial episode of the Bush administration's efforts to develop a post–Cold War grand strategy came when a draft of an internal Pentagon memo, the 1992 Defense Planning Guidance, was leaked to the *New York Times*. Written primarily under the direction of Paul Wolfowitz, then undersecretary of defense for policy, the draft asserted, "Our first objective is to prevent the re-emergence of a new rival . . . that poses a threat on the order of that posed formerly by the Soviet Union." Notably included in this list of potential rivals were long time allies of the United States. Reminiscent of Kennan's focus on centers of military-industrial power, the draft argued: "We must account sufficiently for the interests of the advanced industrial nations to discourage them from challenging our leadership or seeking to overturn the established political and economic order." To do this, the United States not only needed to be powerful enough to counter such challenges, but its might also had to be so overwhelming that it would be capable of "deterring potential competitors from even aspiring to a larger regional or global role." In short, according to the draft, "Our strategy must now refocus on precluding the emergence of any potential future global competitor."[18] Rather than help to build up allies as the United States had tried to do during the Cold War, this document suggested keeping America's allies as well as its enemies weak to ward off any potential challenges to U.S. global primacy. The draft Defense Planning Guidance also offered an internal administration challenge to the Bush administration's multilateralism, especially its commitment to bolstering the United Nations. Instead of looking to formal international institutions, "we should expect future coalitions to be ad hoc assemblies, often not lasting beyond the crisis being confronted."[19]

As a draft of an internal Defense Department paper, the document had little official status. Indeed, following the controversy raised by the draft, the 1992 Defense Planning Guidance was quickly reworked, and when the official version came out in April, the most contentious parts of the draft had been eliminated or significantly toned down. This was done not just to quiet a public relations crisis—the arguments of the draft were also controversial within the administration itself. When the Bush administration was set to hand over power to the incoming Clinton team, it prepared a foreign policy transition memo that bore little resemblance to the draft Defense Planning Guidance. The transition memo, written under the supervision of the secretary of state, Lawrence Eagleburger, stressed multilateralism and nontraditional security issues rather than state-centered threats.[20]

In summary, whereas President Bush has been described by a member of his own foreign policy team as having an "anti-grandness gene,"[21] and whereas the Bush administration was more concerned with safely ending the Cold War than grappling with the complexities of the post–Cold War era, Bush did not leave a blank slate to his successors. Instead, he bequeathed an optimistic worldview famously encapsulated in Francis Fukuyama's argument about the "end of history,"[22] stemming from the triumph of U.S. liberal democratic ideals over that of its ideological competitors, an emphasis on the value of multilateralism, and an appreciation for, if not an answer to, the more complex threat environment of a post-Soviet world. Even the redacted arguments of the draft 1992 Defense Planning Guidance would not be forgotten but would return a decade later when another Bush occupied the Oval Office.

Clinton and Engagement

In his run for the White House in 1992, Bill Clinton's chief criticism of George H. W. Bush's foreign policy was that Bush was spending too much time on it. Basing his campaign on the mantra "it's the economy stupid," candidate Clinton promised not to change U.S. foreign policy but to reduce it. In a major foreign policy speech during the campaign, Clinton noted that he "agreed with President Bush on a number of foreign policy questions," but he prefaced the remark with the criticism that President Bush had "devoted his time and energy to foreign concerns and ignored dire problems here at home."[23] His speech accepting the Democratic Party's nomination contained 4,250 words, only 141 of which were devoted to foreign affairs, and even those few words stressed that America's "strength begins at home."[24] In a historical estimation heavily based on his view of the Johnson administration, the newly elected President Clinton worried that foreign policy can only ruin a presidency, it cannot make one great.[25] To Lee Hamilton, the incoming chair of the House Foreign Relations Committee, the former governor of Arkansas insisted that no one cared about foreign policy except a few journalists.[26] Clinton did not return most of the congratulatory phone calls he received from abroad following his inauguration, delegating that responsibility to others.[27] As the new president bluntly told an early interviewer, "Foreign Policy is not what I came here to do."[28]

To oversee his administration's foreign policy, Clinton appointed as secretary of state the experienced but far from dynamic Warren Christopher, whose bland personality was captured in one inside-the-beltway quip that described him as "so lifelike."[29] At an early cabinet meeting that discussed the Clinton administration's priorities for its first 100 days, foreign policy issues had no place on the agenda.[30] Christopher, along with new secretary of defense, Les Aspin and national security adviser, Anthony Lake, had to plead with the president to get just one hour of his time every week, a request the president granted only when he found it possible to fit it into his schedule.[31] James Woolsey, the new president's first director of Central Intelligence estimated that he met with Clinton only twice in the two years he held the job as principal intelligence adviser to the president.[32] In the estimate of longtime presidential adviser David Gergen, Clinton spent only one-quarter as much time as his predecessors on foreign policy.[33] Contrasting presidential memoirs, Zbigniew Brzezinski estimates that whereas George H. W. Bush's memoirs focus almost exclusively on foreign policy, only about 15 percent of Clinton's memoirs focuses on international affairs.[34]

This lack of attention to foreign affairs was partly a reflection of the personality of the young governor from Arkansas who had virtually no foreign policy experience before coming to the Oval Office, but it was also a reflection of the political mood of the country. Indeed, President Clinton's most influential political opponents at home also largely accepted the subordination of U.S. foreign policy to domestic concerns. Of the ten planks put forward by House Republicans as part of their "Contract with America," only one related to foreign policy and the part of that plank that got the most attention was its opposition to placing U.S. troops under United Nations commanders. When Clinton's top foreign policy aides asked to meet with the members of the new Republican leadership following their victory in the 1994 congressional elections, they, like the president they opposed, decided that they had no time to devote to foreign policy discussions.[35] A major reason why the administration and Congress were able to take such a laissez-faire attitude toward foreign policy was that the global situation was seen as relatively benign for the United States, which made neglect a viable policy option.

This reduced attention to foreign affairs did not change the core national interests of the United States. The Clinton administration's first National Security Strategy document started off with a traditional rendering of U.S. interests, offering a triad of goals, which were "To credibly sustain our security," "To bolster America's economic revitalization" and "To promote democracy abroad."[36] The end of the Cold War did, however, change the U.S. conception of what the potential threats to those interests were. Now that the Soviet threat could no longer play the principal organizing role for U.S. grand strategy that it had played during the containment era, the United States had to redefine its security perimeter and determine what threats existed and how to prioritize among those potential threats.[37]

A DIVERSE SECURITY PERIMETER

Giving voice to the universal aspirations of the new administration, Lake averred, "I want to work to end every conflict" and "I want to work to save every child."[38] In attempting to operationalize the security perimeter of the United States, however, the best the Clinton administration could offer was a long and disparate list of potential threats. With the Soviet threat gone, the United States could no longer build its grand strategy against a specific rival or overarching threat. Instead, in the administration's assessment, the United States "confronted a complex array of new and old security challenges." These potential challenges included the possible failure of political and economic reforms in the former Soviet sphere, the question of China's future direction, the proliferation of weapons of mass destruction, rogue states with aggressive regional intentions, violent extremists, militant nationalists, ethnic and religious conflict, environmental degradation, natural resource depletion, rapid population growth, refugee flows, terrorists, organized crime, and drug trafficking. If that extensive list were not daunting enough, the administration also stressed that, given developments in modern technologies that allowed "information, money and ideas to move around the globe at record speed," the security perimeter of the United States could not be geographically bounded. As a result, any potential distinctions between perimeter and strong-point grand strategies were seemingly rendered obsolete by a technology-driven universalism.[39]

Formulating a coherent strategy to deal with such a diverse, nonprioritized list posed a significant challenge. One way the Clinton administration grappled with this challenge was to attempt to unify these varied potential threats under the common heading of globalization. Rather than seeing these as isolated threats, the administration argued that what held this list together was that all these security challenges stemmed from or were exacerbated by the phenomenon of globalization, which the administration defined as "the process of accelerating economic, technological, cultural and political integration."[40] The concept of globalization eventually became so central to Clinton's approach to foreign affairs that the administration's final National Security Strategy document was titled, "A National Security Strategy for a Global Age."[41] Putting a disparate list of threats under the common heading of globalization did not, however, solve the administration's prioritization problem because the concept of globalization itself was so amorphous and, by definition, universal. Putting globalization at the center of U.S. national security strategy still did not provide a clear answer to the question of how the United States could best prioritize the use of its resources. Rather than answer the question, it rephrased it—which of the potential problems of globalization were most pressing for the United States and thus merited a greater expenditure of effort and which could be relegated to secondary status? Brzezinski, for example, was quite critical of Clinton's embrace of globalization, arguing that it offered him a "seemingly coherent theme while freeing him of the obligation to pursue a disciplined foreign policy strategy."[42]

Michael Mandelbaum, another critic of Clinton's grand strategy, charged the administration with attempting "to turn American foreign policy into a branch of social work," citing U.S. interventions in Somalia, the Balkans, and Haiti. These interventions, in Mandelbaum's view, focused the United States on the international periphery rather than the core, on internal developments rather than international relations, and on U.S. values rather than U.S. interests. In its place Mandelbaum recommended an approach similar to Kennan's strongpoints, arguing that the United States still needs to be principally concerned "with the maintenance of an American military presence in Europe and in the Asia-Pacific region," the prevention of the spread of nuclear weapons, and the promotion of international trade.[43] More recently, Richard Betts similarly criticized the Clinton approach to U.S. foreign policy as having "an instinct for the capillaries" rather than the jugular.[44] By Clinton's definition of the post–Cold War security perimeter of the United States, however, dealing with collapsing government structures and civil wars was central to U.S. interests, not peripheral. Globalization was going to create winners and losers and put increasing stress on weak governmental structures, which could spawn or at least exacerbate all the threats Clinton believed the United States needed to be concerned about. In dealing with the political resentments fueled by the perceived inequities and disruptions of globalization the United States was pushed, in Clinton's view, to the geographic periphery rather than to the traditional core states of Western Europe and East Asia.

Also at play in this push to the periphery in U.S. grand strategy was the logic of the domino theory, which survived the end of the Cold War. Responding to Mandelbaum's critique of the Clinton administration's foreign policy, Stanley Hoffmann countered: "We live in a world in which apathy about what happens in 'far away countries of which we know nothing' can all too easily lead—through contagion, through the message such moral passivity sends to troublemakers, would-be tyrants and ethnic cleansers elsewhere—not to the kind of Armageddon we feared during the Cold War but to a creeping escalation of disorder and beastliness that will, sooner or later, reach the shores of the complacent, the rich and the indifferent."[45] U.S. grand strategy was right back to the logic of National Security Council Report 68 (NSC-68) (complete with a reference to appeasement and the Munich analogy), stressing the importance of credibility and worrying that a moral defeat anywhere could lead to defeat everywhere.

EXPLORATORY CRUSADING

Beyond the question of where to draw the security perimeter of the United States, the debate between Mandelbaum and Hoffmann was also a debate about the proper role of America's values in its foreign policy. Like his predecessors and successors in office, Clinton believed that U.S. values and interests were inextricably linked in a virtuous circle so that advancing U.S. interests would also advance its values, and advancing U.S. values would also advance its interests. As his 1995 National Security Strategy summarized it, "We believe that our goals of enhancing our security, bolstering our economic prosperity, and promoting democracy are mutually supportive."[46] Whereas few in the United States would reject the proposition that the world would be a better place the more democracy spread, it was of course possible to reject the explicit promotion of democracy as a core part of U.S. foreign policy. Echoing the earlier worries of John Quincy Adams, doubters could argue that although doing things like trying to make Bosnia into a multiethnic democracy might be a noble goal, it was not a wise or attainable goal for U.S. foreign policy. For such critics, such goals were simply too costly and open-ended and U.S. efforts were too likely to be counterproductive.

The strong relative power position of the United States, however, made crusading a tempting possibility in the post–Cold War world. During the 1970s and into the 1980s, worries about the decline of the United States were on the rise. The collapse of the Soviet Union, economic stagnation in Japan, and the return of robust economic growth in the United States meant that by the early 1990s, instead of decline, the United States seemed further ahead of the rest of the world than at any time in history, with the exception of the immediate post–World War II years. In the assessment of the chairman of the joint chiefs of staff, General John Shalikashvili, "today the difference, or 'delta' between [the] capabilities of our military forces and the military forces of those who would wish us ill is greater than at any time in my 39 years of service." The United States, General Shalikashvili continued, was able to achieve this positive delta even as Washington was "spend[ing] less of a percentage of our national wealth on defense than at any time since before World War II."[47] More broadly, Madeleine Albright, Clinton's pick to represent the United States at the United Nations, characterized the United States "as the world's sole remaining superpower, leading economy, and foremost democracy."[48] Washington seemingly had security and resources to spare, so why not take advantage of this opportunity to reshape the world in the image of the United States? The United States had always possessed the motive, did the end of the Cold War mean that it also now had the opportunity and the means?

For Clinton, however, even the world's sole remaining superpower had limited means to expend on foreign affairs. Candidate Clinton had criticized his predecessor for spending too much time on international issues, and the absence of a clearly defined threat further sapped Clinton's ability to generate domestic support for any potentially expensive foreign policy agenda, especially one that would entail a loss of U.S. lives. Being the world's sole remaining superpower combined with being a superpower that was unwilling to expend many resources in the international arena led the Clinton administration to what its critics have derided as "cruise missile hegemony" or a belief in "immaculate coercion."[49] If the United States faced a problem overseas, Washington would lob a small number of cruise missiles at the problem, an approach that risked no American lives and few foreign ones, and also cost little. Under Clinton, the United States engaged in what could be characterized as exploratory crusading. Washington would embrace sometimes ambitious foreign policy goals, but would only be willing to expend limited means to achieve them. If those crusades became too costly, the Clinton administration was willing to walk away from them.

Somalia is an excellent example of exploratory crusading. Inheriting from the first Bush administration a humanitarian mission to alleviate the potential for mass starvation, Clinton expanded the mission in Somalia to include the bolder goal of building a functioning Somali state. As the Clinton administration saw it, providing food was only a Band-Aid solution that failed to deal with the root of the problem, which was the dysfunctionality of Somali politics. To prevent similar crises in the future, Clinton's team believed that a more representative and competent government needed to be established in Mogadishu. As soon as that more ambitious state-building mission began to cost U.S. lives, captured most dramatically in the Black Hawk Down incident, the Clinton administration was willing to back away from this crusade and pull the United States out of Somalia.

Similarly in Iraq, although Congress had passed the Iraq Liberation Act calling for the overthrow of Saddam Hussein and authorizing funds for that purpose, Clinton requested only a small fraction of those funds, downplayed his administration's enthusiasm for regime change, and resisted efforts such as training expatriate Iraqis to challenge the regime in Baghdad.[50] The same type of cost-sensitive crusading led to slow-motion involvement in Bosnia, a negotiated resolution in Haiti, cruise missile strikes following the U.S. Embassy bombings in Africa, a four-day Desert Fox air campaign against Iraq, a favoring of trade with China over pushing Beijing on human rights, air-only U.S. involvement in the war over Kosovo, and perhaps most conspicuous, the failure to do anything as Rwanda descended into genocide. Coming on the heels of the loss of U.S. lives on the streets of Mogadishu, Lake considered any potential intervention in Rwanda "inconceivable,"[51] and President Clinton later admitted that "we never even had a staff meeting on it."[52]

In conceiving the proper place of U.S. values in U.S. foreign policy, exploratory crusading adapted ends to means rather than means to ends.[53] Crusades might be launched, but if the costs of those crusades got too high, the administration was content to retreat into the Promised Land rather than expend more resources. By the end of Clinton's eight years in office, the costs of even limited forays into crusading had put the administration squarely in the camp of the Promised Landers: "Much as John Winthrop set a standard for early colonists that we 'be as a city upon a hill,'" President Clinton's last National Security Strategy asserted, "nearly four centuries later we still seek to demonstrate the power of our democratic ideals and values by our example." The United States, a more experienced Clinton concluded, is "a nation leading by the authority that comes from the attractiveness of its values and force of its example, rather than the power of its military might to compel by force or sanction."[54]

Exploratory crusading left Clinton's foreign policy vulnerable to criticisms from both ends of the Promised Land–Crusader State spectrum. For critics of crusading, Clinton's rhetoric of the United States as the "indispensable nation" suggested that Washington believed not only that the United States could be a force for good in the world but also that it was the only potential source of good in the world, which put the United States on a path, in the eyes of these critics, for costly and endless efforts to remake the world in its image.[55] For the advocates of crusading, Clinton's policies were tentative and inadequate. William Kristol and Robert Kagan, for example, warned against "succumb[ing] to the charming old metaphor of the United States as a 'city on a hill.'" To John Quincy Adams's caution that the United States not go "abroad in search of monsters to destroy," they asked: "Why not? The alternative is to leave monsters on the loose, ravaging and pillaging to their hearts' content, as Americans stand by and watch. . . . Because America has the capacity to contain or destroy many of the world's monsters, most of which can be found without much searching, and because the responsibility for the peace and security of the international order rests so heavily on America's shoulders, a policy of sitting atop a hill and leading by example becomes in practice a policy of cowardice and dishonor."[56]

Clinton, however, was not too worried about the lack of resources that the United States was putting, or could put, toward foreign policy for two primary reasons. First, his commitment to multilateralism encouraged him to believe that other states could pick up some of the slack by devoting more of their resources to global security problems. Second, his conviction that time was on America's side convinced him that a great expenditure of U.S. resources was not needed because history was moving in a direction that favored the United States on its own.

THE DECLINE OF ASSERTIVE MULTILATERALISM

One reason Clinton believed the United States could safely reduce the resources it put into foreign policy was that "our allies are able to and should shoulder more of the defense burden." As part of his plan to "shift that burden to a wider coalition of nations," candidate Clinton supported the creation of "a U.N. Rapid Deployment Force that could be used for purposes beyond traditional peacekeeping, such as standing guard at the borders of countries threatened by aggression, preventing attacks on civilians, providing humanitarian relief; and combating terrorism and drug trafficking."[57] This policy of "assertive multilateralism" faced challenges from Clinton's earliest days in office, particularly over the issue of potential multilateral command of U.S. forces. As a result, backing for a standing rapid deployment force under the United Nations was quickly downsized to support for a more extensive peacekeeping staff at UN Headquarters to which national military units could be supplied in a time of crisis.[58]

In her position as U.S. ambassador to the United Nations, Madeleine Albright described the dilemma the Clinton administration was facing in foreign policy: "We are being importuned—by allies and former foes alike—to intensify our global security leadership at the very time when the enemy is much harder to identify, when our vital interests are threatened in more subtle and remote ways, and when our budget is so strained." Multilateralism provided one way to ease this dilemma because it would allow the United States to remain active in international affairs, without excessive costs. Global security, Albright maintained, did not require that the United States act "as the world's policeman, only that there should be policemen and that we take a hand in assuring their effectiveness." To do this, the United States should "work energetically to strengthen the capacity of the United Nations and other multilateral organizations to conduct peace-keeping, preventive diplomacy, peace-making, peace-enforcement, humanitarian security, and similar operations." Specifically, Albright called for "a substantial enlargement and reorganization of the peace-keeping headquarters' staff" at the United Nations.[59] The president seconded these plans in a speech at the General Assembly, calling for preparing "U.N. peacekeeping for the 21st Century" by supporting "the creation of a genuine U.N. peacekeeping headquarters with a planning staff, with access to timely intelligence, with a logistics unit that can be deployed at a moment's notice, and a modern operations center with global communications."[60]

Clinton's speech, however, was given just days before the battle of Mogadishu in which eighteen U.S. servicemen were killed as part of the UN operation in Somalia and some of their bodies were dragged through the streets. As a result of troubles in Somalia and difficulty getting any allied agreement on action to stop the growing violence in the former Yugoslavia, when Clinton issued his first National Security Strategy, although he still emphasized that the United States could not achieve its goals unilaterally, his discussions of multilateralism were less assertive and more characterized by limitations, hedges, and questions. "The lesson we must take away from our first ventures in peace operations is not that we should foreswear such operations," the document concluded, "but that we should employ this tool selectively and more effectively."[61]

This increasingly less-assertive multilateralism mirrored a broader grand strategic scaling back from enlargement to engagement. When National Security Adviser Lake first attempted to offer an overarching foreign policy statement, the term at center stage was enlargement, with the more modest engagement playing a supporting role. Stating explicitly that the United States was the globe's "dominant power" with "the world's strongest military, its largest economy, and its most dynamic, multiethnic society," Lake argued that "The successor to a doctrine of containment must be a strategy of enlargement—enlargement of the world's free community of market democracies."[62] The Clinton administration's first-term National Security Strategy documents, however, paired enlargement with engagement, with engagement coming first. By Clinton's second term, the term enlargement was being used only to talk about specific issues like the expansion of NATO or the European Union and was no longer being used to characterize Clinton's approach to foreign policy as a whole. Instead, the documents talked about the "Imperative of Engagement." The administration's last two National Security strategies talked explicitly about the "Strategy of Engagement" and made no mention of any strategy of enlargement.[63]

The core argument behind enlargement was that "All of America's Strategic Interests—from promoting prosperity at home to checking global threats abroad before they threaten our territory—are served by enlarging the community of democratic and free market nations."[64] This strategy was based on the three core ideas of liberalism as an approach to international politics, positing that democracies were less likely to go to war with each other, that free trade was a path to a more peaceful and prosperous world, and that international cooperation could support both peace and prosperity.[65] In this view, increasing the number of market democracies in the world would kick start a virtuous circle and support all U.S. core interests.

The virtuous circle, however, proved more problematic in practice than in theory. Spreading democracy in places like Somalia, Haiti, and the former Yugoslavia was proving to be both doubtful and costly.[66] Even if stable democracies were less likely to go to war with each other, transitions to democracy could lead to increased violence in the short term.[67] Furthermore, many of America's most important allies in places like the Middle East were hardly democratic. The link between democracy and free trade was also not straightforward because China's lack of democracy was not hindering its integration into the world economy, but populist reactions in democracies against the costs of globalization did pose a threat to further economic integration. Free trade was creating winners and losers both in the United States and abroad, and this increased security threats because the losers of globalization could turn to violence. Finally, whereas international institutions could add legitimacy to U.S. actions and provide resources and expertise, obtaining agreement on multilateral actions was time consuming and seemed as likely to lead to gridlock as to effective action. The costs and uncertain prospects of enlargement led the Clinton administration to the more reserved strategy of engagement. Instead of talking about enlarging the community of democracies, the 1999 National Security Strategy spoke more modestly of trying to "influence the actions of other states and non-state actors, to provide global leadership, and to remain a reliable security partner for the community of nations that share our interests."[68] This more modest approach was sufficient, Clinton believed, because of a final key component of his grand strategy—his conviction that time was on America's side.

THE TRAVAILS AND ULTIMATE TRIUMPH OF GLOBALIZATION

For the Clinton administration globalization was a two-edged sword, but one that ultimately cut in favor of the United States and its interests. Whereas globalization was a source of potential threats in the near term, for Clinton it also "offered unprecedented opportunities to avert those threats and advance our interests."[69] Over time, Clinton and his team believed that the positive aspects of globalization would outweigh the negative, thus ushering in a more peaceful, prosperous, and democratic world. The Clinton administration trusted in a "teleology of technology," in the words of Josef Joffe, and believed that the spread of information and technology would inexorably advance U.S. interests. History was on America's side and at most needed a bit of a push from Washington to keep it heading in the right direction. "The Clintonites bestowed upon themselves the role of midwife," Joffe continues, not driving the creation of this new world, but simply monitoring the birthing process to deal with any complications that arose.[70]

As globalization was primarily an economic phenomenon, the Clinton administration put more emphasis on foreign economic policy than the administrations of his predecessors. In his first days in office, President Clinton created a new National Economic Council, which he staffed before staffing his National Security Council.[71] Similarly, two of the greatest political risks that Clinton took in relation to foreign policy dealt with the economics of globalization: he pushed approval of the North American Free Trade Agreement against the consensus of his party and he oversaw a bailout of the Mexican economy in the face of congressional opposition.[72]

Although the term "globalization" did not appear in any of Clinton's National Security Strategies until 1998, his belief in the positive long-term influence of globalization trends was present from the start. His administration's first National Security Strategy avowed: "The dynamism of the global economy is transforming commerce, culture, and global politics, promising greater prosperity for America and greater cooperation among nations."[73] Although it still pointed out the short-term dangers that globalization posed for the United States and global security, Clinton's 1998 National Security Strategy asserted that the central duty of the United States lay in "harnessing the forces of global integration for the benefit of our own people and people around the world."[74] Clinton's final National Security Strategy made his administration's teleology explicit, contending that, "Globalization, which has drawn our economic and security interests closely together, is an inexorable trend in the post–Cold War international system." In language more evocative of new-age mysticism than national strategy, Clinton argued that given the relentless march of globalization, it was America's job "to capture its positive energy and to limit its negative outcomes, where they exist."[75]

Like the expectation that other states would start doing more as the United States did less, the belief that world politics was moving in the right direction through the forces of globalization made it safe for the United States to take a less active role in the international arena, especially when that role came with significant costs. The United States would be better off husbanding its resources and reaping the benefits of globalization's "positive energy."

In the waning years of his administration, unlike in its opening years, President Clinton took a far more personal role in foreign affairs. Overseeing a war in Kosovo and attempting to play the role of direct mediator for Israeli–Palestinian negotiations, Clinton left office far more engaged in foreign policy than when he had entered. This increased presidential attention, however, did not translate into a particularly activist foreign policy. Chastened by early failures in crusading, less confident in the potential of multilateralism, and still relatively serene about the overall direction of international politics, Clinton's foreign policy remained modest. One key grand strategic issue that did not change during Clinton's eight years in the Oval Office was his administration's continued difficulty delineating a clear security perimeter for the United States. Many threats remained, but they were amorphous. George Tenet, Clinton's second-term director of Central Intelligence explained the administration's priorities to Congress by arguing that there are "10 or 15 things that matter most to American Security."[76] When priorities remain too numerous to accurately count, however, it is hard to count them as priorities.

Opportunity Lost or Resources Husbanded?

The first two attempts by the United States to develop a post–Cold War grand strategy were both tentative. The presidency of George H. W. Bush was preoccupied with ending the Cold War and had little time to answer the question of what would come next. Moreover, its dispositional caution made it more conservative than revolutionary. The presidency of Bill Clinton was, initially at least, preoccupied with the economy at home and devoted to foreign policy only when the president had time left over. Moreover, the administration's sensitivity to the costs of its foreign policy initiatives also made it more cautious than bold in the international arena. In the absence of a clear overarching threat, U.S. grand strategy became less grand. Perhaps it is the containment era that should be seen as the anomalous period in U.S. foreign policy. Without the Soviet threat to drive it, U.S. foreign policy became more diffuse.

Overall the United States had little to show for its first decade as the world's sole remaining superpower. Nothing the United States did in the 1990s matched the activity and boldness of U.S. foreign policy in the first years after World War II, which, beyond the formulation of containment, saw the establishment of the United Nations, the North Atlantic Treaty Organization (NATO), the World Bank, the International Monetary Fund, and the General Agreement on Tariffs and Trade (GATT). If the period immediately following victory in great power war is the time when the victor is in the best position to reshape the international order,[77] the results of U.S. foreign policy in the decade after the Cold War are relatively meager. If anything, U.S. foreign policy seemed more focused on fine-tuning remnants of the Cold War, such as expanding NATO, moving from the GATT to the World Trade Organization, and reforming the United Nations, than in developing the institutions that would be needed to confront a new era. As Richard Haass lamented, "the overriding theme of recent U.S. foreign policy is underachievement and squandered potential. . . . Clinton inherited a world of unprecedented American advantage and opportunity and did little with it. Few relationships or institutions bear his imprint; no consensus exists at home on U.S. purposes in the world or how they should be pursued."[78]

On the other hand, the United States avoided any costly and draining conflicts, retained its position as the world's preeminent power in a way that avoided the creation of any overt counterbalancing coalition, and enjoyed a decade of relative peace and prosperity. In a more positive evaluation of Clinton's limited foreign policy, Josef Joffe concludes: "This is hardly the worst grand strategy for a power that enjoys primacy, . . . economy of force is the better part of valor because its superiority is neither overwhelming nor guaranteed forever. Nor can the United States count on the automatic succor of allies abroad and the electorate at home. Power must not be expended wantonly or provocatively so as not to tempt the lesser players to coalesce in countervailing coalitions. So, power must be invested wisely if primacy is not to wither soon."[79]

The opening of America's second decade as the world's sole remaining superpower would see another Bush in the White House. In his initial months in the Oval Office, George W. Bush appeared to be following largely in the footsteps of both his father and President Clinton, overseeing a less-grand grand strategy for the United States. After the terrorist attacks of September 11, 2001, however, the second President Bush would depart from the model of his predecessors and pursue a far more ambitious foreign policy agenda, this one built around terrorism, in the same way that containment had been built around the Soviet threat. The questions with which Washington had grappled throughout the 1990s about U.S. grand strategy in the absence of an overarching threat and in an era of constrained resources, however, were not answered. Instead they were pushed to the side in a war on terrorism that the administration of Bush the younger was determined to find the means to fight. Pushing these questions to the side did not make them go away. Indeed, George W. Bush's successor in office would have to wrestle with even more severely limited means, given the costs that the War on Terror would impose, and he would have to confront a threat picture just as amorphous as that confronted in the 1990s. U.S. foreign policy in the George W. Bush years, the subject of the next chapter, might therefore be more accurately characterized not as the start of a new era in U.S. grand strategy, but as a temporary interlude in the ongoing post–Cold War attempts of the United States to forge a grand strategy in the context of a complicated threat environment and with only limited means.

The Rise and Fall of the War on Terror in U.S. Grand Strategy

Although new presidential administrations offer one potential source for change in U.S. foreign policy, sometimes changes within one administration can be just as sweeping, if not more so. In these cases, the source of change is not variation in personnel, but variation in the thinking of the existing personnel or variation in the influence of current advisers because the same policy makers are forced to grapple with new problems or respond to unexpected developments. The foreign policy of the George W. Bush administration fits the latter template. His campaign for the presidency and his initial months in office put him squarely in the mold of his two post–Cold War predecessors. The most significant changes in U.S. grand strategy came not when George W. Bush was inaugurated, but in response to the terrorist attacks of September 11, 2001.[1] The deaths of close to three thousand Americans in lower Manhattan, at the Pentagon, and in rural Pennsylvania not only increased the influence of certain foreign policy advisers at the expense of others but also greatly affected the thinking of the most important foreign policymaker—the president. This resulted in far-reaching changes in U.S. grand strategy under the banner of the War on Terror. The grand strategy of the George W. Bush administration would also undergo further, if less dramatic changes, in its final years as the costs of the War on Terror, especially on the Iraqi front, continued to mount.

Bush's Pre-9/11 Foreign Policy

Like President Clinton, George W. Bush came to the presidency with little background in foreign policy. In preparing his run for the Oval Office, Bush confided in Condoleezza Rice, who would become his closest foreign policy counselor and first national security adviser: "I don't have any ideas about foreign affairs." As a governor, also like his predecessor, "This isn't what I do."[2] Given the limited and secondary role to which foreign policy had been demoted in the post–Cold War era, it was no longer much of a disadvantage to be a candidate, who in his own words, was "not going to play like a person who's spent hours involved with foreign policy."[3]

In the Bush team's criticisms of their immediate predecessor, they tried to stake out positions different from Clinton in their definition of the U.S. security perimeter, in the balance they wanted to strike between unilateralism and multilateralism, and in the role they thought U.S. values should play in foreign policy. Echoing critics who derided Clinton's foreign policy as social work, Condoleezza Rice, in the Bush campaign's most elaborate statement of the candidate's foreign policy views, argued that Clinton failed to separate "the important from the trivial," singling out U.S. operations in Haiti as a particularly grievous example. Instead of frittering away U.S. resources in peripheral arenas, Washington needed "to focus U.S. energies on comprehensive relationships with the big powers, particularly Russia and China."[4] This appeared to be an attempt to move U.S. grand strategy toward a strong-point approach focusing on the great powers and away from the more universalist strategic perimeter of the Clinton years, which focused on dealing with the worldwide effects of globalization. Any move to a strong-point approach was undermined, however, by continued uncertainty about the precise nature of the most important threats facing the United States in a post–Cold War world. In talking about threats, candidate Bush argued confusingly, "When I was coming up it was a dangerous world and we knew exactly who the 'they' were. It was us versus them. And it was clear who 'them' was. Today, we're not so sure who the 'they' are, but we know they're there."[5] Even his more prepared remarks were similarly vague in defining threats, arguing that "The Empire has passed, but evil remains."[6]

Terrorism, the problem that would consume much of the administration's foreign policy, merited little consideration in the opening months of Bush's tenure. Clinton had reformed the National Security Council to deal with global issues such as terrorism, and he had paid increasing attention to the issue throughout his eight years in office. Richard Clarke, who was the counterterrorism czar during the Clinton era, had his position downgraded in the new administration and did not get a chance to speak to the president about the al-Qaeda threat until after the horror of 9/11.[7] The president reportedly diminished other briefings he received about the terrorist threat from the Central Intelligence Agency, calling them "cover your ass briefings."[8] Whereas responsibility for the failure to prevent the attacks of 9/11 has become a highly politicized issue, perhaps the fairest assessment has been offered by Derek Chollet and James Goldgeier, who note that although the Clinton administration came to focus much rhetorical attention on terrorism, it "did not pursue a strategy commensurate with the language it was using internally" and they also note that initially "the Bush administration lumped terrorism into the category of 'Clinton issues' that they believed were a sideshow to core American interests."[9]

Rice also criticized the Clinton administration for not finding the right balance between unilateralism and multilateralism, arguing that the Clinton team had been so "anxious to find multilateral solutions to problems that it has signed agreements that are not in America's interests." In talking about efforts to stop the proliferation of nuclear weapons, Rice placed the word "norm" in quotes to question the existence of any such thing and more broadly argued that "the Clinton administration's attachment to largely symbolic agreements and its pursuit of, at best, illusory 'norms' of international behavior has become an epidemic."[10] Consistent with this more unilateral bent, the Bush administration dramatically "unsigned" the Rome Statute creating the International Criminal Court, rejected a verification protocol to the Chemical Weapons Convention, and dismissed the Kyoto Accords designed to deal with climate change—without offering any alternative international solutions.[11]

In delineating the proper role of U.S. values in its foreign policy, Rice criticized the Clinton administration for being too concerned with launching crusades that would spread U.S. ideals. Even as she rejected any "sharp line between power politics and a principled foreign policy based on values" and maintained, along with many of her predecessors, that "American values are universal," she nevertheless insisted that whereas "there is nothing wrong with doing something that benefits all humanity" this "is, in a sense a second-order effect." Speaking the language of the Promised Landers, Rice argued that furthering the more concrete security and economic interests of the United States "will create conditions that promote freedom, markets, and peace."[12] This was consistent with the rhetoric of candidate Bush, who attempted to place himself even deeper in the Promised Land camp than President Clinton had. He reproached his predecessor for getting the United States involved in protracted nation-building activities in places like Haiti, Bosnia, and Kosovo, deriding them as "missions without end."[13] When asked during one of the presidential debates about what he thought of nation building, he wondered, "Maybe I'm missing something here. I mean, we're going to have kind of a nation-building corps from America? Absolutely not."[14]

One area in which candidate Bush was in full agreement with his predecessor was in his conviction that time was on America's side. Serving as the Promised Land would be sufficient for the United States because, in the words of then Governor Bush, "There is a direction in events, a current in our times. 'Depend on it,' said Edmund Burke. 'The lovers of freedom will be free.'" "We firmly believe," Bush continued, that "our nation is on the right side of history."[15] Although less enamored with the term "globalization" than Clinton's advisers had been, Condoleezza Rice similarly argued, "Powerful secular trends are moving the world toward economic openness and—more unevenly—democracy and individual liberty." "As history marches toward markets and democracy," rogue states like Iraq, North Korea, and Iran "have been left by the side of the road." With time working in favor of the United States, Washington could afford strategic patience. "These regimes are living on borrowed time, so there need be no sense of panic about them," Rice concluded, even if they were to develop nuclear weapons.[16]

It is difficult to read the administration's early foreign policy statements without thinking about what Bush's foreign policy was to become, especially its eventual decision to launch a preventive war against Iraq and the costs that would entail. Indeed, it is especially ironic to read the Bush team's criticisms of the Clinton administration for actions that they too would soon commit. "The president must remember," Rice chided, "that the military is a special instrument. . . . It is not a civilian police force. It is not a political referee. And it is most certainly not designed to build a civil society." Rice's critique of Clinton's handling of the former Yugoslavia would not be out of place in the many criticisms that the Bush administration would later face over their handling of the Iraq War: "That President Clinton was surprised at Milošević's tenacity is, well, surprising. If there is any lesson from history, it is that small powers with everything to lose are often more stubborn than big powers, for whom the conflict is merely one among many problems. The lesson, too, is that if it is worth fighting for, you had better be prepared to win. Also, there must be a political game plan that will permit the withdrawal of our forces."[17] At the time these words were written, however, the attacks of 9/11 had yet to occur and the War on Terrorism and the war in Iraq were beyond America's strategic horizon.

9/11 and U.S. Grand Strategy

By early September 2001, the Bush administration had been in office for approximately eight months and was reportedly well on its way to writing, approving, and issuing its first National Security Strategy. After the terrorist attacks of 9/11, however, those initial efforts were largely abandoned because of the need to respond to the shock of that day's events. More like a lightning bolt than an earthquake, in the fitting image offered by Josef Joffe, those attacks did not restructure international politics, but instead shone a bright, fleeting light on the existing landscape. The result was a series of significant changes in the Bush administration's approach to U.S. grand strategy.[18] As Vice President Cheney saw it, "all our assumptions about our own security had changed. It was a fundamental shift. . . . We were in a new era and needed an entirely new strategy to keep America secure."[19]

One important facet of U.S. foreign policy that did not change was the Bush administration's conception of fundamental U.S. national interests.

Similar to his predecessors, President Bush offered the traditional triad of security, economic progress, and the spread of U.S. values, by putting forth the goal of creating "decades of peace, prosperity, and liberty." Also similar to his predecessors, Bush saw these goals as inextricably linked in a virtuous circle that "reflects the union of our values and our national interests" and would "make the world not just safer but better."[20] In other ways, however, the 2002 National Security Strategy that followed the attacks of 9/11 was a significant departure from its predecessors. It radically reprioritized the threats that the United States was facing, advocated crusading for U.S. values, argued that although history remained on America's side, time did not, and it furthered the administration's already existing preference for unilateralism.

A PRIORITY THREAT, BUT AN UNLIMITED SECURITY PERIMETER

Perhaps the most difficult grand strategic problem the United States had been grappling with since the end of the Cold War involved how to define and prioritize the threats the United States was facing. In the decade after the collapse of the Soviet Union, presidents tended to offer a laundry list of potential threats but with little sense of prioritization to guide strategic choices. Following 9/11, the Bush administration combined two of the threats on those lists and vaulted that amalgamation to the top of U.S. security concerns. The potential proliferation of weapons of mass destruction and the dangers of terrorism had appeared on all threat lists that the United States had produced in the 1990s, but these were just two among many threats that Washington seemingly had to be concerned about. Because of the demonstrated willingness of terrorist groups to cause mass casualties that were on gruesome display in the rubble of the Twin Towers, the Bush administration concluded that terrorists with access to weapons of mass destruction were now the most important threat the United States faced and that U.S. grand strategy had to be directed toward conducting a war on terror. "The gravest danger our nation faces lies," the 2002 National Security Strategy averred, "lies at the crossroads of radicalism and technology."[21]

This definition of the most pressing threat the United States faced was in important ways a direct refutation of the logic George Kennan had used to define the security perimeter of the United States at the outset of the Cold War. Only a state capable of producing military-industrial power on a massive scale, Kennan had reasoned, would be capable of crossing oceans and inflicting significant damage on the United States. As a result, Kennan concluded, the United States had to be principally concerned with the most powerful states in world politics and could afford to pay less attention to the poorer and weaker regions of the world. In the aftermath of 9/11, according to the Bush team, Kennan's logic no longer applied. "Enemies in the past needed great armies and great industrial capabilities to endanger America. Now, shadowy networks of individuals can bring great chaos and suffering to our shores for less than it costs to purchase a single tank." Consequently, "America is now threatened less by conquering states than we are by failing ones. We are menaced less by fleets and armies than by catastrophic technologies in the hands of the embittered few."[22] This was a refutation not just of Kennan, but of the Bush campaign's earlier insistence that U.S. foreign policy needed to refocus itself on the world's great powers rather than the international periphery. The periphery had once again become central because "The events of September 11, 2001 taught us that weak states, like Afghanistan, [where al-Qaeda had planned the attacks of 9/11] can pose as great a danger to our national interests as strong states."[23]

Just as you can find discussions of the terrorist threat and the dangers associated with the proliferation of weapons of mass destruction in America's pre-9/11 National Security Strategies, America's post-9/11 National Security Strategy also mentioned other threats beyond the crossroads of radicalism and technology. The difference was one of emphasis and prioritization. Prior to 9/11, terrorism and the proliferation of weapons of mass destruction had not been singled out for particular emphasis. They were just members of a rather long list. In America's first post-9/11 grand strategy, conversely, these threats were singled out in a way that eclipsed all other potential threats.

This new prioritization, however, did little to delimit the security perimeter of the United States, given the amorphous nature of the terrorist threat. In a globalized world, technology can quickly proliferate and political radicalism can arise anywhere. Therefore, the crossroads of radicalism and technology can potentially appear anywhere. As Stephen Biddle observes, the Bush administration's list of potential enemies was "remarkably unspecific." It was a list of categories (terrorists, rogue states, failing states), not of names.[24] As the 2002 National Security Strategy explained, "The enemy is not a single political regime or person, or religion or ideology. The enemy is terrorism."[25] As was noted in an early influential criticism of the War on Terror, wars against common nouns like drugs, poverty, or terrorism are far harder to bound and successfully conclude than wars against proper nouns like Germany or al-Qaeda. The Bush administration had declared war not against any specific terrorist groups, but against the tactic of terrorism and from a strategic perspective, "choosing one's enemies on the basis of their tactics alone has little to recommend it."[26]

Even the domino theory, which had been discredited in public rhetoric because of its association with the costs and ultimate failure of the U.S. war in Vietnam, made a comeback in the post-9/11 world. "Now we understand," argued Bush's deputy director of the Policy Planning Staff, "that a failed state in Central Asia, mistreatment of women under a perverse interpretation of Islam, the curriculum in religious schools in Indonesia, drug trafficking in the Andes, and a virus in the blood stream of millions of Africans can set in place a string of dominos that, once set toppling, can touch our lives here in America in the most immediate ways imaginable."[27] Worries about credibility again meant that even costly endeavors in potentially peripheral areas could not be abandoned. In language reminiscent of earlier defenses of U.S. efforts in Vietnam, the secretary of defense, Donald Rumsfeld, argued that:

> If we left Iraq prematurely—as the terrorists demand—the enemy would tell us to leave Afghanistan. And then withdraw from the Middle East. And if we left the Middle East, they would order us—and all those who don't share their militant ideology—to leave what they call the occupied Muslim lands, from Spain to the Philippines. And then we would face not only the evil ideology of these violent extremists—but an enemy that will have grown accustomed to succeeding in telling free people everywhere what to do. We can persevere in Iraq. Or we can withdraw prematurely, until they force us to make a stand nearer home.[28]

Whereas the domino theory had tended to push America to a universal security perimeter in the Cold War, Kennan's linkage of threats to military-industrial power capabilities pushed in the opposite direction, encouraging a focus on certain core states. A global war on terror offered no such corrective force. The threat had been defined, but it had been defined so broadly that the United States was still confronting a universal security perimeter.

CRUSADING REBORN

The area where the Bush administration's approach to U.S. grand strategy was most affected by the attacks of 9/11 centered on the question of the proper place of American values in U.S. foreign policy. During the campaign Bush had placed himself squarely within the Promised Land camp. He warned that "one way for us to end up being viewed as the ugly American is for us to go around the world saying, 'We do it this way. So should you.'" Instead, he encouraged the United States to be more "humble in how we treat nations that are figuring out how to chart their own course."[29] It is hard to find many traces of that humility in the 2002 National Security Strategy, which opens by characterizing U.S. values not only as triumphant but also as offering "a single sustainable model for national success." Beyond being an exemplar for its values, "the United States will use this moment of opportunity to extend the benefits of freedom across the globe." "We will actively work," the strategy continues, "to bring the hope of democracy, free markets, and free trade to every corner of the world." U.S. values are not just a model the United States offers; they are a set of "non-negotiable demands."[30] The United States as merely a "city on a hill" was too tentative for a president who now favored more active and potentially revolutionary initiatives.[31]

In addressing the "why do they hate us" question that emerged after the attacks of 9/11, Bush averred, "how do I respond when I see that in some Islamic countries there is vitriolic hatred for America? I'll tell you how I respond: I'm amazed. I'm amazed that there is such misunderstanding of what our country is about, that people would hate us. I am, I am—like most Americans, I just can't believe it. Because I know how good we are." This conviction about the goodness that the United States embodied reinforced a crusading outlook, leading Bush to conclude that what the United States needed was to "do a better job of making our case" and, in particular, "a better job of explaining to the people in the Middle East."[32]

Without using the term "nation building," the 2002 National Security Strategy embraced the components of nation building as necessary skills for the United States to have: "we must also be able to help build police forces, court systems, and legal codes, local and provincial government institutions, and electoral systems."[33] This passage is in a section discussing the State Department, but under Bush these missions would be shared across the executive branch. For instance, the Bush administration used its foreign assistance program as a tool of nation building, creating the Millennium Challenge Account, which tied U.S. aid to the ability of recipient countries to meet predefined governance criteria.[34] In the wars in Afghanistan and Iraq it was the military that was thrust into the primary role of nation builders, a mission that candidate Bush had condemned. As the president explained in his memoirs, he had been suspicious of and opposed to nation building as a mission for the military, but "after 9/11, I changed my mind."[35]

The administration's most explicit statement of its crusading impulses is contained in a quote that the 2002 National Security Strategy offers from a speech the president had given at the memorial service held in the National Cathedral for the victims of the 9/11 attacks. "Our responsibility to history is already clear," Bush averred, "to answer these attacks and rid the world of evil."[36] Even Woodrow Wilson, the archetype crusader in U.S. foreign policy (who was in a way present at the speech because his body is interred in the National Cathedral) must have marveled at the audacity of that crusade, making his goal of creating a world safe for democracy seem positively modest by comparison. The president's words that day were consistent with the hymn selected for the service, the "Battle Hymn of the Republic." If the crusaders in U.S. foreign policy had a fight song, this would be it. The "Battle Hymn of the Republic" is not a call for a war of limited goals or a call to serve as a positive example for others to emulate, it is explicitly a call to go to war in God's name. It talks of "the fateful lightning of His terrible swift sword," of crushing the serpent with a heel, and of sounding "forth the trumpet that shall never call Retreat." Just as Christ "died to make men holy" the hymn concludes, "let us die to make men free."

After having criticized his predecessor for having an "overly broad definition of American interests"[37] and undertaking missions without end, the attacks of 9/11 had now led Bush and his administration to embrace the mission of ridding the world of evil. In one famous definition, a neoconservative is characterized as a liberal who has been mugged by reality. In the words of a prominent neoconservative, Charles Krauthammer, after 9/11 the Bush administration was composed of realists who had been mugged by reality.[38] Just as the Black Hawk Down fight on the streets of Mogadishu almost a decade earlier had confirmed the warnings of Promised Landers about the costs and dangers of crusading, after 9/11 it was the crusaders' chance to say "We told you so." After the Soviet withdrawal from Afghanistan events in that country seemed far from U.S. interests. Washington may not have liked the Taliban and those they chose to associate with, but was it the job of the United States to search for monsters in faraway Afghanistan? After the attacks of September 11, 2001, the crusaders answered with a resounding yes. This is what happens, the crusaders argued, if you let monsters roam abroad freely. Eventually those monsters will attack you. To add to U.S. concerns, what if some of those monsters got access to nuclear weapons? Just as the costs of crusading helped push the Clinton administration into the Promised Land, the shock of the attacks of 9/11 jolted the Bush administration into the camp of the crusaders.

The geographical focal point of Bush's crusade was the Middle East. "The opportunity to spread freedom throughout the globe, and particularly in the broader Middle East and in the Muslim world," argued Stephen Hadley, Bush's second national security adviser, "that is, I think for the president, the defining idea of his presidency . . . it is not only a sort of moral duty, it's not only consistent with our principles, it's consistent with our interests, it's actually essential for our national security. . . . For liberty to be secure at home, liberty has to be on the march abroad. Big stuff. Not big. Huge."[39] The White House press secretary, Scott McClellan, similarly argued that what drove the Bush administration to war in Iraq "more than anything else was an ambitious and idealistic post-9/11 vision of transforming the Middle East through the spread of freedom. This view was grounded in a philosophy of coercive democracy, a belief that Iraq was ripe for conversion from a dictatorship into a beacon of liberty through the use of force."[40] The 9/11 attacks had thus reversed the Bush administration's perceived relationship between values and interests. Whereas Rice had argued that the spread of U.S. values would be a "second-order effect" of the pursuit of U.S. interests, now the "defining idea" of the Bush presidency was that securing U.S. interests would instead be an effect of spreading U.S. values. In the Middle East the United States became a revolutionary power, seeking a fundamental reshaping of the region in its image, and, as Anatol Lieven warned, at the risk of "kicking to pieces the hill of which it is the king."[41]

In pursuing a crusade for democracy in the Middle East, the Bush administration was pushing on an open door domestically. The coalition that supported the active spreading of U.S. values went well beyond the neoconservatives and included many liberals who believed in a democratic peace, the universality of democracy, and the limits of sovereignty in the face of massive human rights abuses. The war in Iraq as well as Bush's wider democracy promotion agenda in the Middle East were thus easy to defend on liberal grounds. This is why many Democrats supported the war in Iraq and the ends sought by the Bush administration in the Middle East. Although some did criticize the march to war, that criticism tended to focus on the administration's unilateral conduct of the war rather than the goals of the war.[42]

UNILATERALISM BY PREFERENCE AND BY DEFAULT

The terrorist attacks of 2001 produced a sweeping reversal in the Bush administration's assessment of the proper place of U.S. values in its foreign policy, but when it came to the administration's assessment of the proper role of international law and international institutions in U.S. grand strategy, those attacks served to accentuate a preexisting preference for unilateralism. Well before 9/11 the Bush team had expressed its doubts about the value of multilateralism in U.S. foreign policy. Would those attacks and the subsequent War on Terror influence the way that the administration calculated the relative costs and benefits of working with others as opposed to going it alone?

Writing in the winter of 2001, G. John Ikenberry argued that "the logic of the situation has strengthened the hand of those seeking to pursue American interests through multilateral and alliance-based tools." Doubting "whether the Bush administration's discovery of the virtues of a multilateral coalition in fighting terrorism will spill over to its grand strategy," Ikenberry nevertheless contended that "the long-term demands of a campaign against terrorism," including the need for intelligence sharing and transborder law enforcement, would push the Bush administration "to work with and strengthen rules, laws and institutions."[43] In some ways, Ikenberry's predictions were borne out. The War on Terror changed China and Russia from potential peer competitors into potential allies. Both faced terrorist threats of their own, thus opening the door to a potential great power concert based on opposition to terrorism.[44] Casting a wider net, the Bush administration also set up broader international institutions to help prosecute the War on Terror, such as the Proliferation Security Initiative, which was designed to check the spread of weapons of mass destruction and their delivery vehicles. Ikenberry concluded that by the end of Bush's eight years in office, however, the attacks of 9/11 had not pushed the Bush administration to multilateralism, but far in the opposite direction. "The Bush administration was not simply acting a bit more unilaterally than previous administrations," Ikenberry determined, but "was articulating a new logic of global order" that would be based on U.S. unilateralism, U.S. leadership, and U.S. power rather than multilateral negotiations.[45]

Like its predecessors, Bush's National Security Strategy documents offer vague guidelines rather than strict rules regarding how the United States should make the trade-offs between unilateralism and multilateralism. The 2002 National Security Strategy recognized that "no nation can build a safer, better world alone" and that "Alliances and multilateral institutions can multiply the strength of freedom-loving nations." Overall, it asserted that "America will implement its strategies by organizing coalitions—as broad as practicable." These statements, however, came with the caveat that America "will be prepared to act apart when our interests and unique responsibilities require."[46] Such declarations do not answer the question of how the United States would face the trade-offs between unilateralism and multilateralism, they simply restate the question. How do you determine how broad a coalition is practicable? When do America's "interests and unique responsibilities" push the scale in favor of unilateralism? These general formulations leave a lot of room for case-by-case judgments.

A key variable in making those case-by-case judgments is the administration's assessment of how valuable the contributions of its allies are. Do potential allies bring a lot to the table, so that it is worthwhile to make sacrifices to get them onboard, or do they bring little of tangible value? The Bush administration's answer to this crucial question pushed it to the unilateral end of the spectrum because it saw the potential contributions of its allies as modest at best. The opening line of President Clinton's final National Security Strategy maintained that "Since the end of the Cold War, the United States and its allies have developed a position of extraordinary strength." The corresponding line in President Bush's first National Security Strategy tellingly reshaped that sentence to read: "The United States possesses unprecedented—and unequaled—strength and influence in the world." The obvious difference between these opening lines is that President Bush omitted any mention of what the allies of the United States might bring to the table.[47] Of course the administration would welcome any allied support it could garner, but it saw little to be gained through making sacrifices to secure that support.[48]

Whereas the Clinton administration had talked about maintaining the "delta" between the capabilities of the United States and those of other countries, Bush upped the ante by calling for the military to build "defenses beyond challenge." Not only would the military be asked to be capable of winning any wars the United States engaged in, to deter potential enemies from starting a war, and to reassure allies, but the lead of the United States must also be so large that "Our forces will be strong enough to dissuade potential adversaries from pursuing a military build-up in hopes of surpassing, or equaling, the power of the United States."[49] In other words, the "delta" had to be so great that other states would not even think about developing capabilities that could put them in the same league as the United States. America's power advantages need not be a threat to other states, because, as Secretary of State Colin Powell asserted, the security dilemma itself had been transcended: "The sources of national strength and security for one nation thus need no longer threaten the security of others. An insight of the Enlightenment and a deep belief of the American founders—that politics need not always be a zero-sum competition—has at last been adopted by enough people worldwide to promise a qualitative difference in the character of international relations. If, instead of wasting lives and treasure by opposing each other as in the past, today's powers can pull in the same direction to solve problems common to all, we will begin to redeem history from much human folly."[50]

Bush and his team fervently believed that they were acting on behalf of global interests and universal values. They expected that the rest of the world would eventually accept the war on terror as the administration conceived of it. They did not read their National Security Strategy as a call for unilateralism but as a call for great power cooperation on behalf of common values and interests.[51] Richard Haass, the head of the Policy Planning Staff in the State Department during the early years of the Bush administration, called for "hard-headed multilateralism" or "à la carte multilateralism." In this vision the United States needed to stake out a clear leadership position and then build a series of revolving coalitions around that position.[52] Unilateral U.S. leadership would be a path to multilateral cooperation, not a hindrance to it. As Bush phrased it, "confident action that will yield positive results provides kind of a slipstream into which reluctant nations and leaders can get behind."[53]

Rather than confront the necessary trade-offs between working unilaterally and working multilaterally, this conviction denied them. The United States, under this vision, could define the War on Terror unilaterally and other states would join in that struggle, thus allowing Washington to execute it multilaterally. Because terrorism was a problem facing the entire world, the administration reasoned, why would other states not welcome and be willing to support a global war on terror? The problem, however, is that few other states saw terrorism as their primary security problem and many worried more that U.S. actions would make the security problems they faced worse rather than better. This put the United States on a collision course with some of its allies and putative coalition partners. Washington thought it was providing a public good in its fight against terrorism and that all would welcome it, whereas much of the rest of the world saw U.S. actions as potentially dangerous and destabilizing.[54]

When the administration's optimistic assumption that other states would eagerly embrace the War on Terror was not borne out, it had to face in practice the trade-off that it largely denied in theory. What if you declare a crusade and no one comes? The administration's post-9/11 threat perception and its pre-9/11 skepticism regarding the value of allies answered that question in favor of unilateralism. The United States under Bush, as Ikenberry argues, "showed itself to be not the satisfied protector of the old order but a threatened and insecure power that resisted the bargains and restraints of its own postwar order."[55] The quote that best captures the Bush administration's approach to this question is Rumsfeld's pithy declaration that "you have to let the mission determine the coalition, and you don't let the coalition determine the mission."[56] Although intended as practical policy advice, Rumsfeld's aphorism offered, in beautiful simplicity, an excellent theoretical definition of unilateralism. Bypassing debates over numbers (how many states need to agree before an initiative becomes truly multilateral?) or forums (does multilateralism require approval by the United Nations? NATO? The G-8?),[57] Rumsfeld's phraseology gets to the core issue of whether the United States is willing to take the interests and concerns of others into account when formulating and executing policy. Multilateralism requires a willingness to accommodate the interests of others,[58] accommodations that Rumsfeld and the Bush administration were unwilling to make. You do not let the coalition determine the mission. The United States was going to do what it wanted; if others wanted to enlist in the predefined mission of the United States, they were welcome to join the coalition, but if not, the United States was going to do it anyway. The long list of states that the Bush administration put forward as supportive of the war in Iraq did not impress those who saw multilateralism as more than a matter of numbers, and who characterized it as a "coalition of the anonymous, the dependent, the half-hearted and the uninvolved."[59]

The Bush administration, beyond being unwilling to compromise to placate potential allies, viewed multilateralism more as a trap to be avoided than as a tool to be used. Rumsfeld insisted that one of the key determinants of the post-9/11 repositioning of the U.S. military abroad should be the avoidance of stationing large forces where allies could impose constraints on America's freedom of action.[60] As the 2005 National Defense Strategy argued, "Our strength as a nation will continue to be challenged by those who employ a strategy of the weak using international fora, judicial processes and terrorism,"[61] thus treating multilateralism as a threat similar to terrorism. As John Bolton, who was appointed by the administration as ambassador to the United Nations, argued in 1999, "Those who think international law really means anything are those who want to constrict the United States."[62]

Even in humanitarian areas where the United States could easily count on multilateral support for U.S. goals, the Bush administration preferred to act unilaterally. For instance, when President Bush decided to vastly expand Washington's efforts to confront the HIV/AIDS epidemic, the secretary-general of the UN, Kofi Annan proposed a Global Fund to fight HIV/AIDS, tuberculosis, and malaria. Bush was persuaded to contribute some money to the Global Fund, but he put the bulk of America's resources into a U.S. program, which became the President's Emergency Plan for AIDS Relief (PEPFAR). As Bush explained this decision, "I considered the UN to be cumbersome, bureaucratic, and inefficient. . . . I couldn't stand the idea of innocent people dying while the international community delayed. I decided it was time for America to launch a global AIDS initiative of our own. We would control the funds. We would move fast. And we would insist on results." So although the Bush administration contributed $500 million to the Global Fund, it asked for appropriations of $15 billion for PEPFAR.[63]

The experience of fighting as part of a coalition in Afghanistan and Iraq only added to the administration's concerns about multilateralism. General Dan McNeill, commander of the NATO-led International Security Assistance Force (ISAF) in Afghanistan, kept a chart in his office denoting all military missions that units under his command would not carry out due to the national "caveats" that allies placed on their troops.[64] General James Jones, as the head of NATO, called these national caveats "NATO's operational cancer," and U.S. troops joked that ISAF really stood for "I Saw Americans Fight."[65] As the costs of the war in Iraq mounted, President Bush concluded that multilateralism was part of the problem, not part of the solution. "It was clear we needed to adjust our strategy," Bush argued. "The multilateral approach to rebuilding, hailed by so many in the international community, was failing."[66] In his farewell address as secretary of defense, Rumsfeld maintained: "Ours is a world of many friends and allies, but sadly, realistically friends and allies with declining defense investment and declining capabilities, and, I would add, as a result, with increasing vulnerabilities."[67]

Under George W. Bush the United States found itself in the odd position of claiming to be fighting on behalf of international order, but largely ignoring the other members of that order in formulating and executing policy. Convinced of America's righteousness, Bush assumed others would eventually agree to follow, and confident in the power of the United States, he was relatively untroubled when they did not. As the president explained to his advisers in the days after the 9/11 attacks, "At some point, we may be the only ones left. That's okay with me, we are America."[68]

HISTORY IS ON AMERICA'S SIDE, BUT TIME IS NOT

Flowing directly from the Bush administration's confidence in the universality and efficacy of U.S. values was the certainty that history was on America's side. The attacks of 9/11 did not dent this conviction. Defining the terrorist threat to a Joint Session of Congress in September 2001, the president argued, "We have seen their kind before. They are the heirs of all the murderous ideologies of the 20th century . . . they follow in the path of fascism, and Nazism, and totalitarianism. And they will follow that path all the way, to where it ends: in history's unmarked grave of discarded lies."[69] If history was on America's side, could Washington simply wait out its terrorist enemies? Kennan had based the containment strategy on the premise that history was on the side of the U.S. model rather than the Soviet one, but would a policy of containment be similarly appropriate against terrorists who were also offering an unsustainable political model? For the Bush administration, the answer was no. While convinced that history was on the side of the United States, the attacks of 9/11 also convinced the Bush administration that time was not.[70]

During the 2000 presidential campaign, Rice had argued that states like Iraq were "living on borrowed time" and that "there need be no sense of panic about them" even if they did develop nuclear weapons.[71] After 9/11, the Bush administration concluded that the danger of additional attacks, especially attacks with weapons of mass destruction, meant that potential threats could not simply be waited out but had to be confronted immediately. As the president argued in his first State of the Union Address after the 9/11attacks, "Time is not on our side. I will not wait on events while dangers gather. I will not stand by as peril draws closer and closer."[72] A year later, in the run-up to the war in Iraq, Bush returned to the same theme, calculating the damage inflicted by hijackers armed with box cutters and extrapolating what other enemies of the United States could do with more advanced weapons, especially weapons of mass destruction. "Imagine those 19 hijackers with other weapons and other planes—this time armed by Saddam Hussein. It would take one vial, one canister, one crate slipped into this country to bring a day of horror like none we have ever known. We will do everything in our power to make sure that day never comes."[73] Given such dangers, the Bush administration was unwilling to just act defensively and wait for the collapse of its enemies, but preferred to go on the offensive to try to prevent those attacks. The belief that time was not on America's side and that the country would be better off confronting potential threats now rather than later was central to the administration's case for preventive war, or what it preferred to call "preemptive war." It was now time to panic.

The conviction that time was working against the United States, even as history favored it, was prevalent throughout the administration. A central lesson that President Bush took from the attacks of 9/11 was that it was better to act "too early than waiting until it was too late."[74] Discussing the war in Afghanistan, Vice President Cheney maintained: " 'Time is *not* on our side.' Every day that al Qaeda and its supporters went without a major defeat, the danger to the United States grew."[75] National Security Adviser Rice concisely summed up the key lesson that the administration took from 9/11, which was to "Take care of threats early."[76] When a senator asked Secretary of Defense Rumsfeld why the United States had to go to war with Iraq now, Rumsfeld replied: "What's different is 3,000 people were killed, I suggest that any who insist on perfect evidence are back in the 20th Century and still thinking in pre-9/11 terms."[77] The administration's preference for action over delay is well captured by the vice president's argument, "If there is a one percent chance that Pakistani scientists are helping al-Qaeda build or develop nuclear weapons, we have to treat it as a certainty in terms of our response. It's not about our analysis or finding a preponderance of evidence, it's about our response."[78]

As Marc Trachtenberg has noted, the concept of preventive war has a long pedigree in U.S. foreign policy and tends to recur whenever policymakers fear that waiting could damage U.S. interests.[79] This was precisely the situation in which the Bush administration saw itself after 9/11. Arguing against waiting out the Saddam Hussein regime, President Bush asked, "after 11 years of living with this problem, why do we need to confront it now?" Answering his own question, he argued, "We've experienced the horrors of September the 11th. . . . America must not ignore the threat gathering against us. Facing clear evidence of peril, we cannot wait for the final proof—the smoking gun—that could come in the form of a mushroom cloud."[80] Prior to September 11, the Bush administration was thinking about how sanctions could be better crafted to contain Iraq, but after 9/11, according to the president, "the doctrine of containment just doesn't hold any water."[81]

In the early 1960s Richard Hofstadter produced his classic study of what he termed the "paranoid style in American politics."[82] In Hofstadter's account, excesses like those associated with McCarthyism during the Cold War were not novel, but part of a U.S. tradition similar to earlier fears such as how sympathizers with the French Revolution could undermine U.S. democracy, or worries about Roman Catholic or Masonic plots against U.S. freedom. Hofstadter's description of the paranoid style in American politics offers a surprisingly accurate portrayal of how the Bush administration would react to the attacks of 9/11, highlighting a continuous thread in U.S. politics running from the Alien and Sedition Acts through the Patriot Act. As Hofstadter notes, the paranoid style is often elicited by a catastrophe, and for the Bush administration, 9/11 was that catastrophic catalyst. The characteristics that Hofstadter sees as descriptive of the paranoid style include a perceived threat to a culture or a way of life (the terrorists hate us because of our values); a predilection for conspiracy thinking (worries about sleeper cells in the United States or cooperation between Iraq and al-Qaeda); a tendency to reject the give and take of normal politics in favor of prosecuting a crusade against evil; and an affinity for unattainable goals (ridding the world of evil).

In a passage that is hard not to read in light of the debates that were to arise about the Bush administration's handling of intelligence regarding Iraq's weapons of mass destruction program, Hofstadter notes that whereas the paranoid style puts great emphasis on finding evidence, a leap of imagination is always needed to move from that evidence to desired policies. As

Hofstadter explains, "What distinguishes the paranoid style is not, then, the absence of verifiable facts (though it is occasionally true that in his extravagant passion for facts the paranoid occasionally manufactures them), but the rather curious leap in imagination that is always made at some critical point in the recital of events."[83] For the Bush administration, that curious leap was from the mixed, confusing, contradictory, and relatively stable intelligence on Iraq's weapons of mass destruction program to the need to reverse a decade of containment in favor of immediate regime change. As one official postmortem concluded following the failure to find the expected large arsenal of weapons of mass destruction in Iraq, the raw intelligence produced on Iraq did not change after 9/11, but estimates of how threatening that intelligence was did change.[84]

Post-Iraq Course Corrections

Dramatic events that alter U.S. grand strategy can come in two forms, a sudden jolt (the attack on Pearl Harbor) or a protracted crisis (U.S. efforts in Vietnam). The foreign policy of George W. Bush experienced both types of events. The terror strikes of 9/11 represented the former, and the large and largely unanticipated costs and difficulties of the U.S. campaign in Iraq represented the latter. Just as the Bush administration had to reevaluate U.S. grand strategy after September 11, 2001, it also had to perform another reevaluation after the costs of the Iraq War grew. Convinced of the universality of U.S. values, the Bush administration radically underestimated the costs and difficulties involved in installing a more democratic government in Iraq. Believing that democracy was natural, the administration also believed it would be easy to install once the corrupt and authoritarian leadership blocking it was removed. If, on 9/11, it was the realists who had been mugged by reality, as the costs of the war in Iraq mounted, it was now the neoconservatives' turn to get mugged by reality.[85]

The rising costs of the war in Iraq exposed a divide in the Bush administration over how much the United States should be willing to pay in pursuing the president's democratization agenda. Just after offering the job of secretary of defense to Donald Rumsfeld, President-elect Bush asked Andy Card, "Is this a trapdoor?"[86] In Iraq, that trapdoor opened. If the president, as originally intended, wanted a secretary of defense who could oversee a massive transformation of the U.S. armed forces, Rumsfeld was a logical choice. As it turned out, however, what the president needed was a secretary of defense to oversee an ambitious, costly, and time-consuming democratization project in Iraq. For this task, Rumsfeld was an extremely poor fit. The result was a disjuncture in the administration's grand strategy because the man put in charge of the war effort favored transforming U.S. military forces over pursuing the president's political goals in the war.[87]

No neoconservative, Rumsfeld instead represented a faction in the administration that Ivo Daalder and James Lindsay categorized as "assertive nationalists." This group was willing to take down Saddam Hussein's regime in Iraq as a show of U.S. might and a warning to those who might be tempted to cross the United States, but it had little interest or confidence in any democratization project in the Middle East.[88] In the lead-up to the wars in Afghanistan and Iraq, Rumsfeld maintained that even if the United States eliminated the sitting governments in Kabul and Baghdad, it did not mean that Washington had the responsibility of installing new governments there, much less democratic ones. Whereas critics derided this as foreign policy by drive-by shooting, Rumsfeld doubted the feasibility of democratizing Afghanistan and Iraq, resisted the huge price tag associated with the attempts, and preferred the more limited goal of demonstrating that enemies of the United States could be quickly dispatched.[89] Throughout the wars, whenever confronted with the choice of doing more or less, Rumsfeld preferred to do less.[90]

Initially, Rumsfeld's vocal role in defending and enunciating the Bush administration's response to the attacks of 9/11 cloaked this disjuncture. Rumsfeld had run into early difficulties in implementing his vision for a transformed U.S. military, and his celebrated post-9/11 press conference performances suggested to some "that Donald Rumsfeld may not have been a very good secretary of defense, but he is a remarkable secretary of war."[91] Over time, however, the distance between the president's democratization agenda and his secretary of defense's vision for the proper use of the U.S. military grew and the war in Iraq exposed the fissure. Preferring the transformation of the U.S. military to the transformation of Iraq, Rumsfeld prosecuted the war in Iraq to further and justify his campaign for a smaller, more agile, more precise, and more lethal force structure rather than to build a democratic state in Iraq. As one of General George Casey's advisers saw it, Rumsfeld did not approach the war in Iraq asking "What does it take to win?" but asking "How little can I use to try to win?" Using as little as possible would bolster the secretary's preexisting campaign to transform the U.S. military. As Rumsfeld explained, "People said there is no way you can have a major transformation program and simultaneously be involved in a war. I said just the opposite . . . That's the time you've got the best opportunity to make the changes." Andy Card, the president's chief of staff, argued that Rumsfeld "had an expectation of what his job would be as secretary of defense, and it probably centered around transformation. . . . And the war got in the way. Transformation had been a labor of love for him. The war became a labor of responsibility. It was the beautiful siren of transformation that had attracted him to the job, but the shoals ended up being the shoals of war."[92]

The president, rather than give up on his goals for Iraq, was eventually persuaded to give up on his secretary of defense. Instead of continuing to fight the war with as few troops as possible, as Rumsfeld and many of his military advisers preferred, Bush opted for a "surge" of troops to implement a more manpower-intensive counterinsurgency strategy.[93] The surge succeeded in dramatically lowering the level of violence in Iraq and creating some political space for the new government of Iraq to stabilize its rule. From the perspective of U.S. grand strategy, what did the surge mean for the feasibility and sustainability of Bush's post-9/11 foreign policy? Did it show that the president's bold agenda could be successful if sufficiently resourced and properly implemented? Or was Iraq's future after the surge still too uncertain and were the costs of the war in Iraq far too high to make this a model worth emulating? In its final years the Bush administration answered these questions by leaning more toward caution and restraint than toward boldness. The administration pushed negotiations rather than force in dealing with North Korea's nuclear program; it left the question of Iran's nuclear program largely to its successor, and the administration declined to act when provided evidence that Syria was building a secret nuclear reactor. Even in a post-surge Iraq, when President Bush left office the United States was on a path to withdrawal rather than to continued efforts at state building.

After eight years in power, Condoleezza Rice again took to the pages of *Foreign Affairs* to offer her assessment of U.S. grand strategy, this time not as an aspirant for power, but as an experienced practitioner. What had the Bush administration learned in its eight years at the helm? The title of her article, "Rethinking the National Interest," is telling. As a foreign policy adviser to then Governor Bush in 2000, Rice had spoken confidently of "Promoting the National Interest." What she was confident of "promoting" in 2000, after two terms in power, she was now "rethinking."[94]

Parts of that rethinking were consistent with changes the Bush administration had made to U.S. grand strategy after 9/11. In defining the security perimeter of the United States and judging whether time was on America's side, Rice argued that as a result of the terrorist attacks on New York and Washington, DC, "the United States was swept into a fundamentally different world. We were called to lead with a new urgency and with a new perspective on what constituted threats." Similarly, the area where Rice recognized the most significant changes in her thinking centered on the proper place of U.S. values in its foreign policy. Rather than merely seeing the spread of U.S. values as at best "a second-order effect" of the pursuit of America's more material security and economic interests, as she had in 2000, in 2008 she insisted that "democratic state building is now an urgent component of our national interest."[95] In assessing U.S. alliance relationships, in 2008 Rice placed much greater emphasis on shared values than she had in 2000. Distancing herself from Lord Palmerston's quip that Britain had no permanent allies, only permanent interests, Rice argued that "the United States does have permanent allies: the nations with whom we share common values." Further, Rice argued that "the defining geopolitical event of the twenty-first century" will not be the rising power of China, but the "broader rise of an increasingly democratic community of Asian states."[96]

Other parts of Rice's "rethinking" flowed from the costs of the Iraq War. One effect of those costs was that it reinforced the importance of multilateralism. In 2000 she had criticized the Clinton administration for being too "anxious to find multilateral solutions to problems," had decried his administration's concerns with "the international community," and had spoken derisively of "illusory 'norms' of international behavior," but in 2008 she spoke comfortably about "habits of cooperation," a "vision of international order," and the "norms and values of the international community."[97] This rhetoric was consistent with a move toward greater multilateralism in the later years of the Bush administration, with an increased reliance on NATO in Afghanistan, a prominent role for key European states in negotiations with Iran over its nuclear program, and an emphasis on the six-party talks regarding North Korea.[98]

The war in Iraq also shaped Rice's assessment of the proper role of U.S. values in U.S. foreign policy. "The cost of this war, in lives and treasure, for Americans and Iraqis," Rice conceded, "has been greater than we ever imagined." Rice defended the decision to go to war and to try to bring greater democracy to the Middle East, but she also stressed that democratization is "never fast or easy," "is likely to be messy and unsatisfactory," and "will be a difficult, generational task."[99] Rice recognized the dilemma this posed for U.S. foreign policy. She saw that the spread of U.S. values was necessary for U.S. security, but also that attempts to spread those values promised to be costly and time consuming. As she squarely posed the question, "Is the United States up to the challenge, or, as some fear and assert these days, is the United States a nation in decline?"[100]

To ease this dilemma, Rice moved a bit closer to the Promised Landers. She ended her article in the same way that Kennan had ended the X-Article, by looking inward. She confidently asserted that the United States could meet its challenges because of the "dynamism, vigor, and resilience of American society" and, more important, because of what she called "our imagination," by which she meant a combination of American values and interests that "has freed America to imagine that the world can always be better—not perfect, but better—than others have consistently thought possible." In words that any advocate of America as the Promised Land could applaud, Rice argued: "We support democracy not because we think ourselves perfect but because we know ourselves to be deeply imperfect. This gives us reason to be humble in our own endeavors and patient with the endeavors of others."[101]

Patience, however, still had its limits for Rice and her conviction that history needs the United States to give it a push in the right direction kept her within the camp of the crusaders. America is "an incredibly impatient nation. We live in the future, not the past. We do not linger over our own history. This has led our nation to make mistakes in the past, and we will surely make them in the future. Still, it is our impatience to improve less-than-ideal situations and to accelerate the pace of change that leads to our most enduring achievements, at home and abroad."[102] Rice wanted to reduce the costs of these active attempts to "accelerate the pace of change" by limiting the role of the military in these efforts, going back to her argument from the 2000 presidential campaign that the military should not be the primary tool of nation building, but in her vision, American nation building efforts must continue.[103]

The question of the affordability and feasibility of democratic nation building is an appropriate place to end this discussion of the post-9/11 U.S. grand strategy because it was central to the Bush administration's conception of how to prosecute the War on Terror. Even if Iraq is accounted a victory, how many such victories could the United States withstand? The pairing of an ambitious foreign policy agenda with a domestic focus on cutting taxes threatened an imbalance between means and ends in U.S. grand strategy. As David Hendrickson asked about a foreign policy largely financed through deficit spending, "If he [Bush] is not willing to pay for his own doctrine, who will be?"[104] That would be a central question with which Bush's successor would have to grapple.

"Don't Do Stupid Stuff"

Grand Strategy Debates under Obama

In his first visit to the Pentagon as commander in chief, Barack Obama reportedly likened being president to parallel parking. Inheriting a floundering economy, a bleak fiscal situation, a war on terror, and wars in Afghanistan and Iraq, Obama explained that when it came to foreign policy, he did not have an open street to park in but, instead, had "to carefully find his spot between existing commitments."[1] Although this is true for all U.S. presidents, none of whom inherit a blank slate for their grand strategy, Obama was not just inheriting a series of commitments, but a relatively novel set of commitments. Just as Eisenhower had to decide how many of Truman's Cold War policies he was willing to sustain, Obama too had to decide how many of George W. Bush's War on Terror policies he was willing to sustain. Like democracies, which need to undergo a peaceful transition of power between competing parties before they can be considered stable, grand strategy commitments similarly need to survive changes of administration and changes of party if they are to be considered stable. In some areas of U.S. grand strategy President Obama has largely continued the policies of his predecessor and in other areas his approach is taking the United States in a different direction.

Parallel Parking in the War on Terror

Many of the similarities between the foreign policies of George W. Bush and Barack Obama stem from broader continuities across U.S. foreign policy. A definition of U.S. interests is a key starting point for all grand strategic choices, and President Obama's conception of U.S. interests differs little from that of any of his recent predecessors. Echoing the U.S. Constitution's injunction that it is the job of government to "provide for the common defense, promote the general welfare, and secure the blessings of liberty," the 2010

National Security Strategy offers the same triad of interests calling for the protection of "The security of the United States," "A strong, innovative, and growing U.S. economy," and "Respect for universal values at home and around the world." President Obama, however, attempts to add a fourth member to this club, by defining "An international order advanced by U.S. leadership that promotes peace, security, and opportunity through stronger cooperation to meet global challenges" as a similarly core U.S. interest.[2]

This addition is problematic. To justify its inclusion, the National Security Strategy stresses how a favorable international order can increase U.S. security and prosperity and support the expansion of U.S. values abroad. Note how parts of the traditional trio of interests are embedded in the definition of international order ("peace, security, and opportunity"). This suggests that a favorable international order is more properly thought of as a means to U.S. ends rather than an end in itself. Conflating means and ends is an all too common strategic mistake and elevating the promotion of international order to the level of a core national interest risks doing just that. Moreover, strategic choices often entail making trade-offs between interests. It is possible to enumerate cases in which the United States pursued policies that sacrificed certain core interests in order to advance other interests. For instance, the United States paid an economic and civil-liberty price as a result of homeland security measures enacted in the War on Terror, but those sacrifices were deemed appropriate because of the additional security they offered. In other cases, for example, in regard to the close relationship of the United States with Saudi Arabia, U.S. policymakers have judged that the economic advantages of that relationship outweigh Riyadh's lack of democracy and its earlier role in supporting groups like al-Qaeda. The U.S. intervention in Somalia offered more security and economic costs than benefits, but was judged worth attempting on humanitarian grounds. Can "international order" reach the level of a core U.S. interest on these grounds? That is, would it ever make sense for the United States to pursue a policy that advanced international order but undermined U.S. security, prosperity, and values? If the answer is no, this also suggests that international order is more properly thought of as a tool to pursue U.S. interests, not an interest itself.

To be clear, this criticism is not intended to suggest that building a favorable international order is not in the interest of the United States. Instead, the argument is that even if one accepts the idea that institution building internationally could be a useful means of advancing U.S. interests, it remains a means, maybe even an important means, not an end. Elevating international order to a core U.S. interest is a recipe for strategic confusion rather than clarity. Whereas its inclusion on the list of enduring U.S. interests helps to differentiate President Obama from his immediate predecessor on the central issue of unilateralism versus multilateralism in U.S. grand strategy and sends a strong signal that the Obama administration intends to put more emphasis on working with allies, other powers, and international organizations, it does little to clarify the logic of U.S. grand strategy. America's core interests remain unchanged.

Also unchanged is the conviction that in the long term all U.S. interests coincide with and reinforce one another. Indeed, this conviction that all good things go together in U.S. grand strategy makes it easy to blur the distinction between means and ends because each of America's three fundamental ends (peace, prosperity, and liberty) is also seen as a means of advancing the other two. Obama's National Security Strategy contains an explicit assertion of this virtuous circle, arguing that "each of these interests is inextricably linked to the others . . . [and] positive action in one area will help advance all."[3] Like his predecessors, however, President Obama would also find it difficult to translate this grand strategic conviction into practice because particular foreign policy problems often present the trade-offs that such assertions deny. How does one weigh the benefits of increased port security with the economic costs such measures entail? How does one balance the long-term benefits of fiscal health against the current needs of military preparedness? Events in the Middle East presented these trade-offs most starkly to the Obama administration. The Arab Spring could potentially bring increased democracy to the region, but upheaval also risked undermining the most important security partner of the United States in the Arab world, Mubarak's Egypt, and potentially risked disastrous economic consequences if revolts spread to U.S. allies in the Gulf. Whereas early on Vice President Biden could confidently aver: "There is no conflict between our security and our ideals. We believe they are mutually reinforcing," and President Obama could argue: "We reject the false choice between our security and our ideals," events in the Arab world showed the limits of such rhetoric in the context of confronting immediate foreign policy dilemmas.[4]

Given such conflicting interests, U.S. foreign policy was equally conflicted as the United States made case-by-case assessments in extremely fluid circumstances. Tunisia was considered small and insignificant enough for the United States to shed few tears for the end of the Ben Ali regime. Egypt, however, was a considerably more consequential player and as a result the Obama administration was far more hesitant to see a similarly sudden end for the Mubarak regime. Only after the administration became convinced that Mubarak's days were numbered did it move toward a policy of protecting the relationship of the United States with a post-Mubarak Egypt. These efforts were complicated by the sometimes violent competition between electorally potent Islamist forces, which were generally suspicious of ties with the United States, and the military, which enjoyed close ties to Washington. In Yemen, the United States was content to let the Gulf Cooperation Council take the lead in easing President Saleh out of power. For the Gulf monarchies themselves, however, the United States was less willing to run the risk of what popular uprisings could lead to; it therefore backed Saudi-led efforts to help the Gulf monarchs weather the Arab Spring, including playing down the use of force by the Bahraini regime, with Saudi and other Gulf Cooperation Council support, to put down the protest movement Manama was facing.

Whereas these continuities spanned all U.S. post–Cold War administrations, the Obama administration also inherited the more specific War on Terror. President Obama, consistent with his parallel parking metaphor, did not abandon the counterterrorism policies he inherited, but modified what was already in place, as he sought "to carefully find his spot between existing commitments." The War on Terror President Obama inherited, it is worth noting, had been evolving for some time. President Bush had already implemented several post–Iraq War course corrections. Thus, many of the similarities between the foreign policies of President Bush and those of Obama stem from Bush's later years in office. Indeed, there are arguably more similarities between President Bush late in his second term and President Obama than there are between the President Bush of 2007 and 2008 and the President Bush of 2002 and 2003.

One important modification Obama pursued was to downplay the centrality of the War on Terror in U.S. grand strategy.[5] As John Brennan, the administration's adviser for counterterrorism, explained, "the fight against terrorists and violent extremists has been returned to its right and proper place: no longer defining—indeed, distorting—our entire national security and foreign policy, but rather serving as a vital part of those larger policies." The Obama administration also attempted to change the language associated with counterterrorism, preferring to talk about combating violent extremists rather than conducting a global war on terror.[6] As the 2010 National Security Strategy put it, "this is not a global war against a tactic—terrorism or a religion—Islam. We are at war with a specific network, al-Qa'ida, and its terrorist affiliates who support efforts to attack the United States, our allies, and partners."[7] This change of terminology, however, did little to bound the problem the United States was facing. The inclusion of al-Qaeda "affiliates" who might target "our allies and partners" meant that this definition omitted few terrorist groups.

President Obama accepted a key inheritance from the War on Terror—the Bush administration's argument that the growing destructiveness of modern weapons, combined with the type of enemies the United States faced, whether called terrorists or violent extremists, forced the United States to pursue a new set of foreign policy instruments. "After 9/11," President Obama explained, "we knew that we had entered a new era—that enemies who did not abide by any law of war would present new challenges to our application of the law; that our government would need new tools to protect the American people, and that these tools would have to allow us to prevent attacks instead of simply prosecuting those who try to carry them out."[8] Many of these new tools raised controversial political and legal issues, such as the rights of enemy combatants being held at Guantanamo, the use of "enhanced" interrogation techniques that critics saw as a euphemism for torture, extraordinary rendition of prisoners to jurisdictions outside the United States, the ability of the executive branch to order targeted killings overseas (including of U.S. citizens) in drone strikes, and the balancing of privacy rights with expanded intelligence programs. Under Obama, "enhanced" interrogation techniques were further limited, Guantanamo has shrunk but remained open, renditions have continued, and drone strikes have increased.[9] The most noteworthy of the administration's antiterrorism activities took place on May 2, 2011, when U.S. special operations forces raided Osama bin Laden's compound in Pakistan and killed the man behind the 9/11 attacks. The surveillance programs put into place after 9/11 underwent a similar process of parallel parking. Responding to leaks regarding intelligence programs that gathered massive amounts of so-called metadata on phone calls and overseas e-mails, President Obama maintained that whereas he came into office "with a healthy skepticism about these programs," he further explained: "My team evaluated them. We scrubbed them thoroughly. We actually expanded some of the oversight, increased some of [the] safeguards. But my assessment and my team's assessment was that they help us prevent terrorist attacks. And the modest encroachments on the privacy that are involved in getting phone numbers or duration without a name attached and not looking at content, that on net, it was worth us doing."[10]

Perhaps the most striking difference in Obama's use of these antiterrorism tools, in contrast to his predecessor, is how less controversial the continuation of these policies has been, compared to their origins. In part, this is due to the self-corrective nature of the U.S. governmental system of checks and balances. Many of the most controversial parts of the legal regime that the Bush administration put into place in the early days of the War on Terror had already been significantly modified by the time Bush left office, as a result of opposition from inside the executive branch, Supreme Court rulings, and congressional legislation.[11] President Obama also benefited from a liberal counterpart to the "only Nixon could go to China" effect, which could be termed the "only Obama could keep Guantanamo open" argument. Just as Nixon's credentials as a staunch anticommunist protected him from criticisms of being soft on communism, Obama's credentials as a liberal law school professor who had been openly critical of many of the Bush administration's policies have largely insulated him from criticisms of overreaching the constitutional powers of his office.

The most controversial foreign policy tool that the Bush administration highlighted in its War on Terror was the preventive, or what the administration preferred to call the preemptive, use of force. As Bush explained in his 2002 National Security Strategy, "Given the goals of rogue states and terrorists, the United States can no longer solely rely on a reactive posture as we have in the past. The inability to deter a potential attacker; the immediacy of today's threats, and the magnitude of potential harm that could be caused by our adversaries' choice of weapons do not permit that option. We cannot let our enemies strike first."[12] The argument for prevention thus has two key components. First, the sheer destructiveness of weapons of mass destruction means that if one simply responds to an attack after it takes place, it is already too late to avoid horrific casualties. Weapons of mass destruction, however, had been around for some time. Why was prevention necessary in the War on Terror, when it had not been necessary against the Soviets during the Cold War, for example? The second key component of the argument for prevention is the contention that some current enemies of the United States are undeterrable, which makes prevention the only acceptable policy option. This preventive war argument was a central part of the Bush administration's case for war in Iraq.

The 2010 National Security Strategy is conspicuously quiet about the preventive use of force. This omission is striking, considering how controversial the inclusion of this argument was in the 2002 National Security Strategy. Obama's National Security Strategy neither directly rejects nor endorses the argument for prevention; it largely ignores it. One reason for this silence is that even as the Obama administration has continually criticized the preventive war in Iraq as a mistake, it has remained convinced of the value of the preventive use of force against specific terrorist groups. As President Obama later elaborated, "a strategy that involves invading every country that harbors terrorist networks is naïve and unsustainable." "Direct action," like drone strikes or capture operations against potential terrorists, however, remain "necessary to protect ourselves. When we have actionable intelligence, that's what we do."[13]

Another reason for this silence is that President Obama does not want to take the preventive war option off the table, even against states. Consider the administration's policies toward Iran and its nuclear program. The 2010 National Security Strategy stresses that the administration will "work to prevent Iran from developing a nuclear weapon," but stresses nonmilitary means of prevention, such as diplomacy, international pressure, and economic sanctions.[14] The Obama administration has also continued a program started under the Bush administration to use cyber-attacks to slow down Iran's nuclear program. Whereas these cyber-strikes are less overt than kinetic strikes, they occupy a zone somewhere between covert action and the preventive use of force.[15] If U.S. policy is to prevent Iran from developing a nuclear weapon, does it, however, imply a willingness to more directly use force if these efforts fail? According to the president, the answer is yes:

> We all prefer to resolve this issue diplomatically. Having said that, Iran's leaders should have no doubt about the resolve of the United States. . . . I have said that when it comes to preventing Iran from obtaining a nuclear weapon, I will take no options off the table, and I mean what I say. That includes all

elements of national power: A political effort aimed at isolating Iran; a diplomatic effort to sustain our coalition and ensure that the Iranian program is
monitored; an economic effort that imposes crippling sanctions; and yes, a
military effort to be prepared for any contingency. Iran's leaders should understand that I do not have a policy of containment; I have a policy to prevent Iran from obtaining a nuclear weapon. And as I have made clear time
and again during the course of my presidency, I will not hesitate to use force
when it is necessary to defend the United States and its interests.[16]

Having options on the table is quite different from exercising those options,
however. The Obama administration may see the threat of force as a necessary
component of its efforts to dissuade Iran from developing nuclear weapons,
but if this coercive policy fails, the administration could still decide to accept a nuclear-armed Iran rather than to attempt a preventive military
strike. If faced with this choice, a key part of the debate will be whether the
United States views the regime in Tehran as deterrable. This is why comments by the chairman of the Joint Chiefs of Staff, General Martin E. Dempsey,
generated so much attention, and criticism in some quarters, when he argued
that "the Iranian regime is a rational actor."[17] Rationality suggests that Iran
is deterrable, and if so, deterrence becomes a more attractive option than a
preventive military strike. In an interview where President Obama reiter-
ated that "I don't bluff" and that "it is unacceptable for Iran to have a nuclear
weapon," when he was directly asked about General Dempsey's assessment that the Iranian regime was rational, the president responded: "they
care about the regime's survival" and "they are able to make decisions based
on trying to avoid bad outcomes from their perspective. So if they're presented with options that lead either to a lot of pain from their perspective,
or potentially a better path, then there is no guarantee that they can't make
a better decision."[18] Although less direct than Dempsey's formulation, the
president's comments similarly suggest a perception of a regime that is capable of the calculations of nuclear deterrence. All of this together suggests
that even though military preemption is no longer highlighted in the National Security Strategy, the United States has not seen the end of debates
about the proper role of the preventive use of force in its grand strategy.

A New Era of Engagement

One way in which candidate Obama differentiated himself from the out-
going president was that he stressed analytical agility over consistency.
Trained as a lawyer, Obama was more comfortable applying standards to
particular cases than thinking in terms of broad generalizations. In his 2006
book, *The Audacity of Hope*, he denied having "grand strategy in my back
pocket," but outlined a series of principles that would guide his foreign

policy.[19] As he put it more bluntly in one of his major foreign policy speeches during the 2008 campaign, "If you want rigid ideology, I'm not your man."[20] Well into his second term, the president remained adamant, saying "I don't really even need George Kennan right now."[21] His aides have attempted to summarize his overall approach to foreign policy with the phrase "Don't do stupid stuff."[22]

In dealing with the tension inherent in the need for grand strategy to provide consistency across time and space versus the need to tailor particular policies to specific circumstances, President Obama favors the tailoring end of the spectrum. As a result, similar to the problem of the Clinton administration in finding a suitable winner for the Kennan sweepstakes, the problem of the Obama administration in capturing grand strategy in a single term, such as "containment" has also proved difficult.[23] Just as Clinton eventually settled on "engagement" to describe his grand strategy, the Obama administration has also found itself talking about "a new era of engagement" or "a new chapter of American engagement."[24] Although the name has not gotten wide circulation, in part because of the understandable hesitation of any administration to link itself too closely with its predecessors, it is as apt a description as any for the Obama administration's grand strategy, which bears many similarities to the approach taken by the United States in the first decade after the end of the Cold War.

Whereas Obama's foreign policy has stressed case-by-case judgments rather than ideological consistency, it is possible to discern some core principles underlying those judgments—principles that reveal his administration's positions on the four grand strategic debates running throughout this book. Specifically, the Obama administration has emphasized a universal and complicated threat picture that warns against an overemphasis of any one threat, such as terrorism; has greatly emphasized multilateralism; has affirmed the conviction that time is on the side of the United States; and has embraced America's role as the Promised Land, resisting urges to launch crusades to spread U.S. values. Although these stances differ greatly from those taken by the George W. Bush administration immediately after the attacks of 9/11, they are strikingly similar to approaches of the first Bush and the Clinton administrations to these issues in the 1990s.

A RETURN TO THREAT LISTS

After defining interests, the next step in formulating a grand strategy is to assess potential threats to those interests. As discussed in chapter six, assessing and prioritizing threats proved particularly troublesome for the United States in the decade after the collapse of the Soviet Union. Instead of a clearly preeminent threat, the Clinton administration saw "a complex array of new and old security challenges" and presented a long list of potential threats with no clear priority among them.[25] After the attacks of September 11, 2001, the Bush administration combined two of the threats from that list, terrorism and the proliferation of weapons of mass destruction, and placed the combination at the forefront of U.S. concerns. On this front, President Obama moved U.S. grand strategy back to the threat lists of the 1990s rather than the more narrow focus of the United States on the "crossroads of radicalism and technology,"[26] which dominated the post-9/11 threat picture.

The terrorism/weapons of mass destruction threat has not gone away, but in the assessment of the Obama administration, it has lost its preeminent status. In his Nobel Peace Prize acceptance speech, President Obama reminded his audience that "modern technology allows a few small men with outsized rage to murder innocents on a horrific scale."[27] For the Obama administration, however, this threat should be seen as just one member of a broader threat list. Although the 2010 National Security Strategy accepted that the United States faced "no greater or more urgent danger than a terrorist with a nuclear weapon," it also insisted that the War on Terror is "only one element of our strategic environment and cannot define America's engagement with the world." Terrorism, Obama argued, is just "one of many threats that are more consequential in a global age."[28]

As the use of the word "global" indicates, Obama sees the U.S. security perimeter in universal terms. As a presidential candidate, then Senator Obama argued:

> In today's globalized world, the security of the American people is inextricably linked to the security of all people. When narco-trafficking and corruption threaten democracy in Latin America, it's America's problem too. When poor villagers in Indonesia have no choice but to send chickens to market infected with avian flu, it cannot be seen as a distant concern. When religious schools in Pakistan teach hatred to young children, our children are threatened as well. Whether it's global terrorism or pandemic disease, dramatic climate change or the proliferation of weapons of mass annihilation, the threats we face at the dawn of the 21st century can no longer be contained by borders and boundaries.[29]

As president, Obama continued to define the U.S. security perimeter globally: "When a financial system weakens in one country, prosperity is hurt everywhere. When a new flu infects one human being, all are at risk. When one nation pursues a nuclear weapon, the risk of nuclear attack rises for all nations. When violent extremists operate in one stretch of mountains, people are endangered across an ocean."[30]

Instead of seeing a clearly predominant threat that rises above all others, the Obama administration sees a varied and extensive set of threats that all merit consideration. As General James Jones, Obama's first national security adviser, explained, "the challenges that we face are broader and more diverse than we ever imagined, even after the terrible events of 9/11." In enumerating what he assesses as only "a few" of "the wider array of existing threats," Jones lists terrorism, the struggle on the Afghanistan/Pakistan border, the proliferation of weapons of mass destruction, America's "overdependence on fossil fuels," "Protracted tribal, ethnic and religious conflicts," "Poverty, corruption, and disease," "Narco-terrorism that provides the economic fuel for insurgencies," and "an economic crisis."[31] The 2010 National Security Strategy offers a similar list, including "a broad and complex array of challenges to our national security" that includes terrorism and the proliferation of weapons of mass destruction, the global economic crisis, climate change, the global food supply, regional conflict, pandemic diseases, rogue states, failed states, global criminal networks, and U.S. reliance on space and cyberspace assets.[32]

One way the Obama administration has attempted to prioritize the U.S. security perimeter is with its "pivot" to Asia.[33] The costly wars in Afghanistan and Iraq, combined with the robust economic growth of East and South Asia, led the Obama team to call for a *rebalance toward the Asia-Pacific region.*[34] More difficult than calling for the investment of more U.S. foreign policy resources in Asia, however, is figuring out which regions of the world deserve less U.S. attention. Whereas the aspirations of the rebalance recognize "the national security imperative of deficit reduction through a lower level of defense spending," it is unclear where potential savings would come from to execute the pivot because the threats and potential military missions in other regions remain largely unchanged. In the Middle East, the same document that calls for a rebalancing to Asia also insists that *"the United States will continue to place a premium on U.S. and allied military presence in—and support of—partner nations in and around this region."* Moreover, it describes Europe as America's "principal partner in seeking global and economic security" and talks about the need for the posture of the United States in Europe to *"evolve,"* which is not the same as to reduce. The document further pledges that "Across the globe we will seek to be the security partner of choice, pursuing new partnerships with a growing number of nations—including those in Africa and Latin America." The only concrete reduction specified, interestingly one that closely parallels President Bush's pre-9/11 warnings about avoiding "missions without end," is that *"U.S. forces will no longer be sized to conduct large-scale prolonged stability operations."*[35] Thus, the U.S. security perimeter, beyond avoiding future Afghanistan and Iraq-type missions, remained universal and weakly prioritized, even with the pivot to Asia.

As had the Clinton administration, the Obama administration has also attempted to make this extensive list of potential threats more coherent by placing all of them under the heading of challenges wrought by globalization. The concept of globalization, central to the thinking of the Clinton administration, disappeared from George W. Bush's first National Security Strategy (2002), but returned in his 2006 version, where he added a new chapter that called on Washington to "Engage the Opportunities and Confront the Challenges of Globalization."[36] The 2010 National Security Strategy made the comeback complete, putting globalization again onto center stage as a way of framing the challenges the United States faces. As Washington discovered in the 1990s, however, placing diverse threats under the heading of globalization does not answer questions of prioritization. Because strategy inevitably entails making choices regarding where to put limited resources, such a diversity of threats poses a problem with which U.S. grand strategy grappled from the fall of the Berlin Wall to 9/11: How do you implement a coherent grand strategy against such varied and numerous threats? So far, President Obama has been no more successful in solving this problem than were his predecessors in the 1990s. One way to avoid this problem is to select one or two threats from the list and build a strategy against them, but what if the threats chosen are the wrong ones or are too narrow? This is precisely what troubled many about the central place afforded to the War on Terror after 9/11. Perhaps this should not be seen as a grand strategic problem to be solved but as a condition to be lived with. A muddled and diverse threat picture might be the norm for a great power in a globalized world, and the Soviet-focused era in U.S. foreign policy might be the anomaly.

MULTILATERALISM AS THE OBAMA DOCTRINE

At an early press conference President Obama was asked what an "Obama Doctrine" might look like. The first principle the new president offered in response was multilateralism. "The United States remains the most powerful, wealthiest nation on earth," Obama explained, "but we're only one nation." "The problems that we confront," the president continued, "whether it's drug cartels, climate change, terrorism, you name it, can't be solved just by one country. And I think if you start with that approach, then you are inclined to listen and not just talk."[37] This is the area in which President Obama has drawn the starkest distinctions between his approach to foreign policy and that of his immediate predecessor. From the early days of his candidacy Obama has portrayed multilateralism as a way of extending rather than limiting U.S. power. Referring to the multilateral aspects of U.S. post–World War II grand strategy, he argued: "Leaders like Harry Truman and George Marshall knew that instead of constraining our power, these institutions magnified it."[38] Although Obama has been criticized for "leading from behind" (a line attributed to an Obama adviser and one the administration tried to distance itself from[39]), he sees working multilaterally as a way of "renewing American leadership,"[40] not diminishing it.

This commitment to multilateralism came with the standard caveat that "The United States must reserve the right to act unilaterally if necessary to defend our nation and our interests."[41] One distinction the president subsequently offered is that on issues "where our core interests demand it," the unilateral use of military force might remain necessary. He defined these as instances "when our people are threatened, when our livelihoods are at stake, [or] when the security of our allies are in danger." But only collective action would be appropriate for what he characterized as "issues of global concern" that "stir our conscience or push the world in a more dangerous direction but do not directly threaten us."[42]

Part of what drove the Obama administration toward multilateralism was a sense of the limited resources of the United States. Whereas the National Security Strategy of his predecessor talked confidently of America's "unprecedented—and unequaled—strength" and of its ability to build "defenses beyond challenge,"[43] Obama's National Security Strategy is far less sanguine about the resources Washington can afford to devote to foreign policy. "The burdens of a young century cannot fall on American shoulders alone," the 2010 National Security Strategy insists as it warns against "sap[ping] our strength by overextending our power," stressing that the United States is just "emerging from the most devastating recession that we have faced since the Great Depression" and that "[y]ears of rising fiscal and trade deficits will also necessitate hard choices in the years ahead." Limited resources make multilateralism critical because "Our national security goals can only be reached if we make hard choices and work with international partners to share burdens."[44]

Multilateralism, however, requires more than a willingness to let others share your burdens, it also means being willing to share the burdens of others and taking their interests into account when formulating policy. Asked directly how he thought his foreign policy principles differed from his predecessor's, President Obama explained that what he has tried to do "is to communicate the notion that America is a critical actor and leader on the world stage, and that we shouldn't be embarrassed about that, but that we exercise our leadership best when we are listening; when we recognize that the world is a complicated place and that we are going to act in partnership with other countries."[45] Using more direct language, Secretary of State Hillary Clinton defined "the heart of America's mission in the world today" as "exercis[ing] American leadership to solve problems in concert with others" and criticized America's post-9/11 approach by arguing that "we will not tell our partners to take it or leave it, nor will we insist that they're either with us or against us. In today's world, that's global malpractice."[46] Implicitly rejecting Donald Rumsfeld's famous aphorism that the United States should not let the coalition determine the mission, President Obama countered that "in order for us to work collectively, all parties have to compromise and that includes us."[47] Such compromises are worth making, the 2010 National Security Strategy calculates, because "America has not succeeded by stepping outside the currents of international cooperation."[48] In this logic, allies are not just valuable, they are necessary for success.

As President Clinton discovered with his assertive multilateralism, however, the requirements of multilateralism can often undermine the possibility for assertiveness. What if U.S. allies or key international institutions just say no? As the 2010 National Security Strategy recognizes, "In order for collective action to be mobilized, the polarization that persists across region, race, and religion will need to be replaced by a galvanizing sense of shared interests." Is such a transformation possible in a world with a growing number of influential actors, all with their own particular interests? What goals might the United States need to abandon or curtail because of a lack of international support? What problems will be impossible to address in a broad multilateral manner because of political disputes between or within states?[49] Furthermore, if part of what is driving this move to multilateralism is a desire to share costs with others, what states will be willing and able to be buckcatchers?[50] The relative inaction of the Obama administration on the climate change front internationally and the difficulty in securing broad international agreement on a policy toward the bloody civil war in Syria are both examples of limits that President Obama's multilateralism has not been able to overcome. Those who favor unilateralism in U.S. foreign policy tend to believe that the United States is powerful enough to get most of what it needs on its own and is benevolent enough that it can find whatever international support is needed without much effort. In contrast, those who favor multilateralism tend to believe that interests are common enough to allow for jointly determined ends and that international institutions can be effective enough to realize those common interests. The reason the debate between unilateralism and multilateralism persists in U.S. foreign policy is that neither side's beliefs are fully justified or completely unjustified.

BENDING THE ARC

One of President Obama's favorite quotes is Martin Luther King's paraphrase of the abolitionist Theodore Parker's argument that "The arc of the moral universe is long, but it bends toward justice."[51] This quotation encapsulates two key parts of President Obama's approach to U.S. grand strategy. The first is his assumption that time is on the side of the United States and that therefore U.S. grand strategy would be better served by patience than by precipitate action. Obama's use of this metaphor also captures his assessment of the proper place of values in U.S. foreign policy; it expresses a preference for modest efforts to bend the arc in the right direction over revolutionary crusades.

Addressing terrorism in his inaugural address, President Obama argued that "for those who seek to advance their aims by inducing terror and slaughtering innocents, we say to you now that our spirit is stronger and cannot be broken—you cannot outlast us, and we will defeat you." Addressing rogue states, the president warned: "To those who cling to power through corruption and deceit and the silencing of dissent, know that you are on the wrong side of history."[52] Such statements would not have been out of place in speeches given by George W. Bush, who was also convinced that history was on the side of the United States. Where Obama differs from Bush is in his related conviction that time is also on the side of the United States. Bush stressed the immediacy of threats and the need to act now to counter them. In contrast, Obama stresses the danger of precipitate action, overreaction, and panic. Obama assumes not only that history is on America's side, but time is as well.

Critiquing the legal regime set up to conduct the War on Terror, President Obama argued: "Unfortunately, faced with an uncertain threat, our government made a series of hasty decisions. . . . [A]ll too often our government made decisions based on fear rather than foresight."[53] Making the case for strategic patience in the struggle against terrorism, the president reasoned that "the threat will not go away soon, but let's be clear: Al Qaeda and its affiliates are small men on the wrong side of history. . . . We need not give in to fear every time a terrorist tries to scare us. . . . We are the United States of America, and we have repaired our union, and faced down fascism, and outlasted communism. We've gone through turmoil, we've gone through Civil War, and we will come out stronger—and we will do so once more."[54] Accepting his Nobel Peace Prize, Obama wrestled with the dilemma that whereas "war is sometimes necessary," it is also "an expression of human folly." To reconcile these conflicting positions, he recommended strategic patience over bold action. Quoting President Kennedy, who was, ironically, a leader often on the side of bold action rather than patience, Obama sought "a more practical, more attainable peace, based not on a sudden revolution in human nature but on a gradual evolution in human institutions."[55] That gradual evolution will be in the favor of the United States, the president affirmed, because history is on the side of U.S. values. Quoting the Declaration of Independence "that all men are created equal, that they are endowed by the Creator with certain unalienable rights that among these are life, liberty and the pursuit of happiness," Obama asked: "Can anybody doubt that this belief will be any less true—any less powerful—two years, two decades, or even two centuries from now?"[56] The Obama administration adopted a similar policy of "strategic patience" with regard to North Korea and its nuclear weapons program; containing Pyongyang, not recognizing it as a nuclear weapon state, and waiting for an internally driven change of regime.[57] Similar calculations informed the president's decision to start the process of normalizing U.S.–Cuban relations: "I do not expect the changes I am announcing today to bring about a transformation of Cuban society overnight. But I am convinced that through a policy of engagement, we can more effectively stand up for our values and help the Cuban people help themselves as they move into the 21st century."[58]

History, however, will not move in this direction purely on its own. President Clinton believed that globalization might need an occasional shove in the right direction, and so too does Obama, who said, referring to the U.S.

arc: "It doesn't bend on its own. It bends because all of us are putting our hand on the arc and we are bending it in that direction. And it takes time. And it's hard work. And there are frustrations. And if everybody here is reminded of that fact, then I'm absolutely confident that America's arc is going to be bending in the direction of justice and prosperity and opportunity."[59] How much the United States puts its hands on that arc goes back to the fundamental debate between Promised Landers and Crusaders in U.S. foreign policy. Can the United States best bend the arc by serving as an example of the success of U.S. values, or must it bend the arc more directly by forcibly converting or defeating those who reject core U.S. values? Although he insists that U.S. values are universal and accepts that the United States has a responsibility to spread those values,[60] President Obama's conception of the U.S. mission is consistently clothed in the rhetoric of the Promised Landers, not the Crusaders.

In *The Audacity of Hope*, Obama expressed doubts about crusading in U.S. foreign policy, noting that "there are few examples in history in which the freedom men and women crave is delivered through outside intervention" and instead calling for "perfecting our own democracy and leading by example."[61] In his major speech during the campaign on the war in Iraq, then Senator Obama argued that getting out of Iraq would support the advancement of U.S. values better than getting into it did: "When we end this war in Iraq, we can once again lead the world against the common challenges of the 21st century. . . . When we end this war, we can reclaim the cause of freedom and democracy. We can be that beacon of hope, that light to all the world."[62] Speaking as an adherent of America as the Promised Land, candidate Obama insisted that "To lead the world, we must lead by example. . . . [W]e'll be the country that credibly tells the dissidents in the prison camps around the world that America is your voice, America is your dream, America is your light of justice."[63]

The United States as the Promised Land remained a strong part of President Obama's rhetoric into his presidency. "There is no force in the world more powerful than the example of America," President Obama affirmed as he recalled John Winthrop's city on a hill sermon that "the eyes of all people in all nations are once again upon us."[64] President Obama speaks as confidently as his predecessors about the universality of U.S. values and the role of the United States in spreading those values, but he does so in the language of America serving in a supporting role as "beacon," a "light," or "a voice."[65] President Obama also explicitly rejects the path of the crusaders, averring that "America will not seek to impose any system of government on any other nation." Technical assistance for programs that encourage good governance might be appropriate, but ultimately "The essential truth of democracy is that each nation determines its own destiny."[66] This is the path outlined as well in the 2010 National Security Strategy. Insisting that the "United States believes certain values are universal and will work to promote them worldwide," it also characterizes America's role as an exemplar, explaining that the United States is "promoting universal values by living them at home, and will not seek to impose these values through force."[67]

As an advocate of the United States as the Promised Land, President Obama views U.S. values as something to which the nation must continually aspire. Talking about existing problems and faults is not a bar to America's serving as a model for other nations; it is a necessary step in working to improve these imperfections, which is what makes the United States worthy of emulation. In addressing the United Nations General Assembly on the crises in Syria and Ukraine, terrorism, a spreading Ebola epidemic, Iran's nuclear program, a stalemated Israeli–Palestinian conflict, and the growing threat of climate change, President Obama took time out of his speech to address the racial tensions in the United States:

> I realize that America's critics will be quick to point out that at times we too have failed to live up to our ideals; that America has plenty of problems within its own borders. This is true. In a summer marked by instability in the Middle East and Eastern Europe, I know the world also took notice of the small American city of Ferguson, Missouri—where a young man was killed, and a community was divided. So, yes, we have our own racial and ethnic tensions. . . . But we welcome the scrutiny of the world—because what you see in America is a country that has steadily worked to address our problems, to make our union more perfect, to bridge the divides that existed at the founding of this nation.

It is by correcting these faults, not denying them, the president concludes, that the United States and U.S. values "can help light the world."[68] The president took a similar view when the Senate Select Committee on Intelligence released a damning report detailing some of the country's post-9/11 detention and interrogation programs. Admitting that significant parts of these programs "were inconsistent with our values as a nation," he supported the release of the report because "one of the strengths that makes America exceptional is our willingness to openly confront our past, face our imperfections, make changes, and do better."[69]

Just as the attacks of September 11, 2001, boosted the arguments of the crusaders, the costs of U.S. attempts at state-building in Iraq and Afghanistan undermined those arguments. Obama came to office determined to end the country's costly involvement in both. In Iraq, Obama continued the post-surge drawdown and had all U.S combat forces out by December 2011. After approving a similar surge of combat troops for Afghanistan in late 2009, U.S. drawdowns commenced in 2011 and were completed by the end of 2014. Even as President Obama announced the surge in Afghanistan he made clear that he was not launching "a nation-building project. . . . I reject this course because it sets goals that are beyond what can be achieved at reasonable cost, and what we need to achieve our security interests."[70] Obama's

Promised Land convictions also influenced his approach to other important issues, such as U.S.–China relations, where in a speech in Shanghai the president affirmed that the United States does not "believe that the principles that we stand for are unique to our nation" and that "America will always speak out for these core principles around the world," but also affirmed: "We do not seek to impose any system of government on any other nation."[71]

It was in the Middle East, however, where President Obama would most directly have to calibrate the proper role of U.S. values in its foreign policy. As uprisings and potential uprisings swept through Iran, North Africa, and much of the Arab world, President Obama has preferred a generally modest role for the United States, consistent with his conception of the country as an exemplar rather than as a Crusader State. In his speech at Cairo University, to set the stage for his policy toward the region, Obama argued that the values the United States believes in "Are not just American ideas; they are human rights" and "we will support them everywhere," but he explicitly renounced any intentions of forcibly spreading U.S. values: "I know there has been controversy about the promotion of democracy in recent years, and much of this controversy is connected to the war in Iraq. So let me be clear: No system of government can or should be imposed by one nation by [sic] any other."[72]

This approach to the region met its first test in Iran, when thousands of Iranians took to the streets in the summer of 2009 to protest what they saw as the fraudulent reelection of President Mahmoud Ahmadinejad. Since the United States had hostile relations with the Islamic Republic, these protests did not pose the dilemma that later democratic movements in the region would present when they threatened close allies. Even here, however, President Obama adopted a circumspect policy. Fearing that any statements regarding the protests would be used by the regime to accuse the United States of meddling in Iranian affairs, Obama was hesitant and restrained in his comments. In the face of domestic criticisms that his administration was doing too little to support the opposition movement, President Obama condemned the government's crackdown and voiced support for the democratic aspirations of the Iranian people, but continued to insist that the United States respected Iran's sovereignty and was not trying to meddle in their electoral process, and that the outcome would be determined by the Iranian people, not the United States.[73]

When the Arab Spring later swept through North Africa and much of the Middle East, U.S. policy was equally circumspect, especially because some of the regimes threatened by democratization movements were important allies.[74] Whereas the United States did little to support the initial uprising in Tunisia, it also did nothing to try to save the Ben Ali regime. The administration was willing to give the Mubarak regime in Egypt more time to save itself, but as events in Cairo escalated the Obama administration calculated that direct support for Mubarak was a losing proposition and the United

States took the pragmatic approach of working with the military after Mubarak was deposed, working with the short-lived Morsi government, and then again working with the military as it sought to oversee a second transition to a post-Mubarak era. In Yemen the Obama administration let the Gulf States take the lead in encouraging a handover of power from President Saleh to his vice president. In the Gulf itself the United States offered some muffled criticisms of Bahrain's crackdown on its protestors, but kept its close relationship with King Hamad.

One place in which the United States accepted a more direct and forceful role in the Arab Spring was Libya, where the United States used military force to unseat the Qaddafi regime. Although this would undoubtedly be put onto the crusading side of the ledger, it was also a narrowly defined and limited crusade. Several factors combined to make the use of force an acceptable option for the United States in Libya. The first factor was the danger that Qaddafi would carry out mass killings of his own people. The United States was not only worried about preventing a humanitarian disaster but also concerned about the message this would send to other governments in the region facing similar protests if Qaddafi had been allowed to carry out a massacre of the Libyan people. Qaddafi's international isolation also made it easy to garner multilateral support for military action against Libya. The Arab League called for international action against Qaddafi and the United Nations Security Council followed suit, passing Resolution 1973, giving its support to a no-fly zone over Libya that could be expanded to protect civilian life. Finally, the weakness of the Qaddafi regime and the relative isolation of Libya from regional politics also created a permissive environment for the use of force.

Even in such a permissive environment, President Obama attempted to keep U.S. commitments limited. From the beginning he ruled out the use of any U.S. ground forces, he was eager to see the operation turned over to NATO control (which did occur before the end of March 2011), and he denied that regime change in Libya was the goal of the military operation, claiming that its mandate was a humanitarian one to protect the Libyan people. Regime change however, was the ultimate result as rebel forces took Tripoli in August 2011 and captured Sirte and executed Qaddafi in October 2011, whereupon NATO ended its military operation. As President Obama explained his case-specific reasoning:

> It's true that America cannot use our military wherever repression occurs. And given the costs and risks of intervention, we must always measure our interests against the need for action. But that cannot be an argument for never acting on behalf of what's right. In this particular country—Libya—at this particular moment, we were faced with the prospect of violence on a horrific scale. We had a unique ability to stop that violence: an international mandate for action, a broad coalition prepared to join us, the support of Arab countries, and a plea for help from the Libyan people themselves. We also

had the ability to stop Qaddafi's forces in their tracks without putting American troops on the ground.

As for those who criticized the administration for not going far enough in its efforts to oust Qaddafi, "we went down that road in Iraq," Obama recounted, "regime change there took eight years, thousands of American and Iraqi lives, and nearly a trillion dollars. That is not something we can afford to repeat in Libya."[75] In short, in the case of Libya, the Obama administration's resistance to crusading was outweighed by the fear of a humanitarian disaster, the promise of limited liability, and the administration's commitment to multilateralism.

The civil war in Syria, however, has presented the Obama administration with its most persistent and difficult problem in the Middle East. As civilian casualties mounted, the Obama administration resisted early calls for more forceful U.S. or international actions seeking regime change in Damascus. Fear of weapons ending up in the hands of terrorist groups made the administration wary of providing military aid to those seeking the overthrow of Bashar al-Assad. Even when Assad used chemical weapons, after being warned not to by the president, Obama eschewed unilateral military action and instead pursued a multilateral initiative to have Syria's chemical weapons stockpile be declared, taken out of the country, and destroyed. In the summer and fall of 2014, when a group calling itself the Islamic State (IS)[76] took over large portions of Syria and Iraq, however, the Obama administration responded by launching air strikes in both countries, boosting the U.S. military's advisory mission in Iraq, and taking an active and leading role in attempting to build up groups in Syria that would oppose both IS and the Assad regime.

This change in policy, however, did not lead the administration to embrace crusading, and the president, speaking in particular about his actions in Iraq, insisted: "I will not allow the United States to be dragged into fighting another war in Iraq."[77] With regard to Syria, distancing himself from his predecessor's rhetoric about ridding the world of evil, Obama argued that "we can't erase every trace of evil from the world" and stressed how "this effort will be different from the wars in Iraq and Afghanistan." In making that case he stressed he would not be sending in U.S. combat troops, but would instead rely on U.S. air power and support for local allies on the ground. Tellingly, he likened his actions in Iraq and Syria to the policies "we have successfully pursued in Yemen and Somalia for years."[78] In both places, the United States has focused on limited counterterrorism missions and avoided any pretenses of state building.

Also being consistent with his overall approach to U.S. grand strategy, President Obama ensured that his actions had multilateral support, especially from regional actors. In 2013, when contemplating military action in Syria because of the regime's use of chemical weapons, the United States would have been forced to go in mostly alone because even Great Britain declined to support military actions at the time. In contrast, in 2014, when the Obama administration announced air strikes in Syria, it was part of a coalition that included five Arab allies. In terms of local allies on the ground, in Iraq the United States could work with the Iraqi government and Kurdish forces, but in Syria the United States is just in the beginning stages of trying to create local forces with which it can ally itself. If fully pursued, this project promises to long outlive the Obama administration.

Conclusion

As of this writing the Obama administration's grand strategy is still a work in progress, but its outlines are clear. Compared to previous U.S. grand strategies, it is probably closest to the engagement strategies of the 1990s. Whereas it adopts certain parts of the War on Terror, it has submerged the threat of terrorism into a more complex and diffuse threat picture, it has put great emphasis on multilateralism, it is based on the conviction that time is on the side of the United States, and although it generally prefers to take the role of exemplar rather than crusader in spreading U.S. values, limited crusades remain a possibility. Looking toward what an Obama administration grand strategy might be in its closing years, there is little reason to expect any of these positions to change drastically, barring unforeseen dramatic crises.

One foreseeable crisis with which the Obama administration will have to grapple in its final years is the question of U.S. fiscal health and its potential effect on U.S. grand strategy. As argued above, the 2010 National Security Strategy accepts the reality of limited U.S. resources and admits that "Years of rising fiscal and trade deficits will also necessitate hard choices in the years ahead."[79] The administration did little in its first term, however, to get the fiscal house of the United States in order. Because of the administration's fear that a large decrease in public spending would deal a serious blow to an already sputtering economic situation, the U.S. fiscal position has worsened. Similarly unwilling or unable to raise taxes, the Obama administration has thus continued what Thomas Friedman and Michael Mandelbaum have termed America's "war on math" that began under the George W. Bush administration.[80] Ending the war in Iraq, ending the war in Afghanistan (albeit after a surge), narrowing the war on terror, limiting intervention in Libya and Syria, and relying more on allies for burden sharing have helped stop some of the fiscal bleeding, but the United States remains on an unsustainable fiscal path. Although foreign policy spending may play only a partial role in that poor fiscal picture, a sudden deterioration in U.S. economic health as a result of a fiscal crisis could have large ramifications for future U.S. foreign policy. As songwriters Mick Jagger and Keith Richards point out, it is always better to walk before they make you run.[81] The more gradually the United States can step away from its untenable fiscal situation the less influence it will have on U.S. foreign policy. If the United States waits until the crisis fully hits before acting, however, drastic changes to its role in the world cannot be ruled out. What the experience of the Obama years and the entire experience of U.S. grand strategy as explored in this book mean for the future of U.S. grand strategy are the subject of the conclusion.

Conclusion
Balancing the Pendulum?

The Past and the Future of U.S. Grand Strategy

It might seem appropriate to conclude a book devoted to four central and recurring debates in U.S. grand strategy by declaring a winner in each debate. Proclaiming winners, however, would provide poor guidance for the future of U.S. foreign policy. Indeed, the very reason these debates recur is that their competing answers have enduring value. In some cases, going it alone might offer more benefits than working with partners, in others, multilateralism may be the better option. Some crusades might be worth pursuing, others not. Except for the anomalous Cold War years, debates about the most pressing security threats facing the United States have been the norm, not the exception. On some issues time may be working in favor of the United States, in others against. Debates about these questions have been a constant thread throughout the U.S. approach to grand strategy precisely because they have no obvious and eternal right answers.

Although these grand strategic debates have no single right answer, the pendulum swings in U.S. foreign policy that often follow dramatic grand strategic failures suggest that wrong answers are not only possible but, unfortunately, common. At the outset of the Cold War Reinhold Niebuhr warned the United States about "the ironic tendency of virtues to turn into vices when too complacently relied upon; and of power to become vexatious if the wisdom which directs it is trusted too confidently."[1] A core conclusion of this book is that U.S. foreign policy is most likely to go astray not when the debates examined here are most contested, but when any particular answer is uncritically accepted without a proper appreciation for its limits and the virtues of alternative approaches. Whereas a core purpose of grand strategy is to bring some measure of coherence across time and space for the many foreign policy choices of the United States, grand strategy should be thought of as a starting point for thinking about particular problems, not an ending point; as an aid to judgment, not an instructional manual. Translating grand strategic convictions into concrete policy decisions requires that each response be tailored to the particular circumstances at hand. The most successful grand strategists are likely to be those who offer balanced rather than dogmatic answers to these recurring questions.

Achieving that balance, especially in a democracy, also requires a certain amount of domestic political skills. In assessing Ronald Reagan's foreign policy performance, Colin Dueck notes: "Part of the secret of his success was no doubt the ability to convince supporters of his core convictions while simultaneously pursuing policies that were actually more circumspect and less interventionist than would have been obvious from his rhetoric."[2] This is a useful way of thinking about grand strategy. It requires core convictions, but it also requires circumspection in application. A balanced and circumspect assessment is important for the United States in its future thinking about how to address the grand strategic debates covered in this book; it should also be based on America's past approaches to these questions.

Multilateralism, Unilateralism, and the Future of U.S. Foreign Policy

As discussed throughout this book, a continuous source of debate in U.S. foreign policy has involved finding the proper balance between working alone and working with others. As defined here, multilateralism is not simply a matter of numbers, but a measure of how willing the United States is to accommodate the interests of others in order to gain their assistance in carrying out particular policies.[3] At its core, this debate in U.S. foreign policy is over what costs to America's freedom of action are acceptable in return for the added resources, expertise, and legitimacy that allies can bring. There is also a strong temporal aspect of this debate because the costs of multilateralism are usually immediate and clear (the United States has to go more slowly and accommodate its allies at the outset); however, its benefits are more long term and diffuse (legitimacy and burden sharing as missions get costly). The opposite case is unilateralism, which typically has immediate benefits and more long-term and diffuse costs.[4]

Looking to the future of U.S. foreign policy there are good reasons to argue that the United States would be better served in its grand strategy by favoring the multilateral end of the spectrum. First, as the United States faces greater fiscal constraints the resources that other countries can put toward solving shared global problems can be one way of filling the gap created by lower U.S. expenditures. Although other countries are unlikely to happily embrace the role of "buck-catcher" as the United States adapts its foreign policy to its new fiscal environment,[5] the reality of fewer U.S. resources will offer Washington's allies an incentive to help fill this void in their own interests. The less frequently the buses run, the harder it is to be a free-rider. Whereas America's enemies are also likely to attempt to increase their influence at the expense of the United States, this too can be seen as an argument for rather than against multilateralism because the resources of allies will be important in countering such threats.

Second, the nature of many of the dangers the United States is likely to face in the future also favor multilateralism. Consider potential threats such as climate change, infectious diseases, or even terrorism and the proliferation of weapons of mass destruction. Even assuming unlimited resources, such problems are unamenable to unilateral solutions. No U.S. policy toward climate change can have a decisive influence unless those efforts are part of a broader international effort. Given the speed and extent of international travel, no country can wall itself off from the dangers of epidemics. Some unilateral actions could certainly be taken against terrorists as well as to stem the tide of proliferation, but even efforts in those areas are likely to benefit greatly from international coordination. As Joseph Nye prudently warns, too great an emphasis on protecting U.S. freedom of action "mistakes the abstractions of sovereignty for the realities of power" in a globalized world.[6]

Finally, even given its deteriorating fiscal position, the United States is likely to remain the most powerful state in the world for the foreseeable future. Allowing other states a say in how U.S. power is used as part of broad multilateral efforts will help the United States to be seen as a valuable partner rather than a potential threat. One goal of U.S. grand strategy, as Richard Haass sees it, should be to convince other countries "that it is neither wise to work against the United States, given its strength, nor necessary to work against it, given its intentions."[7] Multilateralism, by providing an opening for other states to help shape the international agenda, offers a means for achieving this goal. A central challenge for future American policymakers will lie in framing a multilateral agenda that can accommodate the interests of the United States and its potential allies.[8]

In keeping with this chapter's emphasis on balance rather than on answers "too complacently relied upon," it is also important to recognize the limits of multilateralism for U.S. foreign policy. As the most powerful state in the world, the United States cannot become just another state at the global negotiation table. International consensus on pressing issues is unlikely to arise without concerted U.S. efforts to build such a consensus. For the future of U.S. grand strategy, American leadership and multilateralism should be seen as complementary, not as opposite. If multilateralism is not to become the "isolationism of the internationalist,"[9] it cannot be an excuse for inaction; it must be a spur to coalition and institution building. Moreover, multilateralism need not be tied to a particular institution, even institutions as important as the United Nations and the North Atlantic Treaty Organization. Thinking in terms of "multi-multilateralism," "à la carte" multilateralism," or "a coalition of the relevant," according to which the United States conducts its policies through multiple formal institutions and multiple ad hoc coalitions,[10] will allow the United States the take advantage of the benefits of multilateralism, while also providing U.S. policymakers the flexibility that implementing grand strategy requires.

U.S. Values and the Future of U.S. Foreign Policy

U.S. policymakers have generally agreed on the benefits of spreading U.S. values, but they have disagreed regarding the best means of doing so. Should the United States go abroad in search of monsters to destroy in active attempts to impose its values on others, or should it simply serve as a model for others, letting the intrinsic attraction of its values do most of the work. This debate continues to hold a central position in U.S. foreign policy. How far should the United States go in seeking a more democratic solution to the civil war in Syria? Should the United States actively support those seeking to overthrow nondemocratic rulers abroad or should the United States stand on the sidelines, offering moral support, but only limited physical support? Such questions consistently arise about U.S. policy toward the Kim regime in North Korea, the clerical regime in Iran, and the military rulers in Myanmar, for example. When states are in danger of collapsing or turning against a significant portion of their own people (for example, in Somalia or Sudan), should the United States actively attempt to build functioning democratic institutions in those places, or simply try to contain the problem and let the domestic actors work out their own fate, offering a potential model but not active involvement?

At first glance this might look as if it is an easy dispute to adjudicate because the most costly and controversial foreign policy failures of the United States, such as the wars in Vietnam and Iraq, stemmed in part from overambitious attempts to actively spread U.S. values. Conversely, the collapse of Soviet-allied regimes in Eastern Europe, and indeed the collapse of the Soviet Union itself, demonstrated the power of the U.S. and West European models to achieve impressive foreign policy successes through the power of example rather than direct force. Combining that track record with an increasingly tight fiscal situation makes the arguments that Washington should take on new state-building campaigns look problematic at best. Forswearing crusading would not, of course, require the United States to lessen its commitment to its values or reject its historical optimism regarding the eventual spread of those values, but it would require the United States to be less directly involved and more patient.

On the other hand, some of America's greatest successes as a world power have come from crusades.[11] The democratization of Germany and what that meant for the pacification of Europe and the democratization of Japan and what that meant for the spread of liberal values throughout Asia still stand as perhaps the most important grand strategic successes of the United States. It is important to note that neither of these success stories was launched as a crusade first. The United States did not go to war with Japan and Germany in the 1940s to turn those states into democracies. Once the United States was involved in those wars, however, its attempt to change the domestic structure of those enemy regimes proved the most effective way of advancing long-term U.S. interests in both Europe and Asia. The crusades came, but only after the United States had already found itself in the midst of costly and difficult struggles. Whereas both Germany and Japan were unique cases that obviously did not prove to be valid guides for many subsequent U.S. state-building efforts, that observation does not settle the debate over the proper place of U.S. values in its foreign policy, it only reframes it to ask when crusading might be an appropriate part of U.S. grand strategy. Similarly, U.S. failures to act as Cambodia, Rwanda, and Darfur descended into genocide or to take more forceful actions against al-Qaeda and its Taliban allies in the 1990s suggest that avoiding any actions that have the whiff of a crusade about them can also come with costs. Again, the United States needs a balanced answer to this debate, rather than an unbending commitment to either side of the continuum.

In the pattern of U.S. foreign policy, crusading has expanded along with perceptions of U.S. power, and the appeal of the United States as the Promised Land has grown as U.S. ambitions have encountered more serious obstacles. Woodrow Wilson was initially more willing to put his weight behind state-building ventures in relatively weaker Latin America instead of Europe; the privatized crusade of the 1920s turned inward with the Great Depression; the Kennedy and Johnson administrations' confidence in their ability to wield U.S. power put the United States on the path to the Vietnam War; the costs of that war and the economic troubles of the 1970s caused another turn inward; America's position as the sole remaining superpower made crusading an attractive option for the United States in the 1990s, until the costs of those crusades grew; the George W. Bush administration's sense of unparalleled U.S. power caused it to embark on three wars with crusading components (Afghanistan, Iraq, and the War on Terror); and the costs of those wars and the economic downturns following the 2008 financial crisis have dampened enthusiasm for crusading.[12]

To adapt a phrase used more often in the debate about multilateralism, the tendency of the United States on the value question has been to crusade when it can (when it has a seeming surplus of power), but to act as the Promised Land when it must (when its resources are more limited). The analysis offered in this book suggests that the United States would be better off flipping this approach on its head. Rather than adopt crusading when it can and settle for being the Promised Land when it must, the United States would be better off adopting the role of the Promised Land whenever it can and crusading only when it must. If the United States has a seeming surplus of power, it is likely to be secure enough to exercise strategic patience and let domestic developments overseas take their own course, assisted modestly by the force of U.S. example. Only when the severity of the threat justifies bearing significant costs should crusading become a key part of U.S. grand strategy. Because crusades are never likely to be cheap and easy, unless the United States is willing to pay the necessary costs, it should avoid crusades if possible. When faced with severe threats, however, as the United States was in World War II, crusading may be a necessary part of any U.S. response. This is not a call for isolationism or an argument against taking early prudent and potentially cheap preventive actions to ward off threats, but an argument that crusades are unlikely to ever be prudent and relatively cheap preventive actions.

Given the absence of a clear overarching threat that would justify the costs or necessitate the use of crusading, U.S. grand strategy in the coming years should therefore lie closer to the Promised Land end of the spectrum. China's power is already too great and its intentions still too unknown to justify any crusade in Beijing; moreover, even a nuclear-armed Iran, for example, would be better handled by a policy of containment and deterrence than by an attempt to change the regime in Tehran. This, however, takes us to the third recurring debate discussed in this book about determining the principal threats facing the United States.

Assessing Threats and the Future of U.S. Foreign Policy

Delineating the security perimeter of the United States has perhaps been the most vexing problem facing U.S. grand strategy over the past twenty years. With the Soviet Union defunct, what are the most dangerous threats the United States has had to confront? The expansive and unprioritized lists of potential threats that characterized the National Security Strategies of the 1990s and those of the Obama administration offer little guidance for the key strategic task of allocating scarce foreign policy resources. Conversely, the immediate post-9/11 focus on the nexus of terrorism and the proliferation of weapons of mass destruction proved a relatively narrow basis for U.S. grand strategy. Current and future U.S. grand strategists must face the core challenge of conceiving a security perimeter that avoids both problems: it must be specific enough to provide guidance for resource allocation decisions, but it must also be broad enough to respond adequately to a multi-faceted threat environment.

Although the term "security perimeter" evokes a geographical image, assessing threats on a primarily geographic basis—by attempting to identify "geopolitical pivots," a "Global Balkans," "pivotal states," "buffer states," or a "core versus the gap" dichotomy—is likely to be inadequate for grand strategy.[13] The chief limitations of such approaches are twofold. First, they tend to favor state-centric approaches to security in an era where threats are increasingly non–state-based (climate change and infectious diseases, for example). Second, technological advances and globalization have made geography less important. My intent here is not to resurrect the myth of America's free security and bemoan the fact that technology has destroyed the security barriers that oceans once afforded the United States. Indeed, as Anne-Marie Slaughter has noted, America is still favored by its geographical position, which will help buffer it from conflicts exacerbated by climate change, reduce its exposure to pollutants created by other states, and limit refugee flows.[14] Instead, the point worth stressing is that in a globalized, high-tech world, threats are unlikely to be neatly circumscribed geographically. The recognition that dangerous threats to the United States can potentially originate from any geographical location, however, offers little strategic guidance for the allocation of U.S. attention and resources. In offering some guidance for clarifying America's strategic perimeter, three general rules are helpful for thinking about the potential threats that the United States should focus on, and just as important, the potential threats that merit less attention and resources.

The first of these guidelines is to ask whether a potential threat can be deterred or contained. A driving insight of Kennan's approach to U.S. grand strategy after World War II was his assessment that the Soviets were deterrable. This meant that there was no reason to risk prohibitively costly measures that would have sought an immediate eradication of the Soviet threat. Containing that threat was the less dramatic but strategically sounder course. Speaking more broadly, former national security adviser Sandy Berger concluded that although "containment is aesthetically displeasing" it is often "strategically sufficient."[15] Given the growing fiscal constraints on U.S. foreign policy, and the multitude of potential threats the United States could be facing, a key part of any grand strategic threat assessment should be to determine which threats are containable and which require immediate attention.

Using this yardstick, stateless groups with political agendas hostile to the United States and with potential access to weapons of mass destruction merit a high level of U.S. attention. Whereas a war on terror is a narrow base for an entire grand strategy, any U.S. grand strategy will have to include some components of a war on terror. The willingness of certain terrorist groups to inflict mass casualties, and the difficulties of deterring stateless groups that present few targets for retaliation, make concerted prevention efforts a wise investment. The logic of this prioritization, however, also pushes other concerns off the top of the list of America's most important foreign policy worries. For the same reason that stateless terrorist groups with potential access to weapons of mass destruction merit so much attention, hostile states with weapons of mass destruction merit less attention. States, which have far more to lose in a retaliatory U.S. strike, can be deterred and contained. Such policies are certainly not cost free, but they are far less taxing than attempts at preventive war. Whereas a nuclear-armed North Korea or a potentially nuclear-armed Iran is certainly problematic for the United States, both are far lesser threats than a nuclear-armed al-Qaeda.

This logic similarly pushes concerns about the potential rise of a great power competitor lower on the list of current U.S. priorities. Even if such a peer competitor were to arise, the logic of deterrence would help to limit that competition. In addition, each of the potential future great powers, with China and the European Union as perhaps the two most prominent possibilities, still face significant hurdles in their attainment of superpower status and neither has yet posed a fundamental challenge to the current U.S.-led global order. The emergence of a near-peer competitor that did seek to overthrow the current international system would jump to the front of U.S. concerns, as the Soviet Union did during the Cold War. However, that is not the situation the United States is likely to be facing any time soon. Attempts to incorporate growing powers into the existing international order would be a more cost-effective strategy than active attempts to stifle their growth, and even if those efforts failed, the United States could still fall back on deterrence and containment.

A second guideline for thinking about America's future security perimeter borrows a metaphor from economics and conceives of the United States as the security provider of last resort. In the financial world, a lender of last resort may be necessary in times of crisis to stave off economic ruin, but a lender of last resort need not be deeply involved in all day-to-day transactions during more normal times. The classic case that may require intervention by the lender of last resort is when a liquidity crisis risks generating a run on the banks. By providing money to troubled banks to assure investors that their investments are protected, a lender of last resort helps to ensure that normal economic activity can continue. Transplanting this concept into U.S. grand strategy suggests that the United States should attempt to delegate most day-to-day security transactions to local actors but should remain prepared to intervene whenever local or regional forces find themselves in danger of being overwhelmed.[16] Whether the issue is a potential regional hegemon, a failing state, a rogue state, or ethnic cleansing, the United States should first allow local and regional actors to take the lead in tackling and containing these problems, offer support in areas of exceptional U.S. capabilities (global airlift and communications, for example), but take on a more prominent role only if those local efforts are in danger of failing catastrophically.

Thinking of the United States as the security provider of last resort would not only help husband U.S. foreign policy resources, it is also consistent with the arguments for multilateralism discussed above. Contrary to the arguments of the offshore balancers, effectively playing the role of security provider of last resort will require maintaining some U.S. presence overseas, not dismantling it. Advocates for offshore balancing argue that the United States should strive to maintain its dominance in the Western hemisphere while simultaneously preventing any other state from achieving a similarly hegemonic status in its home region, especially in critically important areas like Northeast Asia, the Persian Gulf, or Europe. As part of this strong-point strategy, the offshore balancers further posit that the United States should remove its physical presence in those regions and let local actors pay the costs of balancing, intervening only if local forces are clearly overmatched and a regional hegemon is threatening to emerge. Why not let the South Koreans provide the needed balance against the North because the North's actions are a far greater threat to Seoul than to Washington? For the offshore balancers, a continued U.S. presence overseas allows U.S. allies to be free-riders and to avoid paying the costs for their security, and a U.S. withdrawal would compel, for example, the Japanese and the Koreans to step up their balancing efforts against the Chinese. Similarly, offshore balancers would prefer that Germany or a German-led alliance, instead of NATO, provide a check on a potentially resurgent Russia.[17]

For many of the same reasons discussed in the section on multilateralism, however, U.S. security would be better served by keeping some level of forward presence and some level of multilateral commitments as part of U.S. grand strategy.[18] A lender of last resort without any physical presence, which might unilaterally deem that a particular bank run does not rise to the level of a financial crisis (for it), is likely to be far less reassuring to the market than one that has a more obvious physical presence and an institutionalized mechanism for jointly deciding how to respond to crises that do arise. America's more limited resources, due to fiscal constraints, will not only make the support of other countries more important for achieving U.S. foreign policy goals but also will provide a disincentive of its own for free-riding. In addition, offshore balancing is designed to counter one important security threat (the rise of a potential peer competitor), but offers little guidance about other potential threats such as climate change, infectious diseases, and policing cyberspace that will require multilateral solutions. Nothing in the logic of offshore balancing requires not cooperating in these areas but, in practice, it will be hard to draw distinct lines between collaboration on these issues and existing U.S. security commitments. Can the United States simultaneously tell allies that they are on their own with regard to what they see as their most important security threats (a nearby threatening regional power) and ask for increased cooperation in areas Washington defines as more pressing? As Bradley Thayer warns, the offshore balancers "think that the current system can be maintained without the current amount of U.S. power behind it. . . . Without U.S. power, the liberal order created by the United States will end."[19] Because key parts of that liberal order will need to be strengthened rather than weakened to deal with newly emerging threats, the United States should be seeking to buttress the current international order rather than distance itself from it.

A third useful guideline for thinking about the security perimeter of the United States in the coming years is to focus on building flexible institutions rather than countering specific threats. Instead of building single-purpose tools to counter particular threats, Washington's goal should be to build multipurpose institutions that can respond to a wide array of threats. As John Ikenberry cogently argues, "if all we know is that the security threats of tomorrow will be shifting, diffuse and uncertain, we should want to create a flexible and capable political system that can meet and defeat a lot of complex threats."[20] America's grand strategy during the Cold War was a positional one: the goal was to stay ahead of the Soviet Union. The future is likely to call more for what Ikenberry describes as a milieu-based grand strategy structured around the type of global environment the United States would like to help construct.[21] This approach to thinking about U.S. security is also consistent with arguments for multilateralism.

These guidelines do not offer a neat list of threat priorities. Indeed, such a goal is probably beyond the realm of the possible in the current security environment. Again, perhaps the clarity of the Cold War years is the anomaly rather than the rule in having such a clear threat picture. What these guidelines do offer, however, is a way to think strategically about the threats the United States faces; they offer a way to help determine where the United States should put its limited foreign policy resources and to decide which issues are better left to others or better ignored.

Time and the Future of U.S. Foreign Policy

The final of the four core questions for U.S. grand strategy considered in this book is the question of whether time is on America's side or not. Contrary to the conventional wisdom that the United States has a congenitally short attention span, U.S. grand strategy has had its successes in pursuing long-term goals. The forty-five-plus years of containment during the Cold War is perhaps the best example, but even outside of that era, continuities in U.S. grand strategy across administrations has been at least as striking as the discontinuities. This is not to say that the United States has always used time effectively as a grand strategic tool. Errors on this front have come in two primary but contradictory forms: panic induced by fear that time was working against the United States, and inaction produced by hopes that since time was on America's side, no costly actions were necessary.

First, consider errors of commission. Fearing that time was working against the United States, U.S. grand strategists have sometimes overreacted to potential threats, for example, by stretching U.S. resources too thinly in attacking overhyped and ultimately transitory threats. The fears of falling dominoes during the Cold War, which helped propel the United States into a protracted war in Vietnam, is a paradigmatic example. The fear that time was working against the United States and that the fall of one domino would send the others toppling made such an intervention seem to be a wise strategic investment. If dominoes did not fall, if instead Soviet gains in places like Vietnam had been seen as limited and transient, the United States could have avoided this costly drain on its resources. Similarly, the George W. Bush administration's post-9/11 fear that time was working on the side of U.S. enemies as they developed more dangerous weapons of mass destruction helped to propel the United States into a protracted war in Iraq. If, however, containment and deterrence were working to keep any threat from Saddam Hussein limited and his regime was living on borrowed time this was also a costly commitment that the United States could have avoided.

"Assuming the worst" might seem to be a prudent approach to foreign policy, but it is an unsustainable and astrategic one. While the fears of any country's imagination may be unlimited, no state's resources are unlimited. The United States has been more successful in its grand strategy when it has recognized both the potential weaknesses and the potential strengths of its enemies. Even though Soviet growth rates were impressive in the early Cold War years, Kennan also stressed the weaknesses and debilities of the Soviet system instead of simply extrapolating those numbers into an indefinite future in which the Soviet Union would outclass the United States. As a result, he developed a strategy that avoided a potentially risky and costly direct confrontation and allowed the Soviet Union to defeat itself. Similarly, a strategy for the United States today that focuses only on China's remarkable recent economic growth and ignores the internal strains and domestic hurdles facing the regime in Beijing would risk many of the same dangers courted by proponents of rollback in the 1950s.[22] Worst-case scenarios may offer compelling thought experiments but as a basis for grand strategy they encourage frenetic, costly, and potentially counterproductive overreactions to threats that are always just about to cascade out of control.

In contrast, the United States has also committed errors of omission, where confidence that time was working for the United States, became an excuse for inaction. The attempt by post–World War I policymakers to pursue an "empire without tears," the relative neglect of foreign policy concerns in the early Clinton years, the lack of concerted action against the growing terrorist threat before 2001, and the failure of U.S. policymakers today to grapple with the long-term effects of continued deficit spending are all cases in point. To continue to assume, for example, that the United States will simply grow its way out of its current debt problems so that "deficits don't matter" as Vice President Cheney reportedly put it,[23] is not beneficial temporal optimism but an abandonment of current responsibilities. Similarly, Aaron Friedberg warns that although both the United States and China believe that time is on their side today, Washington is doing too little to ensure that this belief is justified.[24]

To be successful, U.S. grand strategy needs more than an optimistic belief that time is on America's side, it also requires a willingness to take action today to help ensure that this remains the case. Franklin Roosevelt was not only confident that the United States could emerge from the Great Depression without succumbing to fascism or communism, he explicitly framed his policies with an eye toward stabilizing and ameliorating the domestic front so radical solutions would be less necessary. Dwight Eisenhower did not only believe that the United States would outlast the Soviet Union in the protracted struggle that the Cold War was becoming, he designed his fiscal policies to put the United States in an economically favorable position for that prolonged conflict and refused to be taken off track by short-term setbacks such as the Sputnik launch. The need to balance between the short and the long term is a perpetual strategic problem that has no single solution, but what U.S. experience as a great power demonstrates is that historical optimism needs to be wedded to a desire to make choices and investments today that make the anticipated future outcomes more likely and must not be an excuse for inaction, blindly trusting that it will all work out in the end.

The Value of Recurrent Debates

The purpose of this book has not been to advocate for or against any particular grand strategy for the United States. In short, this is not intended to be another entry in the Kennan sweepstakes.[25] That would require a much closer look at the current state of international politics and the most important trends that will affect the security environment in the future. Instead, this book has looked backward. It has looked at how the United States has conducted itself as a world power, the debates it has had over its foreign policy, how those debates have been translated into policy decisions, and what the results of those policy choices have been.

The purpose of this look backward has been, however, to inform the debates that the United States will continue to have over its grand strategy and to inform the ongoing discussions it needs to have about applying its grand strategic principles to whatever foreign policy issues arise in the future. The four key debates examined in this book, as they have recurred for more than a century, are unlikely to disappear any time soon.

The central lesson that this approach as a whole has to offer for thinking about the present and future of U.S. grand strategy is that heated debates, disagreements, and even some confusion about U.S. grand strategy are not only normal, but beneficial. Observers of U.S. foreign policy should not decry debates over the proper role of the United States in the world or uncertainties about how to respond to any particular problem as definitive evidence for the absence of a grand strategy. Nor should inconsistencies in how the United States treats different issues be seen as conclusive evidence of America's strategic confusion or a dangerous lack of consensus. Even during the height of the containment era, fierce debates continued to exist about how containment should be implemented, and, with little effort, analysts could find inconsistencies in how containment was applied in different cases. Grand strategy at its best offers policymakers a starting point, not an ending point, for thinking about the foreign policy problems their country confronts. Because the implementation of any grand strategy will require adaptation to particular circumstances, debates and inconsistencies do not mean that no grand strategy exists. When used properly, grand strategy informs foreign policy decisions; it does not determine them.

The evidence presented in this book suggests that intense disagreements about U.S. foreign policy are not harmful but beneficial to U.S. interests. The foreign policy debates central to this book recur because the proper answers to these questions are debatable. U.S. foreign policy is most in danger not when these debates are at their most pointed, but when the pendulum swings too far toward any single answer. Considering how controversial the wars in Vietnam and Iraq became, the initial decisions that put the United States on a path to war in both cases engendered strikingly little debate at the outset. Contrast that with the success of the Marshall Plan, combined with the tough domestic sell it required, or the difficulties Ronald Reagan had in convincing members of his own political party that Gorbachev was worth negotiating with.

Analyzing the advantages of democracies over more authoritarian systems, Fisher Ames, one of America's lesser remembered founding fathers, argued: "A monarchy is a merchantman that sails well but will sometimes strike on a rock and go to the bottom; a republic is a raft which will never sink, but then your feet are always in the water."[26] This is an apt description of U.S. grand strategy. The process by which the United States develops and implements its foreign policy is certainly not elegant. The United States has certainly made its share of mistakes. Grand strategy is not a map or an instruction booklet that describes precisely what a state should do. Debates recur, inconsistencies proliferate, America's feet are always in the water. On the other hand, grand strategic principles can and have outlasted multiple administrations and can help in decision making on how best to react to the latest current. Moreover, the ability of the United States to debate and eventually correct its mistakes provides the best long-term security against sinking. The future of global politics will depend to a significant extent on how well the United States, as the most powerful state on earth, plays its role. To play that role most successfully, U.S. policymakers should not shy away from these grand strategic debates or seek pat answers to them, but embrace the dilemmas these debates embody. If the United States is going to navigate the international balance of power effectively, it must first balance the American pendulum. Balancing that pendulum will require not an unquestioned consensus on foreign policy, but ongoing contestation and compromises between competing visions and policies that are informed by grand strategic principles, but not determined by them.

Notes

Introduction

1. For examples of this debate following President Obama's assumption of the office see, Walter Russell Mead, "The Carter Syndrome," *Foreign Policy* 177 (January–February 2010): 58–64; and Christian Brose, "The Making of George W. Obama," *Foreign Policy* 170 (January–February 2009): 53–55. For the author's own attempt at this task, which contains earlier versions of many of the ideas further developed in this book, see Christopher Hemmer, "Continuity and Change in the Obama Administration's National Security Strategy," *Comparative Strategy* 30, no. 3 (2011): 268–77.

2. For diplomatic history, see, for example, Warren I. Cohen, Akira Iriye, Walter LaFeber, and Bradford Perkins, *Cambridge History of American Foreign Relations*, 4 vols. (Cambridge: Cambridge University Press, 1993).

3. For studies that focus on process, see David J. Rothkopf, *Running the World: The Inside Story of the National Security Council and the Architects of American Power* (New York: Public Affairs, 2005); and Alexander L. George and Eric Stern, "Presidential Management Styles and Models," in *Presidential Personality and Performance*, ed. Alexander L. George and Juliette L. George (Boulder, CO: Westview Press, 1998), 199–280.

4. For a book that takes a similar "debate"-centric approach to U.S. foreign policy, although it focuses on a different historical era and a different set of debates, see David C. Hendrickson, *Union, Nation or Empire: The American Debate over International Relations, 1789–1941* (Lawrence: University Press of Kansas, 2009). For a discussion on pendulum swings in U.S. foreign policy, see Geir Lundestad, *The American "Empire" and Other Studies of U.S. Foreign Policy in a Comparative Perspective* (Oslo: Norwegian University Press, 1990), 117–41.

5. Barry Posen, *The Sources of Military Doctrine: France, Britain, and Germany between the World Wars* (Ithaca, NY: Cornell University Press, 1984), 13. See also Paul Kennedy, "Grand Strategy in War and Peace: Toward a Broader Definition," in *Grand Strategies in War and Peace*, ed. Kennedy (New Haven, CT: Yale University Press, 1991), 1–7.

6. For the sake of clarity, when I use the capitalized term "National Security Strategy" I am referring to one of these formal documents. When not capitalized, the term "national security strategy" is intended to refer more generically to grand strategy. On the legal requirements of the National Security Strategy, see Catherine Dale, "National Security Strategy: Mandates, Execution to Date, and Issues for Congress," *Congressional Research Service*, August 6, 2013, 3–4.

7. On defining and operationalizing grand strategy, see also Kevin Narizny, *The Political Economy of Grand Strategy* (Ithaca, NY: Cornell University Press, 2007), 8–10. For a discussion of the institutional challenges of grand strategy and U.S. foreign policy, see Daniel Drezner, ed., *Avoiding Trivia: The Role of Strategic Planning in American Foreign Policy* (Washington, DC: Brookings Institution Press, 2009).

8. See Andrew Goodpaster's forward in Robert R. Bowie and Richard H. Immerman, *Waging Peace: How Eisenhower Shaped an Enduring Cold War Strategy* (New York: Oxford University Press, 1998), vii.

9. Frederick W. Kagan, "Grand Strategy for the United States," in *Finding Our Way: Debating American Grand Strategy*, ed. Michèle A. Flournoy and Shawn Brimley (Washington, DC: Center for New American Security, June 2008), 63; Andrew F. Krepinevich and Barry D. Watts, "Lost at the NSC," *National Interest* 99 (January–February 2009): 64. See also Aaron L. Friedberg, "Strengthening U.S. Strategic Planning," *Washington Quarterly* 31, no. 1 (Winter 2007–8): 47–60. Hal Brands similarly treats grand strategy as a process; see *What Good Is Grand Strategy: Power and Purpose in American Statecraft from Harry S. Truman to George W. Bush* (Ithaca, NY: Cornell University Press, 2014), 4–5, 198–99.

10. Robert D. Blackwill, "The Bush Foreign Policy, Take Two: A Symposium," *National Interest* 84 (Summer 2006): 20–23.

11. I think this is what Stephen Krasner is getting at when he prefers the term "orientating principle" to "grand strategy." See his "An Orientating Principle for Foreign Policy," *Policy Review* (October–November 2010): 3–12.

12. Ronald Reagan, "The National Security Strategy of the United States" (January 1987), 4. This and all National Security Strategies referred to in this book are available at http://nssarchive.us/.

13. On isolationism versus internationalism, or what Stanley Hoffmann calls "quietism versus activism," see his *Gulliver's Troubles, Or the Setting of American Foreign Policy* (New York: McGraw-Hill, 1968), 190–208. Dexter Perkins offers a similar distinction between periods of bellicosity and periods of pacifism in U.S. foreign policy in his *The American Approach to Foreign Policy* (Cambridge, MA: Harvard University Press, 1962), 135–55. See also Thomas M. Magstadt, *An Empire If You Can Keep It: Power and Principle in American Foreign Policy* (Washington, DC: Congressional Quarterly Press, 2004); and Stephen Sestanovich, *Maximalist: America in the World from Truman to Obama* (New York: Knopf, 2014), in which the author distinguishes between maximalists and retrenchers. On the debate as a whole, see David Hastings Dunn, "Isolationism Revisited: Seven Persistent Myths in the Contemporary American Foreign Policy Debate," *Review of International Studies* 31 (2005): 237–61.

14. The one arguable exception might be the brief period in the 1930s under the neutrality acts.

15. On this point, see Alexander Hamilton, "Federalist #63," in *The Federalist Papers*, ed. Clinton Rossiter (New York: Mentor, 1961), 382.

16. On the choice between unilateralism and multilateralism in U.S. foreign policy, see David M. Malone and Yuen Foong Khong, eds., *Multilateralism and U.S. Foreign Policy: International Perspectives* (Boulder, CO: Lynne Rienner, 2003); David A. Lake, *Entangling Relations: American Foreign Policy in Its Century* (Princeton, NJ: Princeton University Press, 1999); and John Gerard Ruggie, *Winning the Peace: America and World Order in the New Era* (New York: Columbia University Press, 1996). For the argument that analysts have tended to overstate the costs of unilateralism, see Stephen G. Brooks and William C. Wohlforth, "International Relations Theory and the Case against Unilateralism," *Perspectives on Politics* 3, no. 3 (September 2005): 509–24.

17. For a copy of Washington's 1796 Farewell Address, see http://avalon.law.yale.edu/18th_Century/washing.asp.

18. For a copy of Jefferson's 1801 First Inaugural Address, see http://avalon.law.yale.edu/19th_Century/jefinau1.asp.

19. Felix Gilbert, *To the Farewell Address: Ideas of Early American Foreign Policy* (Princeton, NJ: Princeton University Press, 1961), 122, 130–31, 139.

20. John Quincy Adams Diary 34, January 1, 1823, June 14, 1824, p. 149 [electronic edition]. Date of entry is November 7, 1823. *The Diaries of John Quincy Adams: A Digital Collection* (Boston: Massachusetts Historical Society, 2005), available at http://www.masshist.org/jqadiaries.

21. For a brief discussion of the origins of the Monroe Doctrine, see Thomas G. Paterson, J. Garry Clifford, and Kenneth J. Hagan, *American Foreign Policy: A History to 1914* (Lexington, MA: D.C. Heath, 1988), 94–99. For a discussion of the Monroe Doctrine that puts it in the context of overall U.S. policy toward Spain and Latin America, see James E. Lewis Jr., *The American Union and the Problem of Neighborhood: The United States and the Collapse of the Spanish Empire, 1783–1829* (Chapel Hill: University of North Carolina Press, 1998), 177–87.

22. For an emphasis on the contested nature of these values themselves in U.S. history, see Rogers M. Smith, "Beyond Tocqueville, Myrdal and Hartz: The Multiple Traditions in America," *American Political Science Review* 87, no. 3 (September 1993): 549–66.

23. See, for example, Henry Kissinger, "The Hinge: Theodore Roosevelt or Woodrow Wilson," in Kissinger, *Diplomacy* (New York: Simon and Schuster, 1994), 29–55 (see also p. 18 where he uses language more consistent with the approach used here); and Magstadt, *An Empire If You Can Keep It*. For an argument that relative power considerations have dominated over value considerations, see Stephen M. Walt, "The Myth of American Exceptionalism," *Foreign Policy* 189 (November–December 2011): 72–75. For broader critiques of the idea of U.S. exceptionalism that stress comparative rather than absolute exceptionalism, see Godfrey Hodgson, *The Myth of American Exceptionalism* (New Haven, CT: Yale University Press, 2009), 61; and Richard T. Hughes, *Myths America Lives By* (Urbana: University of Illinois Press, 2003), 5.

24. See his contribution to a symposium on President Obama's foreign policy. Stephen Krasner, *American Interest* 9, no. 5 (May–June 2014): 43.

25. Walter A. McDougall, *Promised Land, Crusader State: The American Encounter with the World Since 1776* (Boston: Houghton Mifflin, 1997). For a similar distinction regarding what he terms exemplars versus vindicators, see H. W. Brands, *What America Owes the World: The Struggle for the Soul of American Foreign Policy* (Cambridge: Cambridge University Press, 1998). Michael Hunt gets at the same divide in his two visions of national mission, one that stresses the spread of U.S. values through the pursuit of international greatness and the other that stresses restraint abroad and the perfection of liberty at home. See his *Ideology and U.S. Foreign Policy* (New Haven, CT: Yale University Press, 1987), 19–45. See also Trevor B. McCrisken, *American Exceptionalism and the Legacy of Vietnam: U.S. Foreign Policy Since 1974* (New York: Palgrave Macmillan, 2003), 2. For a similar distinction phrased in terms of negative and positive liberty, see Brendan Rittenhouse Green, "Two Concepts of Liberty: U.S. Cold War Grand Strategy and the Liberal Tradition," *International Security* 37, no. 3 (Fall 2012): 9–43.

26. McDougall, *Promised Land, Crusader State*, 205.

27. Abraham Lincoln, "Address to the New Jersey State Senate," February 21, 1861, available at http://www.abrahamlincolnonline.org/lincoln/speeches/trenton1.htm.

28. John Winthrop, "A Modell of Christian Charity," 1630. In this excerpt, the spelling has been updated from Winthrop's original. The entire sermon is available at http://history.hanover .edu/texts/winthmod.html.

29. Thomas Paine, *Common Sense* (London: Penguin Books, 1986), 120.

30. Quoted in Michael Hirsh, *At War with Ourselves: Why America Is Squandering Its Chance to Build a Better World* (Oxford: Oxford University Press, 2003), 243.

31. John Quincy Adams, "Address of July 4, 1821," in *John Quincy Adams and American Continental Empire: Letters, Papers and Speeches*, ed. Walter LaFeber (Chicago: Quadrangle Books, 1965), 45.

32. Robert Kagan, *Dangerous Nation: America's Place in the World from Its Earliest Days to the Dawn of the 20th Century* (New York: Knopf, 2006), 46–47.

33. The weak neighbors and fish quip comes from Jules Jusserand, quoted in Thomas A. Bailey, *A Diplomatic History of the American People*, 7th ed. (New York: Appleton-Century-Crofts, 1964), 4. On free security, see C. Vann Woodward, "The Age of Reinterpretation," *American Historical Review* 66, no. 1 (October 1960): 1–19. For contrary views, see Fareed Zakaria, "The Myth of America's Free Security," *World Policy Journal* 14, no. 2 (Summer 1997): 35–43; and Hendrickson, *Union, Nation, or Empire*, xii.

34. The text of the speech is available at http://georgewbush-whitehouse.archives.gov/news /releases/2002/01/20020129-11.html.

35. Quoted in John A. Thompson, "Exaggeration of American Vulnerability: The Anatomy of a Tradition," *Diplomatic History* 16, no. 1 (Winter 1992): 25–26.

36. Quoted in Stefan Halper and Jonathan Clarke, *America Alone: The Neo-Conservatives and the Global Order* (Cambridge: Cambridge University Press, 2004), 337.

37. Alexander Hamilton, "Federalist #24," in Rossiter, *The Federalist Papers*, 160–61.

38. Andrew Jackson to James Monroe, June 20, 1820, in John Spencer Bassett, ed., *Correspondence of Andrew Jackson*, 7 vols. (Washington, DC: Carnegie Institution of Washington, 1926–35), 3:28–29.

39. Jackson to Aaron V. Brown, February 9, [12], 1843, in Bassett, *Correspondence of Andrew Jackson*, 6:201–2.

40. Niall Ferguson, *Colossus: The Price of America's Empire* (New York: Penguin Press, 2004), 293–95.

41. Thomas Jefferson to John Bacon, April 30, 1803, quoted in Robert W. Tucker and David C. Hendrickson, *Empire of Liberty: The Statecraft of Thomas Jefferson* (New York: Oxford University Press, 1990), 132, 306. For their overall discussion of Jefferson's strategy of playing for time, see pp. 93, 125–35, and 138. See also Hendrickson, *Union, Nation or Empire*, 55–56.

42. See Walter LaFeber, *The American Age: United States Foreign Policy at Home and Abroad since 1750* (New York: Norton, 1989), 11–13.

43. Quoted in Walter A. McDougall, *Let the Sea Make a Noise: A History of the North Pacific from Magellan to MacArthur* (New York: Basic Books, 1993), 225–26.

1. Finding a Place on the World Stage

1. For perhaps the most effective and most noted example of this approach, see Henry Kissinger, *Diplomacy* (New York: Simon and Schuster, 1994), 29–55.

2. Michael H. Hunt, *The American Ascendancy: How the United States Gained and Wielded Global Dominance* (Chapel Hill: University of North Carolina Press, 2007), 44–51.

3. Charles A. Kupchan, *How Enemies Become Friends: The Sources of Stable Peace* (Princeton, NJ: Princeton University Press, 2010), 74.

4. Walter McDougall, *Promised Land, Crusader State: The American Encounter with the World Since 1776* (Boston: Houghton Mifflin, 1997), 117.

5. The key foreign policy portion of Monroe's Annual message to Congress, December 2, 1823, which contains the Monroe Doctrine, is available at http://avalon.law.yale.edu/19th _Century/monroe.asp.

6. See Roosevelt's Fourth Annual Message, December 6, 1904, available at http://www .presidency.ucsb.edu/ws/?pid=29545.

7. Elihu Root, "The Real Monroe Doctrine," *American Journal of International Law* 8, no. 3 (July 1914): 440–41.

8. Ibid., 441.

9. Frank Ninkovich, *The Wilsonian Century: U.S. Foreign Policy Since 1900* (Chicago: University of Chicago Press, 1999), 33.

10. See George C. Herring, *From Colony to Superpower: U.S. Foreign Relations since 1776* (Oxford: Oxford University Press, 2008), 335, 407, 411.

11. Quoted in David C. Hendrickson, *Union, Nation or Empire: The American Debate over International Relations, 1789–1941* (Lawrence: University Press of Kansas, 2009), 187.

12. Quoted in McDougall, *Promised Land, Crusader State*, 119.

13. Quoted in Hendrickson, *Union, Nation or Empire*, 267.

14. Woodrow Wilson, "An Address in Boston," February 24, 1919, in *The Papers of Woodrow Wilson*, ed. Arthur S. Link, vol. 55 (Princeton, NJ: Princeton University Press, 1986), 242–43.

15. For an account of Wilson's foreign policy that moves beyond a realist/idealist dichotomy, see Ross A. Kennedy, "Woodrow Wilson, World War I, and an American Conception of National Security," *Diplomatic History* 25, no. 1 (Winter 2001): 1–31. For an account that stresses the practical limits Wilson imposed upon his crusading, see Lloyd E. Ambrosius, "Woodrow Wilson and

George W. Bush: Historical Comparisons of Ends and Means in Their Foreign Policies," *Diplomatic History* 30, no. 3 (June 2006): 509–43.

16. This entire section relies heavily on McDougall, *Promised Land, Crusader State*.

17. Tony Smith, *America's Mission: The United States and the Worldwide Struggle for Democracy in the Twentieth Century* (Princeton, NJ: Princeton University Press, 1994), 60–83.

18. Michael C. Desch, "Woodrow Wilson's War," *National Interest* 99 (January–February 2009): 87–96.

19. Daniel Larsen, "Abandoning Democracy: Woodrow Wilson and Promoting German Democracy, 1918–1919," *Diplomatic History* 37, no. 3 (June 2013): 476–508; Thomas J. Knock, " 'Playing for a Hundred Years Hence': Woodrow Wilson's Internationalism and His Would-Be Heirs," in *The Crisis of American Foreign Policy: Wilsonianism in the Twenty-First Century*, ed. G. John Ikenberry, Thomas J. Knock, Anne-Marie Slaughter, and Tony Smith (Princeton, NJ: Princeton University Press, 2009), 31–36; and Anne-Marie Slaughter "Wilsonianism in the Twenty-First Century," in Ikenberry et al., *The Crisis of American Foreign Policy*, 92.

20. On the continuity between Wilson's policies to Latin America and later to Europe, see Binoy Kampmark, " 'No Peace with the Hohenzollerns': American Attitudes on Political Legitimacy towards Hohenzollern Germany, 1917–1918," *Diplomatic History* 34, no. 5 (November 2010): 769–91.

21. See, for example, Greg Russell, "Theodore Roosevelt, Geopolitics and Cosmopolitan Ideals," *Review of International Studies* 32 (2006): 541–59; and Stephen G. Walker and Mark Schafer "Theodore Roosevelt and Woodrow Wilson as Cultural Icons of U.S. Foreign Policy," *Political Psychology* 28, no. 6 (December 2007): 747–76.

22. This is a major theme in Robert E. Hannigan's *The New World Power: American Foreign Policy, 1898–1917* (Philadelphia: University of Pennsylvania Press, 2002), 9, 13, 135–36.

23. The Jefferson quote is from Michael Hirsh, *At War With Ourselves: Why America is Squandering its Chance to Build a Better World* (Oxford: Oxford University Press, 2003), 243. The Roosevelt quote is from Hunt, *The American Ascendancy*, 50.

24. Theodore Roosevelt, *Fear God and Take Your Own Part* (New York: George H. Doran, 1916), 406–7.

25. Quoted in James R. Holmes, *Theodore Roosevelt and World Order: Police Power in International Relations* (Washington, DC: Potomac Books, 2006), 22.

26. Theodore Roosevelt, "Fourth Annual Message," December 6, 1904, available at http://www.presidency.ucsb.edu/ws/print.php?pid=29545. On Roosevelt's focusing on more limited crusades than Wilson, see also Elizabeth N. Saunders, *Leaders at War: How Presidents Shape Military Interventions* (Ithaca, NY: Cornell University Press, 2011), 187–91.

27. Michael B. Oren, *Power, Faith and Fantasy: America in the Middle East 1776 to the Present* (New York: Norton, 2007), 344–46; and Ambrosius, "Woodrow Wilson and George W. Bush," 521.

28. Quoted in William Henry Harbaugh, *Power and Responsibility: The Life and Times of Theodore Roosevelt* (New York: Farrar, Straus and Cudahy, 1961), 516.

29. The reference is to the 1741 sermon of Jonathan Edwards titled, "Sinners in the Hands of an Angry God." The text is available at http://edwards.yale.edu/research/major-works/sinners-in-the-hands-of-an-angry-god.

30. Jonathan Monten, "The Roots of the Bush Doctrine: Power, Nationalism and Democracy Promotion in U.S. Strategy," *International Security* 29, no. 4 (Spring 2005): 135–36; and McDougall, *Promised Land, Crusader State*, 104–5.

31. On the labor movement, see Elizabeth McKillen, "Integrating Labor into the Narrative of Wilsonian Internationalism: A Literature Review," *Diplomatic History* 34, no. 4 (September 2010): 647; and Geert Van Goethem, "Labor's Second Front: The Foreign Policy of the American and British Trade Union Movements during the Second World War," *Diplomatic History* 34, no. 4 (September 2010): 675. On increasing religious missionary activity, see Ian Tyrrell, *Reforming the World: The Creation of America's Moral Empire* (Princeton, NJ: Princeton University Press, 2010).

32. Smith, *America's Mission*, 84; and David Ryan, *U.S. Foreign Policy in World History* (New York: Routledge, 2000), 84.

33. Trygve Throntveit, "The Fable of the Fourteen Points: Woodrow Wilson and National Self-Determination," *Diplomatic History* 35, no. 3 (June 2011): 446.

34. For a discussion of Roosevelt's, and other Republicans' ideas on multilateralism in the aftermath of World War I, see Stephen Werthheim, "'The League that Wasn't': American Designs for a Legalist-Sanctionist League of Nations and the Intellectual Origins of International Organization," *Diplomatic History* 35, no. 5 (November 2011): 819, 830, 807.

35. Herring, *From Colony to Superpower*, 429.

36. Michael Mandelbaum, "Bad Statesman, Good Prophet: Woodrow Wilson and the Post–Cold War Order," *National Interest* 64 (Summer 2001): 31–41; and Ninkovich, *The Wilsonian Century*.

37. See Anatol Lieven, "Wolfish Wilsonians: Existential Dilemmas of the Liberal Internationalists," *Orbis* 50, no. 2 (Spring 2006): 243–57.

38. Pierre Hassner, "The United States: The Empire of Force or the Force of Empire," *Chaillot Papers*, no. 54 (September 2002): 43. On the overall comparison of George W. Bush and Woodrow Wilson, see Ambrosius, "Woodrow Wilson and George W. Bush."

39. Tom Parker, "The Realistic Roosevelt," *National Interest* 77 (Fall 2004): 141–47. See also John B. Judis, *The Folly of Empire: What George W. Bush Could Learn from Teddy Roosevelt and Woodrow Wilson* (New York: Scribner, 2004).

40. William Clinton, "Radio Address by the President to the Nation," October 9, 1999, available at http://clinton6.nara.gov/1999/10/1999-10-09-radio-address-by-the-president-on-the-nuclear-test-ban-treaty.html. For the author's earlier attempts to explain U.S. grand strategy in this period, see Christopher Hemmer, "Empire without Tears: The Sequel?," *Brown Journal of World Affairs* 7, no. 2 (Summer–Fall 2000): 163–71.

41. William Clinton, "Press Conference by the President," October 14, 1999, available at http://clinton6.nara.gov/1999/10/1999-10-14-press-conference-by-the-president-on-the-cntbt.html.

42. These numbers come from the Office of the Historian at the U.S. Department of State and are available at http://history.state.gov/about/faq/department-personnel. See also Hunt, *The American Ascendancy*, 70; and Warren Cohen, *Empire without Tears: America's Foreign Relations 1921–1933* (Philadelphia: Temple University Press, 1987), 2.

43. Ninkovich, *The Wilsonian Century*, 90.

44. Philander C. Knox, quoted in Hunt, *The American Ascendancy*, 55.

45. William Mitchell, *Winged Defense: The Development and Possibilities of Modern Air Power, Economic and Military* (1925; repr., Mineola, NY: Dover, 2006), 4.

46. Cohen, *Empire without Tears*, 4–5.

47. Hunt, *The American Ascendancy*, 86.

48. Warren G. Harding, "Inaugural Address," March 4, 1921, available at http://avalon.law.yale.edu/20th_Century/harding.asp.

49. Quoted in Akira Iriye, *The Cambridge History of American Foreign Relations, Volume Three: The Globalizing of America, 1913–1945* (Cambridge: Cambridge University Press, 1993), 98.

50. Hunt, *The American Ascendancy*, 106–9.

51. Cohen, *Empire without Tears*, 11.

52. Iriye, *The Globalizing of America*, 96–97.

53. Harding, "Inaugural Address."

54. Figures from Joan Hoff, *A Faustian Foreign Policy: From Woodrow Wilson to George W. Bush, Dreams of Perfectibility* (New York: Cambridge University Press, 2008), 73.

55. Margot Louria, "The Boldness of Charles Evans Hughes," *National Interest* 72 (Summer 2003): 115–16; Hoff, *A Faustian Foreign Policy*, 71.

56. Thomas L. Friedman, *The World Is Flat: A Brief History of the Twenty-First Century* (New York: Farrar, Straus and Giroux, 2005); Henry R. Luce, "The American Century," *Life*, February 17, 1941; William Thomas Stead, *The Americanisation of the World or The Trend of the Twentieth Century* (London: William Clowes, 1902).

57. Hunt, *The American Ascendancy*, 86.

58. Harding, "Inaugural Address."

59. Cohen, *Empire without Tears*.

60. Quoted in Gene Smith, *The Shattered Dream: Herbert Hoover and The Great Depression* (New York: William Morrow, 1970), 50.

61. For a contrary argument that stresses disillusionment coming out of World War I, see George H. Quester, *American Foreign Policy: The Lost Consensus* (New York: Praeger, 1982), 133–37.

62. Quoted in James Chace and Caleb Carr, *America Invulnerable: The Quest for Absolute Security from 1812 to Star Wars* (New York: Summit Books, 1988), 202. On the effect of the depression as a whole on U.S. foreign policy, see Cohen, *Empire without Tears*, 100–123.

63. See John Lewis Gaddis, *George F. Kennan: An American Life* (New York: Penguin Press, 2011), 114.

64. The quote is from Irving Babbit, cited in H. W. Brands, *What America Owes The World: The Struggle for the Soul of Foreign Policy* (Cambridge: Cambridge University Press, 1998), 107. For this entire period, see pp. 79–108. See also Iriye, *The Globalizing of America*, 131–48.

65. Quoted in Justus A. Doenecke, "The Roosevelt Foreign Policy: An Ambiguous Legacy," in Justus A. Doenecke and Mark A. Stoler, *Debating Franklin D. Roosevelt's Foreign Policy 1933–1945* (Lanham, MD: Rowman and Littlefield, 2005), 69.

66. On this debate, see the contributions of Doenecke and Stoler in their *Debating Franklin D. Roosevelt's Foreign Policy*, with Doenecke stressing FDR's pragmatism and lack of a coherent strategy and Stoler seeing more of a coherent plan. For other discussions of Roosevelt's foreign policy principles for both the war and postwar periods, see Wilson D. Miscamble, "Roosevelt, Truman and the Development of Postwar Grand Strategy," *Orbis* 53, no. 4 (Fall 2009): 555; and Tami Davis Biddle, "Leveraging Strength: The Pillars of American Grand Strategy in World War II," *Orbis* 55, no. 1 (Winter 2011): 6.

67. Quoted in Robert Dallek, *Franklin D. Roosevelt and American Foreign Policy, 1932–1945* (New York: Oxford University Press, 1995), 20.

68. See, for example, Warren F. Kimball, *The Juggler: Franklin Roosevelt as Wartime Statesman* (Princeton, NJ: Princeton University Press, 1991), 180, 186–87. See also Dallek, *Franklin D. Roosevelt and American Foreign Policy*, 546–47, 550; and Doenecke, "The Roosevelt Foreign Policy," 5, 7.

69. FDR to Winston Churchill, April 11, 1945, reproduced in Doenecke and Stoler, *Debating Franklin D. Roosevelt's Foreign Policy*, 215.

70. "President Roosevelt to the Ambassador in Japan (Grew)," January 21, 1941, in *Foreign Relations of the United States, Diplomatic Papers 1941, Volume 4: The Far East* (Washington, DC: Government Printing Office, 1956), 8.

71. Quoted in Colin Dueck, *Hard Line: The Republican Party and U.S. Foreign Policy since World War II* (Princeton, NJ: Princeton University Press, 2010), 43. On FDR's disputes with those who believed a hemispheric defense was still sufficient, see John M. Schuessler, "The Deception Dividend: FDR's Undeclared War," *International Security* 34, no. 4 (Spring 2010): 133–65.

72. Franklin D. Roosevelt, "Fireside Chat," December 9, 1941, available at http://www.presidency.ucsb.edu/ws/index.php?pid=16056&st=&st1.

73. Dallek, *Franklin D. Roosevelt and American Foreign Policy*, 181, 479.

74. Quoted in Patrick Porter, "Beyond the American Century: Walter Lippmann and American Grand Strategy, 1943–1950," *Diplomacy and Statecraft* 22 (2011): 562.

75. On Roosevelt's overall scheme for world order, see Kimball, *The Juggler*, 83–105. For a discussion of FDR's strategy as a potential model for U.S. foreign policy today, see Michael Lind, *The American Way of Strategy: U.S. Foreign Policy and the American Way of Life* (Oxford: Oxford University Press, 2006), 176–83.

76. Kimball, *The Juggler*, 170, 182, 197.

77. Stoler, "The Roosevelt Foreign Policy: Flawed, But Superior to the Competition," 172.

78. Doenecke, "The Roosevelt Foreign Policy," 6.

79. On the neutrality acts in the 1930s, see Ninkovich, *The Wilsonian Century*, 113–30; and Doenecke, "The Roosevelt Foreign Policy," 21.

80. Dallek, *Franklin D. Roosevelt and American Foreign Policy*, 126–37.

81. Brad Simpson, "The United States and the Curious History of Self-Determination," *Diplomatic History* 36, no. 4 (September 2012): 679.

82. David Ekbladh, "Present at the Creation: Edward Mead Earle and the Depression Era Origins of Security Studies," *International Security* 36, no. 3 (Winter 2011–12): 107–41.

83. This issue is explored well in John Gerard Ruggie, *Winning the Peace: America and World Order in the New Era* (New York: Columbia University Press, 1996), 7–27. See also his "The Past as Prologue? Interests, Identity and American Foreign Policy," *International Security* 21, no. 4 (Summer 1997): 94–97.

84. Jean-Jacques Rousseau, "On The Social Contract," Book 1, Chapter 3 in *Jean-Jacques Rousseau: The Basic Political Writings*, ed. and trans. Donald A. Cress (Indianapolis: Hackett, 1987), 143.

2. The Debates Raised by Containment in the Truman Administration

1. John Lewis Gaddis, *Strategies of Containment: A Critical Appraisal of Postwar American National Security Policy*, rev. and exp. ed. (Oxford: Oxford University Press, 2005).

2. Robert Dallek, *The Lost Peace: Leadership in a Time of Horror and Hope, 1949–1953* (New York: HarperCollins, 2010), 68–69.

3. Thomas G. Paterson, "American Expansionism and Exaggerations of the Soviet Threat," in *Major Problems in American Foreign Policy Vol. 2: Since 1914*, 3rd ed. (Lexington, MA: D. C. Heath, 1989), 341.

4. See Warren F. Kimball, *The Juggler: Franklin Roosevelt as Wartime Statesman* (Princeton, NJ: Princeton University Press, 1991), 63–81.

5. Gaddis, *Strategies of Containment*, 8.

6. Melvyn P. Leffler, *A Preponderance of Power: National Security, the Truman Administration and the Cold War* (Stanford, CA: Stanford University Press, 1992), 5.

7. George Kennan, "Résumé of the World Situation (PPS-13)," November 6, 1947, in *Foreign Relations of the United States 1947, Vol.1: General: The United Nations* (Washington, DC: Government Printing Office, 1973), 770–77.

8. Jeffrey M. Cavanaugh, "From the 'Red Juggernaut' to Iraqi WMD: Threat Inflation and How It Succeeds in the United States," *Political Science Quarterly* 122, no. 4 (Winter 2007–8): 559.

9. For U.S. material advantages during and after World War II, see Paul Kennedy, *The Rise and Fall of the Great Powers: Economic Change and Military Conflict from 1500 to 2000* (New York: Vintage Books, 1987), 347–72.

10. For the 1939 figures, see Edward M. Coffman, *The Regulars: The American Army 1898–1941* (Cambridge, MA: Harvard University Press, 2004), 373–74. The post–World War II demobilization figures are from Gaddis, *Strategies of Containment*, 23.

11. The Marshall quote is from Richard Rhodes, *Dark Sun: The Making of the Hydrogen Bomb* (New York: Touchstone, 1995), 282.

12. Kennan, "Résumé of the World Situation (PPS-13)," 770.

13. Ibid., 774.

14. Ibid., 771.

15. For an emphasis on protecting the "American way of life" as the key vital interest of the United States, see Michael Lind, *The American Way of Strategy: U.S. Foreign Policy and the American Way of Life* (Oxford: Oxford University Press, 2006).

16. X (George Kennan), "The Sources of Soviet Conduct," *Foreign Affairs* 25 (July 1947): 566–82.

17. Ibid., 566–71. For an extended discussion that suggests a contrary view, that Roosevelt might have been able to create a partnership with Stalin had he lived, see Frank Costigliola, *Roosevelt's Lost Alliances: How Personal Politics Helped Start the Cold War* (Princeton, NJ: Princeton University Press, 2012).

18. "The Chargé in the Soviet Union (Kennan) to the Secretary of State," March 20, 1946, in *Foreign Relations of the United States 1946, Vol. 6: Eastern Europe, The Soviet Union* (Washington, DC: Government Printing Office, 1969), 721–23.

19. "The Ambassador in the Soviet Union (Harriman) to the Secretary of State," November 22, 1945, in *Foreign Relations of the United States 1945, Vol. 5: Europe* (Washington, DC: Government Printing Office, 1967), 921.

20. John Lewis Gaddis, *We Now Know: Rethinking Cold War History* (Oxford: Oxford University Press, 1997), 23–24.

21. Kennan, "The Sources of Soviet Conduct," 572.

22. Ibid., 574–75.

23. Quoted in Gaddis, *Strategies of Containment*, 48.

24. John Lewis Gaddis goes as far as to say that this was Kennan's "favorite quotation." See his *George F. Kennan: An American Life* (New York: Penguin Press, 2011), 366. For debates between containment and liberation in the early years of the Cold War, see Scott Lucas and Kaeten Mistry, "Illusions of Coherence: George F. Kennan, U.S. Strategy, and Political Warfare in the Early Cold War, 1946–1950," *Diplomatic History* 33, no. 1 (January 2009): 39–66.

25. Kennan, "The Sources of Soviet Conduct," 578.

26. Kennan, "Résumé of the World Situation (PPS-13)," 772.

27. See Joshua Botts, "Nothing to Seek and . . . Nothing to Defend: George F. Kennan's Core Values and American Foreign Policy, 1938–1993," *Diplomatic History* 30, no. 5 (November 2006): 839–66.

28. Kennan, "The Sources of Soviet Conduct," 582.

29. Ibid., 576.

30. Ibid., 580.

31. For debates over how long containment would take and questions about whether the possibility of time working against the United States required a bolder policy of rollback, see Gregory Mitrovich, *Undermining the Kremlin: America's Strategy to Subvert the Soviet Bloc, 1947–1956* (Ithaca, NY: Cornell University Press, 2000), 6–7, 93–94, 178. The Bohlen quote is cited on page 94.

32. Kennan, "The Sources of Soviet Conduct," 575, 576, 581.

33. Ernest May, ed., *America's Cold War Strategy: Interpreting NSC-68* (Boston: Bedford Books, 1993), 124.

34. "We Will Bury You," *Time*, 68, no. 22, November 26, 1956.

35. Melvyn P. Leffler, *For the Soul of Mankind: The United States, the Soviet Union and the Cold War* (New York: Hill and Wang, 2007), 165–74.

36. George F. Kennan, *Memoirs 1925–1950* (New York: Pantheon Books, 1967), 356.

37. Gaddis's *Strategies of Containment* makes a distinction between symmetric and asymmetric approaches to containment. Here I attempt to clarify that distinction by breaking it down into two different issues that are worth distinguishing, regarding how and where to contain the Soviets.

38. Joseph S. Nye Jr., *Soft Power: The Means to Success in World Politics* (New York: Public Affairs, 2004), x.

39. Gaddis, *Strategies of Containment*, 25–31.

40. Quoted in Hal Brands, *What Good Is Grand Strategy: Power and Purpose in American Statecraft from Harry S. Truman to George W. Bush* (Ithaca, NY: Cornell University Press, 2014), 27.

41. On Kennan's struggle to get this argument accepted, see Kennan, *Memoirs*, 462–65. On the more general desire of the United States to create independent centers of power, see Steven Weber, *Multilateralism in NATO: Shaping The Postwar Balance of Power, 1945–1961* (Berkeley: University of California, Berkeley International and Area Studies, 1991); and Steven Weber, "Shaping The Postwar Balance of Power: Multilateralism in NATO," in *Multilateralism Matters: The Theory and Praxis on an Institutional Form*, ed. John Gerard Ruggie (New York: Columbia University Press, 1993), 233–92; and Gaddis, *We Now Know*, 39, 49.

42. Walter Lippmann's critiques were bundled together and published as *The Cold War: A Study in U.S. Foreign Policy* (New York: Harper, 1947). For Kennan's reaction to the reception of the X-Article by Lippmann and others, see Kennan, *Memoirs*, 354–67.

43. On the U.S. response to the dollar gap, see Thomas J. McCormick, *America's Half-Century: United States Foreign Policy in the Cold War* (Baltimore: Johns Hopkins University Press, 1989), 72–98.

44. The GATT was planned to be an interim measure until a more robust World Trade Organization (WTO) could take over this task, but the WTO would not come into force until well after the Cold War was over. For an account of the Cold War and U.S. containment policy that

stresses their economic aspects, see Diane B. Kunz, *Butter and Guns: America's Cold War Economic Diplomacy* (New York: Free Press, 1997).

45. The Truman Doctrine speech is available at http://avalon.law.yale.edu/20th_Century/trudoc.asp.

46. See Jack Snyder, *The Myths of Empire: Domestic Politics and International Ambition* (Ithaca, NY: Cornell University Press, 1991), 41–42. Snyder credits Steven Van Evera for the blowback phrase.

47. Michael H. Hunt, *The American Ascendancy: How the United States Gained and Wielded Global Dominance* (Chapel Hill: University of North Carolina Press, 2007), 211–12.

48. The name NSC-68 comes from the fact that is was the sixty-eighth document created by the newly developed National Security Council. For the document in its entirety, see "NSC-68: Note by the Executive Secretary to the National Security Council on United States Objectives and Programs for National Security," April 7, 1950, in *Foreign Relations of the United States 1950, Vol. 1: National Security Affairs, Foreign Economic Policy* (Washington, DC: Government Printing Office: 1977), 234–92. Both shocks are mentioned in NSC-68, see p. 277.

49. Richard Smoke, *National Security and the Nuclear Dilemma: An Introduction to the American Experience in the Cold War*, 3rd ed. (New York: McGraw-Hill, 1993), 54.

50. Leffler, *A Preponderance of Power*, 325–33, here, 332.

51. Walter LaFeber, *The American Age: United States Foreign Policy at Home and Abroad since 1750* (New York: Norton, 1989), 479. For the overall discussion of the two shocks of 1949 and NSC-68, see pp. 477–82.

52. Paul Nitze, "The Development of NSC-68," *International Security* 4, no. 4 (Spring 1980): 170.

53. "NSC-68," 237, see also 238.

54. Ibid., 241.

55. Ibid., 246–47.

56. Ibid., 290.

57. Ibid., 287.

58. Ibid., 282.

59. Ibid., the precondition quote is from p. 277, the bluff quote is from p. 254.

60. Quoted in Mark Perry, *Partners in Command: George Marshall and Dwight Eisenhower in War and Peace* (New York: Penguin Books, 2007), 246.

61. Mitrovich, *Undermining the Kremlin*, 12.

62. "NSC-68," 256.

63. Ibid., 240.

64. Ibid., 278. See also the almost identical rendering of the same argument on p. 290.

65. Robert J. McMahon, "Credibility and World Power: Exploring the Psychological Dimension in Postwar American Diplomacy," *Diplomatic History* 15, no. 4 (October 1991): 455–72.

66. This was a problem Kennan grappled with because it undermined his more material-based approach to defining U.S. interests, See Gaddis, *George F. Kennan*, 262, 385, 397.

67. "NSC-68," 240.

68. Ibid., 255.

69. Ibid., 284.

70. Gaddis, *Strategies of Containment*, 114.

71. "NSC-68," 280.

72. Dean Acheson, *Present at the Creation: My Years in the State Department* (New York: Norton, 1969), 347.

73. Ibid., 374.

74. Kennan, "Résumé of the World Situation (PPS-13)," 774.

75. Gaddis, *Strategies of Containment*, 96.

76. Ibid., 123–24.

77. "NSC-68," 286.

78. Quoted in James Chace and Caleb Carr, *American Invulnerable: The Quest for Absolute Security from 1812 to Star Wars* (New York: Summit Books, 1988), 251.

79. On the critical impact of the Korean War on how the United States approached containment, see Robert Jervis, "The Impact of the Korean War on the Cold War," *Journal of Conflict Resolution* 24, no. 4 (December 1980): 563–92.

80. Walter LaFeber attributes it to Acheson in *America, Russia and the Cold War 1945–1992*, 7th ed. (New York: McGraw Hill, 1993), 98. Robert L. Beisner argues that it was Nitze, see his *Dean Acheson: A Life in the Cold War* (Oxford: Oxford University Press, 2006), 377, 728.

81. Gaddis, *Strategies of Containment*, 106–8.

82. May, *America's Cold War Strategy*, vii.

83. Rumsfeld "Snowflake," October 16, 2003, available at http://media.hoover.org/documents/0817945423_xxv.pdf.

3. Debating the Implementation of Containment

1. These two speeches are quoted in Elizabeth N. Saunders, *Leaders at War: How Presidents Shape Military Interventions* (Ithaca, NY: Cornell University Press, 2011), 60.

2. Robert R. Bowie and Richard H. Immerman, *Waging Peace: How Eisenhower Shaped an Enduring Cold War Strategy* (New York: Oxford University Press, 1998), 75–77.

3. Thomas Borstelmann, *The Cold War and the Color Line: American Race Relations in the Global Arena* (Cambridge, MA: Harvard University Press, 2001), 85–134. On Eisenhower's caution and general rejection of activism, see Robert A. Divine, *Eisenhower and the Cold War* (New York: Oxford University Press, 1981), 154.

4. "Memorandum of Discussion at the 229th Meeting of the National Security Council, December 21, 1954," in *Foreign Relations of the United States 1952–1954, Vol. 2: National Security Affairs*, part 1 (Washington, DC: Government Printing Office, 1984), 833–34. See also Bowie and Immerman, *Waging Peace*, 176.

5. Colin Dueck, *Hard Line: The Republican Party and U.S. Foreign Policy since World War II* (Princeton, NJ: Princeton University Press, 2010), 121–22.

6. On Solarium and the issue of time being on America's side or not, see Bowie and Immerman, *Waging Peace*, 47, 123–38. See also Melvyn P. Leffler, *For the Soul of Mankind: The United States, the Soviet Union, and the Cold War* (New York: Hill and Wang, 2007), 111, 124; and William Stueck, "Reassessing U.S. Strategy in the Aftermath of the Korean War," *Orbis* 53, no. 4 (Fall 2009): 580–81, 584.

7. Dwight D. Eisenhower, Inaugural Address, January 20, 1953, available at http://www.presidency.ucsb.edu/ws/print.php?pid=9600. On the view of Eisenhower and Dulles on the worldwide interests of the United States and the interdependence of interests in the core and the periphery, see Bowie and Immerman, *Waging Peace*, 51–52, 66.

8. "The President's News Conference of April 7, 1954," *Public Papers of the Presidents*, available at http://www.presidency.ucsb.edu/ws/index.php?pid=10202&st=&st1.

9. See Andrew Goodpaster's forward to Bowie and Immerman, *Waging Peace*, v.

10. Dwight Eisenhower, "The Chance for Peace," April 16, 1953, available at http://www.presidency.ucsb.edu/ws/index.php?pid=9819&st=&st1=.

11. On this point for Eisenhower as well as Truman before him and Kennedy after him, see Aaron L. Friedberg, *In the Shadow of the Garrison State: America's Anti-Statism and Its Cold War Grand Strategy* (Princeton, NJ: Princeton University Press, 2000), 81–148.

12. Dwight Eisenhower, "Farewell Radio and Television Address to the American People," January 17, 1961, available at http://www.presidency.ucsb.edu/ws/print.php?pid=12086.

13. For a good discussion of balancing ends, means, ways, and risks in strategy, see Richard K. Betts, "A Disciplined Defense: How to Regain Strategic Solvency," *Foreign Affairs* 86, no. 6 (November–December 2007): 67–80.

14. See Bowie and Immerman, *Waging Peace*, 189, 200. For Gaddis's discussion of this and other nonnuclear aspects of the New Look, see John Lewis Gaddis, *Strategies of Containment: A Critical Appraisal of Postwar American National Security Policy*, rev. and exp. ed. (Oxford: Oxford University Press, 2005), 149–59.

15. NSC 162/2, "Report to the National Security Council by the Executive Secretary," October 30, 1953, in *Foreign Relations of the United States 1952–1954, Vol. 2: National Security Affairs*, part 1, 583.

16. Quoted in Marc Trachtenberg, *A Constructed Peace: The Making of the European Settlement, 1945–1963* (Princeton, NJ: Princeton University Press, 1999), 147.

17. Gaddis, *Strategies of Containment*, 145.

18. For thinking on the political uses of nuclear weapons, see Thomas C. Schelling's excellent *Arms and Influence* (New Haven, CT: Yale University Press, 1966), which is relied on heavily for this section. For the specific discussion of salami tactics, see pp. 66–69.

19. Eisenhower himself, however, thought about nuclear weapons as distinct and had his doubts about how useful they would be in peripheral conflicts. See Daniel Yergin, *The Quest: Energy, Security and the Remaking of the Modern World* (New York: Penguin Press, 2011), 362; and Bowie and Immerman, *Waging Peace*, 74–75, 250.

20. A. J. Bacevich, *The Pentomic Era: The US Army between Korea and Vietnam* (Washington, DC: National Defense University Press, 1986), 63–70, 103–27. Eisenhower, however, especially after the thermonuclear revolution led to the creation of far more destructive fusion weapons, remained skeptical that any nuclear exchange could be kept limited, see Campbell Craig, *Destroying the Village: Eisenhower and Thermonuclear War* (New York: Columbia University Press, 1998), ix, 60–61.

21. Schelling, *Arms and Influence*, 47.

22. Frank Ninkovich, *The Wilsonian Century: U.S. Foreign Policy since 1900* (Chicago: University of Chicago Press, 1999), 190.

23. On the popular, press, and political reactions in the United States to Sputnik and its influence on the Cold War strategy of the United States, see Walter McDougall, . . . *The Heavens and the Earth: A Political History of the Space Age* (Baltimore: Johns Hopkins University Press, 1997), 141–56. The *Life* magazine article is quoted from p. 150. On Eisenhower's reaction, see Yanek Mieczkowski, *Eisenhower's Sputnik Moment: The Race for Space and World Prestige* (Ithaca, NY: Cornell University Press, 2013).

24. Sean Kay, "America's Sputnik Moments," *Survival* 55, no. 2 (April–May 2013): 125.

25. "NSC 162/2," 581.

26. On the internal debates within the administration and Eisenhower's increasingly conciliatory policies in nuclear crises, see Craig, *Destroying the Village*, 52, 78–89.

27. Quoted in John Nagl, *Learning to Eat Soup with a Knife: Counterinsurgency Lessons from Malaysia to Vietnam* (Chicago: University of Chicago Press, 2005), 49.

28. On the Eisenhower administration's failure to generate enough allied and congressional support to pursue more direct intervention in Vietnam, see Fredrik Logevall, *Embers of War: The Fall of an Empire and the Making of America's Vietnam* (New York: Random House, 2012), 334–49, 362–78, 426–42, 454–509, 549–76.

29. For Eisenhower's ability to limit the capacity of the military to criticize his policies as president, see Donald Alan Carter, "Eisenhower versus the Generals," *Journal of Military History* 71 (October 2007): 1169–99.

30. Inaugural Address of President John F. Kennedy, January 20, 1961, available at http://www.presidency.ucsb.edu/ws/?pid=8032.

31. "Special Message to the Congress on the Defense Budget," March 28, 1961, available at http://www.presidency.ucsb.edu/ws/index.php?pid=8554#axzz1sy4z86JZ.

32. Quoted in Michael H. Hunt, *The American Ascendency: How the United States Gained and Wielded Global Dominance* (Chapel Hill: University of North Carolina Press, 2007), 210.

33. "Inaugural Address," January 20, 1961.

34. Ibid.

35. "Remarks of Senator John F. Kennedy at the University of Minnesota," October 2, 1960, available at http://www.presidency.ucsb.edu/ws/?pid=25918.

36. Borstelmann, *The Cold War and the Color Line*, 138, 178.

37. Henry A. Kissinger, *The Necessity for Choice: Prospects of American Foreign Policy* (New York: Harper, 1960), 6, 9.

38. Quoted in Marilyn B. Young, " 'I Was Thinking, as I Often Do These Days, of War': The United States in the Twenty-First Century," *Diplomatic History* 36, no. 1 (January 2012): 9.

39. The best account of the Kennedy team and its self-image is still David Halberstam, *The Best and the Brightest* (Greenwich, CT: Fawcett Crest, 1973).

40. "Address of Senator John F. Kennedy Accepting the Democratic Party Nomination for the Presidency of the United States" July 15, 1960, available at http://www.presidency.ucsb.edu /ws/?pid=25966 The two quotes used here appear in reverse order in the speech.

41. John F. Kennedy, "Annual Message to the Congress on the State of the Union," January 30, 1961, available at http://www.presidency.ucsb.edu/ws/index.php?pid=8045.

42. John F. Kennedy, "Imperialism: The Enemy of Freedom," July 2, 1957, available at http:// www.jfklink.com/speeches/jfk/congress/jfk020757_imperialism.html.

43. John F. Kennedy, "Commencement Address at American University," June 10, 1963, available at http://www.presidency.ucsb.edu/ws/?pid=9266.

44. Ibid.

45. Francis J. Gavin, "The Myth of Flexible Response: United States Strategy in Europe during the 1960s," *International History Review* 23, no. 4 (December 2001): 850–51.

46. Andrew Bacevich, *Washington Rules: America's Path to Permanent War* (New York: Metropolitan Books, 2010), 63.

47. Robert Kennedy, *Thirteen Days: A Memoir of the Cuban Missile Crisis* (New York: Norton, 1968), 9, 11, 14.

48. The literature on the Cuban Missile Crisis is enormous. Two good places to start, especially with regard to the American side of the crisis, beyond Robert Kennedy's memoir cited above, are Graham Allison and Philip Zelikow, *Essence of Decision: Explaining the Cuban Missile Crisis* 2nd ed. (New York: Longman, 1999); and Ernest R. May and Philip D. Zelikow, *The Kennedy Tapes: Inside the White House during the Cuban Missile Crisis* (Cambridge, MA: Belknap Press of Harvard University Press, 1997).

49. On the influence of the Korean analogy on Vietnam decision making, see Yuen Foong Khong, *Analogies at War: Korea, Munich, Dien Bien Phu, and the Vietnam Decisions of 1965* (Princeton, NJ: Princeton University Press, 1992).

50. The literature on Vietnam is just as extensive as the literature on the Cuban Missile Crisis. For an excellent concise history, see George C. Herring, *America's Longest War: The United States and Vietnam, 1950–1975*, 4th ed. (Boston: McGraw-Hill 2002). For an excellent discussion of Vietnam in the context of the overall strategy of Flexible Response, see Gaddis, *Strategies of Containment*, 235–71.

51. See, in particular, David K. Shipler, "Robert McNamara and the Ghosts of Vietnam," *New York Times Magazine*, August 10, 1997. Overall, see Robert McNamara, *In Retrospect: The Tragedy and Lessons of Vietnam* (New York: Vintage Books, 1996).

52. Fred Kaplan, *The Wizards of Armageddon* (New York: Simon and Schuster, 1993), 330–36.

53. On the domestic side of Johnson's calculations, see Francis M. Bator, "No Good Choices: LBJ and the Vietnam/Great Society Connection," *Diplomatic History* 32, no. 2 (June 2008): 309–40.

54. Halberstam, *The Best and the Brightest*, 620.

55. Gaddis, *Strategies of Containment*, 271.

4. Beyond Containment?

1. See Dan Caldwell, "The Legitimation of the Nixon-Kissinger Grand Design and Grand Strategy," *Diplomatic History* 33, no. 4 (September 2009): 633–52; and Julian Zelizer, "Détente and Domestic Politics," *Diplomatic History* 33, no. 4 (September 2009): 653–70.

2. Michael H. Hunt, *The American Ascendancy: How the United States Gained and Wielded Global Dominance* (Chapel Hill: University of North Carolina Press, 2007), 235.

3. Ibid., 177–78.

4. Bradley Graham, *By His Own Rules: The Ambitions, Successes, and Ultimate Failures of Donald Rumsfeld* (New York: Public Affairs, 2009), 85.

5. See "The Nation: An Interview with the President: The Jury Is Out," *Time* 99, no. 1 (January 3, 1972), available at http://www.time.com/time/magazine/article/0,9171,879011,00.html.

6. Hunt, *The American Ascendancy*, 241.

7. John Lewis Gaddis, *George F. Kennan: An American Life* (New York: Penguin Press, 2011), 622.

8. Richard Nixon, "Speech on Cambodia," April 30, 1970, available at http://vietnam.vassar.edu/doc15.html.

9. Raymond L. Garthoff, *Détente and Confrontation: American-Soviet Relations from Nixon to Reagan* (Washington, DC: Brookings Institution Press, 1985), 521.

10. On the Nixon's administration's approach to the war in Vietnam, especially in getting the Soviets and Chinese to isolate North Vietnam, see George C. Herring, *America's Longest War: The United States and Vietnam, 1950–1975* (New York: Knopf, 1979), 218–21, 239–42.

11. Stephen McGlinchey, "Richard Nixon's Road to Tehran: The Making of the US-Iran Arms Agreement of May 1972," *Diplomatic History* 37, no. 4 (September 2013): 841–60; and Roham Alvandi, "Nixon, Kissinger, and the Shah: The Origins of Iranian Primacy in the Persian Gulf," *Diplomatic History* 36, no. 2 (April 2012): 337–72.

12. Quoted in Caldwell, "The Legitimation of the Nixon-Kissinger Grand Design and Grand Strategy," 644.

13. John Lewis Gaddis, *Strategies of Containment: A Critical Appraisal of Postwar American National Security Policy*, rev. and exp. ed. (Oxford: Oxford University Press, 2005), 287.

14. Henry Kissinger, *Diplomacy* (New York: Simon and Schuster, 1994), 714.

15. On the Offense/Defense Balance, see Stephen Van Evera, "The Cult of the Offensive and the Origins of the First World War," *International Security* 9, no. 1 (Summer 1994): 59–108; and Jack Levy, "The Offensive/Defensive Balance of Military Technology: A Theoretical and Historical Analysis," *International Studies Quarterly* 28 (1984): 219–38.

16. Robert Jervis, *The Meaning of The Nuclear Revolution: Statecraft and the Prospect of Armageddon* (Ithaca, NY: Cornell University Press, 1989), 9.

17. See Garthoff, *Détente and Confrontation*, 1096.

18. On the Nixon's administration's nuclear arms negotiations policies, see David Tal, "'Absolutes' and 'Stages' in the Making and Application of Nixon's SALT Policy," *Diplomatic History* 37, no. 5 (November 2013): 1090–116.

19. Garthoff, *Détente and Confrontation*, 47–50, 1087–88.

20. Mark Mayer, "Grand Strategy after the Vietnam War," *Orbis* 53, no. 4 (Fall 2009): 600.

21. For Kissinger's defense against this dual-headed criticism of détente, see Henry Kissinger, "Between the Old Left and the New Right," *Foreign Affairs* 78, no. 3 (May–June 1999): 99–116.

22. Kissinger, *Diplomacy*, 714.

23. Douglas E. Selvage, "Transforming the Soviet Sphere of Influence? U.S.-Soviet Détente and Eastern Europe, 1969–1976," *Diplomatic History* 33, no. 4 (September 2009): 671–87.

24. Caldwell, "The Legitimation of the Nixon-Kissinger Grand Design and Grand Strategy," 636.

25. Barbara Keys, "Congress, Kissinger and the Origins of Human Rights Diplomacy," *Diplomatic History* 34, no. 5 (November 2010): 823–51.

26. On secrecy as part of Nixon and Kissinger's decision-making style, see Ivo H. Daalder and I. M. Destler, *In The Shadow of the Oval Office: Profiles of the National Security Advisers and the Presidents They Served—From JFK to George W. Bush* (New York: Simon and Schuster, 2009), 57–93. On the contrast between openness regarding strategy and secrecy regarding tactics, see Gaddis, *Strategies of Containment*, 299–305.

27. On the theme of building a domestic consensus for American foreign policy, see Richard H. Melanson, *American Foreign Policy since The Vietnam War: The Search for Consensus from Nixon to Clinton* (Armonk, NY: M. E. Sharpe, 1996), 43–88.

28. Ibid., 90.

29. Daalder and Destler, *In the Shadow of the Oval Office*, 99–100.

30. Quoted in Walter LaFeber, *America, Russia, and the Cold War, 1945–1992*, 7th ed. (New York: McGraw-Hill, 1993), 287.

31. Quoted in Melanson, *American Foreign Policy since the Vietnam War*, 102.

32. Gaddis, *Strategies of Containment*, 344.

33. For an examination of Carter's foreign policy that takes this approach, see Jerel A. Rosati, "Jimmy Carter, a Man Before His Time? The Emergence and Collapse of the First Post–Cold War Presidency," *Presidential Studies Quarterly* 23, no. 3 (Summer 1993): 459–76.

34. Jimmy Carter, "Address at Commencement Exercises at the University of Notre Dame," May 22, 1977, available at http://www.presidency.ucsb.edu/ws/index.php?pid=7552.

35. Jimmy Carter, "State of the Union Address, 1979," January 23, 1979, available at http://www.presidency.ucsb.edu/ws/index.php?pid=32657.

36. Carter, "Address at Commencement Exercises at the University of Notre Dame."

37. Jimmy Carter, "State of the Union Address, 1978," January 19, 1987. available at http://www.presidency.ucsb.edu/ws/index.php?pid=30856.

38. Jimmy Carter, "Inaugural Address," January 20, 1977, available at http://www.presidency.ucsb.edu/ws/index.php?pid=6575.

39. Carter, "Address at Commencement Exercises at the University of Notre Dame."

40. Carter, "Inaugural Address."

41. Carter, "Address at Commencement Exercises at the University of Notre Dame."

42. Ibid.

43. Quoted in Melanson, *American Foreign Policy since the Vietnam War*, 112.

44. Carter, "Address at Commencement Exercises at the University of Notre Dame."

45. LaFeber, *America, Russia, and the Cold War*, 291.

46. Natasha Zaretsky, "Restraint or Retreat? The Debate over the Panama Canal Treaties and U.S. Nationalism after Vietnam," *Diplomatic History* 35, no. 3 (June 2011): 535–62.

47. On the Camp David Accords, see William B. Quandt, *Camp David: Peacemaking and Politics* (Washington, DC: Brookings Institution Press, 1986); and Shibley Telhami, *Power and Leadership in International Bargaining: The Path to the Camp David Accords* (New York: Columbia University Press, 1990).

48. The first quote comes from a December 31, 1979, interview with Frank Reynolds of ABC News, an excerpt of which appears in *Survival* 22, no. 2 (1980), 68. The second quote is from Carter's, "State of the Union Address Delivered before a Joint Session of Congress," January 23, 1980, available at http://www.presidency.ucsb.edu/ws/index.php?pid=33079.

49. On the controversy over the Soviet Brigade in Cuba, see Richard E. Neustadt and Ernest R. May, *Thinking in Time: The Uses of History for Decision Makers* (New York: Free Press, 1986), 92–96. On the rabbit incident, see Brooks Jackson, "Bunny Goes Bugs: Rabbit Attacks President," *Washington Post*, August 30, 1979.

50. X (George Kennan), "The Sources of Soviet Conduct," *Foreign Affairs* 25 (July 1947): 581.

51. Jimmy Carter, "Address to the Nation on Energy and National Goals: 'The Malaise Speech'" July 15, 1979, available at http://www.presidency.ucsb.edu/ws/index.php?pid=32596&st=&st1.

52. Carter, "State of the Union Address," January 23, 1980.

53. George F. Kennan, *Memoirs 1950–1963* (New York: Pantheon Books, 1972), 257.

54. Robert M. Gates, *From the Shadows* (New York: Simon and Schuster, 1996), 176–78. Quoted in James Mann, *The Obamians: The Struggle inside the White House to Redefine American Power* (New York: Viking, 2012), 23.

5. The Culmination of Containment

1. Richard Burt, "Reagan Team Says U.S. Must Deal with Any Threat," *New York Times*, November 13, 1980. For short overviews of the Reagan administration's foreign policy, see Robert W. Tucker, "Reagan's Foreign Policy," *Foreign Affairs* 68, no. 1 (1988–89): 1–27; and Fareed Zakaria, "The Reagan Strategy of Containment," *Political Science Quarterly* 105, no. 3 (Autumn 1990): 373–95.

2. Burt, "Reagan Team Says U.S. Must Deal with Any Threat."

3. Quoted in James Chace and Caleb Carr, *America Invulnerable: The Quest for Absolute Security from 1812 to Star Wars* (New York: Summit Books, 1988), 316.

4. National Security Decision Directive Number 75 (hereafter, NSDD-75), January 17, 1983, p. 1, available at http://www.fas.org/irp/offdocs/nsdd/nsdd-075.htm.

5. Quoted in Raymond L. Garthoff, *Détente and Confrontation: American-Soviet Relations from Nixon to Reagan* (Washington, DC: Brookings Institution Press, 1985), 1051.

6. On the Carter/Reagan buildup, see Richard Smoke, *National Security and the Nuclear Dilemma: An Introduction to the American Experience in the Cold War*, 3rd ed. (New York: McGraw-Hill, 1993), 201–13; James Graham Wilson, *The Triumph of Improvisation: Gorbachev's Adaptability, Reagan's Engagement, and the End of the Cold War* (Ithaca, NY: Cornell University Press, 2013), 18; Thomas J. McCormick, *America's Half Century: United States Foreign Policy in the Cold War* (Baltimore: Johns Hopkins University Press, 1989), 216–20; Richard A. Melanson, *American Foreign Policy Since the Vietnam War: The Search for Consensus from Nixon to Clinton* (Armonk, NY: M. E. Sharpe, 1996), 144–46; and Walter LaFeber, *America, Russia, and the Cold War, 1945–1992*, 7th ed. (New York: McGraw-Hill, 1993), 305–6.

7. *Reagan in His Own Hand: The Writings of Ronald Reagan that Reveal His Revolutionary Vision For America*, ed. Kiron K. Skinner, Annelise Anderson, and Martin Anderson (New York: Free Press, 2001), 442.

8. "National Security Strategy of the United States," January 1987, p. 4. Available at http://nssarchive.us/.

9. Ronald Reagan, *An American Life* (New York: Simon and Schuster 1990), 267.

10. "National Security Decision Directive Number 32," May 20, 1982, p. 1. Available at http://www.fas.org/irp/offdocs/nsdd/nsdd-032.htm.

11. This quote comes from one of his prepresidential speeches, given on June 29, 1979, quoted in John Lewis Gaddis, *Strategies of Containment: A Critical Appraisal of Postwar American National Security Policy*, rev. and exp. ed. (Oxford: Oxford University Press, 2005), 352.

12. James Mann, *The Rebellion of Ronald Reagan: A History of the End of the Cold War* (New York: Viking, 2009), 28–29.

13. NSDD-75, p. 3.

14. Thomas M. Nichols, *Winning the World: Lessons for America's Future from the Cold War* (Westport, CT: Praeger, 2002), 43–45.

15. NSDD-75, p. 8. On Reagan's being torn between wanting to defeat the Soviet Union and wanting to negotiate with the Soviet Union, see also Wilson, *The Triumph of Improvisation*, 13.

16. On the pragmatism and limits of Regan's foreign policy, see Stefan Halper and Jonathan Clarke, *America Alone: The Neoconservatives and the Global Order* (Cambridge: Cambridge University Press, 2004), 157–81.

17. Garthoff, *Détente and Confrontation*, 1011.

18. Ronald Reagan, "Address at Commencement Exercises at the University of Notre Dame," May 17, 1981, available at http://www.presidency.ucsb.edu/ws/index.php?pid=43825. On what he calls Reagan's "transformational" view of the Cold War as opposed to Nixon's more static view, see Mann, *The Rebellion of Ronald Reagan*, 18–23.

19. NSDD-75, p. 1.

20. "National Security Strategy of the United States," January 1987, p. 11.

21. On the efforts of scholars of international relations to deal with the surprise and the suddenness of these events, see Richard Ned Lebow and Thomas Risse-Kappen, eds., *International Relations Theory and the End of the Cold War* (New York: Columbia University Press, 1995).

22. Ronald Reagan, Televised Address by Governor Ronald Reagan, "A Strategy for Peace in the '80s," October 19, 1980, available at http://www.reagan.utexas.edu/archives/Reference/10.19.80.html.

23. Garthoff, *Détente and Confrontation*, 1023–24. See also Wilson, *The Triumph of Improvisation*, 25.

24. On the INF Treaty and U.S. strategy, see Smoke, *National Security and the Nuclear Dilemma*, 225–30, 267–72; and John Lewis Gaddis, "Hanging Tough Paid Off," *Bulletin of Atomic Scientists* (January–February 1989): 11–14.

25. X (George Kennan), "The Sources of Soviet Conduct," *Foreign Affairs* 25 (July 1947): 580.

26. The literature on the end of the Cold War is voluminous. For one-volume histories, see Michael R. Beschloss and Strobe Talbott, *At the Highest Levels: The Inside Story of the End of the*

Cold War (Boston: Back Bay Books, 1994); and Don Oberdorfer, *The Turn: From the Cold War to a New Era, The United States and the Soviet Union 1983–1990* (New York: Poseidon Press, 1991).

27. John Lewis Gaddis, *The Cold War: A New History* (New York: Penguin Press, 2005), 257.

28. Gaddis, "Hanging Tough Paid Off," 14.

29. Gaddis, *Strategies of Containment*, 375. For his overall discussion of Reagan's strategy, see pp. 349–77.

30. Henry Kissinger, *Diplomacy* (New York: Simon and Schuster, 1994), 764, 765–66. For his overall discussion of Reagan's strategy, see pp. 764–85.

31. In offering this positive assessment, however, Kennan ungenerously did not give Reagan credit for being consciously aware of what he was doing. Quoted in Gaddis, *Strategies of Containment*, 377.

32. Richard Ned Lebow and Janice Gross Stein, *We All Lost the Cold War* (Princeton, NJ: Princeton University Press, 1994), 372.

33. John Lewis Gaddis, *George F. Kennan: An American Life* (New York: Penguin Press, 2011), 249.

34. NSDD-75, pp. 6, 8.

35. On the debate over whether the Reagan administration intended to spend the Soviet Union into collapse based on interviews of administration members who take different views on this issue, see Mann, *The Rebellion of Ronald Reagan*, 248–51. See also, Wilson *The Triumph of Improvisation*, which gives more credit to Reagan's concessions than to his buildup but also stresses the reactive rather than the preplanned aspects of Reagan's behavior, pp. 4, 198–200.

36. Jeane Kirkpatrick, "Dictatorships and Double Standards," *Commentary* (November 1979): 37.

37. Nichols, *Winning the World*, 188.

38. NSDD-75, p. 2.

39. On the importance of the 1986 collapse in oil prices, see Daniel Yergin, *The Quest: Energy, Security and the Remaking of the Modern World* (New York: Penguin Press, 2011), 24–25.

40. Quoted in Gaddis, *The Cold War*, 118.

41. Quoted in Melvyn P. Leffler, *For the Soul of Mankind: The United States, The Soviet Union, and the Cold War* (New York: Hill and Wang, 2007), 461.

42. Josef Joffe, "The 'Amazing and Mysterious Life' of Ronald Reagan," *National Interest* (Fall 2004): 85.

43. See Kenneth A. Oye, "Explaining the End of the Cold War: Morphological and Behavioral Modifications to the Nuclear Peace?" in *International Relations Theory and the End of the Cold War*, ed. Richard Ned Lebow and Thomas Risse-Kappen (New York: Columbia University Press, 1995), 57–83.

44. See Beth A. Fischer, *The Reagan Reversal: Foreign Policy and the End of the Cold War* (Columbia: University of Missouri Press, 1997); and Hal Brands, *What Good Is Grand Strategy: Power and Purpose in American Statecraft from Harry S. Truman to George W. Bush* (Ithaca, NY: Cornell University Press, 2014), 104, 124–25.

45. This is the overall theme of Mann's *The Rebellion of Ronald Reagan*. One key adviser who did support Reagan's negotiation efforts, however, was George Shultz, the secretary of state; see Wilson, *The Triumph of Improvisation*, 200–201. Keith L. Shimko's, *Images and Arms Control: Perceptions of the Soviet Union in the Reagan Administration* (Ann Arbor: University of Michigan Press, 1991) argues that Reagan's relatively less complex, yet more contradictory views, made him more open to changing his views on the Soviet Union than many of his advisers. For competing views of the end of the Cold War that agree, however, on the relative unimportance of any shift in the balance of power between the United States and the Soviet Union, see Mark Haas "The United States and the End of the Cold War: Reactions to Shifts in Soviet Power, Policies or Domestic Politics," *International Organization* 61 (Winter 2007): 145–79, which stresses the importance of Gorbachev's domestic reforms; and John Mueller, "What Was the Cold War About? Evidence from Its Ending," *Political Science Quarterly* 119, no. 4 (2004–5): 609–32, which stresses Gorbachev's foreign policy changes.

46. Melvyn Leffler, *For the Soul of Mankind*, 448.

47. Mann, *The Rebellion of Ronald Reagan*, 324–26.

48. George H. W. Bush, "Remarks at the Texas A&M University Commencement Ceremony in College Station," May 12, 1989, available at http://www.presidency.ucsb.edu/ws/index.php?pid=17022&st=&st1.

49. Michael Mandelbawn, *The Ideas that Conquered the World: Peace, Democracy and Free Markets in the Twenty-First Century* (New York: Public Affairs, 2002), 56–57.

50. See Jeffrey A. Engel, "Bush, Germany, and the Power of Time: How History Makes History," *Diplomatic History* 37, no. 4 (September 2013): 655–56; and Ivo H. Daalder and I.M. Destler, *In the Shadow of the Oval Office: Profiles of the National Security Advisers and the Presidents They Served—From JFK to George W. Bush* (New York: Simon and Schuster, 2009), 173–75.

51. Quoted in Beschloss and Talbott, *At the Highest Levels*, 346.

52. George Bush, "Remarks to the Supreme Soviet Republic of the Ukraine in Kiev, Soviet Union," August 1, 1991, available at http://www.presidency.ucsb.edu/ws/index.php?pid=19864&st=&st1.

53. Zbigniew Brzezinski, *Second Chance: Three American Presidents and the Crisis of American Superpower* (New York: Basic Books, 2007), 66–67.

54. Niall Ferguson, *Colossus: The Price of America's Empire* (New York: Penguin Press, 2004), 293.

55. John Lewis Gaddis, "The Rise, Fall and Future of Détente," *Foreign Affairs* 62, no. 2 (Winter 1983): 373.

56. Gaddis, *Strategies of Containment*, 388–89.

57. Ibid., 386.

58. Kennan, "The Sources of Soviet Conduct," 581.

6. Grand Strategy in the Absence of a Clear Threat

1. See Douglas Brinkley, "Democratic Enlargement: The Clinton Doctrine," *Foreign Policy* 106 (Spring 1997): 117–27; and Derek Chollet and James Goldgeier, *America between the Wars: From 11/9 to 9/11, The Misunderstood Years between the Fall of the Berlin Wall and the Start of the War on Terror* (New York: Public Affairs, 2008), 65–68.

2. On this period see Jeremy Suri, "American Grand Strategy from the Cold War's End to 9/11," *Orbis* 53, no. 4 (Fall 2009): 611–27.

3. James Baker, "Democracy and Foreign Policy," March 1990, speech to the World Affairs Council in Dallas, available at http://usinfo.org/enus/government/overview/61.html.

4. George Bush, "Inaugural Address" January 20, 1989, available at http://www.presidency.ucsb.edu/ws/index.php?pid=16610&st=&st1.

5. George Bush, "National Security Strategy of the United States," January 1993, pp. ii, 21. This and all the National Security Strategies cited here are available at http://nssarchive.us/.

6. Richard N. Haass, *War of Necessity, War of Choice: A Memoir of Two Iraq Wars* (New York: Simon and Schuster, 2009), 102.

7. Jeffrey A. Engel, "A Better World . . . but Don't Get Carried Away: The Foreign Policy of George H. W. Bush Twenty Years On," *Diplomatic History* 34, no. 1 (January 2010): 37.

8. For "fostering," see George Bush, "National Security Strategy of the United States," March 1990, p. 2; and Bartholomew H. Sparrow, "Realism's Practitioner: Brent Scowcroft and the Making of the New World Order, 1989–1993," *Diplomatic History* 34, no. 1 (January 2010): 172–73.

9. Bush, "National Security Strategy," January 1993, p. 6.

10. Engel, "A Better World," 34.

11. George Bush, "Address to the Nation Announcing Allied Military Actions in the Persian Gulf," January 16, 1991, available at http://www.presidency.ucsb.edu/ws/index.php?pid=19222&st=&st1.

12. Bush, "National Security Strategy," January 1993, p. 18.

13. George Bush, "National Security Strategy of the United States," March 1990, p. 15 and "National Security Strategy of the United States," August 1991, p. 13.

14. Bush, "National Security Strategy," January 1993, pp. 3, 6.

15. George Bush, "Remarks at the Aspen Institute Symposium in Aspen, Colorado," August 2, 1990, available at http://www.presidency.ucsb.edu/ws/index.php?pid=18731&st=&st1.

16. George Bush, *All The Best: My Life in Letters and Other Writings* (New York: Scribner, 1999), 527–28. I was directed to this source by Hal Brands, *From Berlin to Baghdad: America's Search for Purpose in the Post–Cold War World* (Lexington: University Press of Kentucky, 2008), 90.

17. Bush, "National Security Strategy," January 1993, p. 1.

18. "Excerpts from Pentagon's Plan: 'Prevent the Re-Emergence of a New Rival,'" *New York Times*, March 8, 1992.

19. Quoted in Patrick E. Tyler, "U.S. Strategy Plan Calls for Insuring No Rivals Develop" *New York Times*, March 8, 1992.

20. Chollet and Goldgeier, *America between the Wars*, 43–52.

21. The quote is from Richard Haass, in ibid., 8–9.

22. Francis Fukuyama, "The End of History?," *National Interest* 16 (Summer 1989): 3–18; Fukuyama, *The End of History and the Last Man* (New York: Avon Books, 1992).

23. Bill Clinton, "A New Covenant for American Security," remarks to students at Georgetown University, December 12, 1991, available at http://clintonpresidentialcenter.org/georgetown/speech_newcovenant3.php.

24. Leslie H. Gelb, "Foreign Affairs; A Mere 141 Words," *New York Times*, July 19, 1992. See also Lawrence Freedman, *A Choice of Enemies: America Confronts the Middle East* (New York: Public Affairs, 2008), 275.

25. See Tim Hames, "Searching for the New World Order: The Clinton Administration and Foreign Policy in 1993," *International Relations* 12, no. 1 (April 1994): 112.

26. Warren I. Cohen, *America's Failing Empire: U.S. Foreign Relations since the Cold War* (Malden: Blackwell, 2005), 57.

27. David Halberstam, *War in a Time of Peace: Bush, Clinton, and the Generals* (New York: Scribner, 2001), 193.

28. Peter Beinart, *The Good Fight: Why Liberals—and Only Liberals—Can Win the War on Terror and Make America Great Again* (New York: HarperCollins, 2006), 81–82.

29. See Zbigniew Brzezinski, *Second Chance: Three Presidents and the Crisis of American Superpower* (New York: Basic Books, 2007), 85.

30. Ivo H. Daalder and I. M. Destler, *In the Shadow of the Oval Office: Profiles of the National Security Advisers and the President's They Served—From JFK to George W. Bush* (New York: Simon and Schuster, 2009), 206.

31. Robert J. Lieber, *The American Era: Power and Strategy for the 21st Century* (Cambridge: Cambridge University Press, 2005), 1–2.

32. Tim Weiner, *Legacy of Ashes: The History of the CIA* (New York: Doubleday, 2007), 440.

33. Chollet and Goldgeier, *America between the Wars*, 91.

34. Brzezinski, *Second Chance*, 84–85. Those memoirs are: George Bush and Brent Scowcroft, *A World Transformed* (New York: Knopf, 1998); and Bill Clinton, *My Life* (New York: Vintage Books, 2005).

35. Chollet and Goldgeier, *America between the Wars*, 87, 111. The one foreign policy plank in the Contract with America also called for a National Missile Defense, the enlargement of NATO, and increased defense spending.

36. William Jefferson Clinton, "A National Security Strategy of Engagement and Enlargement," July 1994, p. i.

37. For concise and competing overviews of Clinton's foreign policy, see John Dumbrell, "Was There a Clinton Doctrine? President Clinton's Foreign Policy Reconsidered," *Diplomacy and Statecraft* 13, no. 2 (January 2002): 125–45; Stephen Schlesinger, "The End of Idealism: Foreign Policy in the Clinton Years," *World Policy Journal* 15, no. 4 (Winter 1998–99): 36–40; Stephen Walt, "Two Cheers for Clinton's Foreign Policy," *Foreign Affairs* 79, no. 2 (March–April 2000): 63–79; Richard N. Haas, "Fatal Distraction: Bill Clinton's Foreign Policy," *Foreign Policy* 108 (Fall 1997): 108–23; and Brinkley, "Democratic Enlargement."

38. Quoted in Brands, *From Berlin to Baghdad*, 106.

39. William Jefferson Clinton, "A National Security Strategy of Engagement and Enlargement," February 1996, pp. 1–2.

40. William Jefferson Clinton, "A National Security Strategy for a New Century," October 1998, p. 1.

41. William Jefferson Clinton, "A National Security Strategy for a Global Age," December 2000.

42. Brzezinski, *Second Chance*, 84.

43. Michael Mandelbaum, "Foreign Policy as Social Work," *Foreign Affairs* 75, no. 1 (January–February 1996): 17–18, 28–29.

44. Richard Betts, "From Cold War to Hot Peace: The Habit of American Force," *Political Science Quarterly* 127, no. 3 (2012): 355.

45. Stanley Hoffmann, "In Defense of Mother Teresa," *Foreign Affairs* 75, no. 2 (March–April 1996): 175.

46. William Jefferson Clinton, "A National Security Strategy of Engagement and Enlargement," February 1995, p. i.

47. John M. Shalikashvili, "Maintaining the 'Delta' for Future Military Forces," September 24, 1997, available at http://www.defense.gov/utility/printitem.aspx?print=http://www.defense.gov/speeches/speech.aspx?speechid=788.

48. Madeleine K. Albright, "A Strong United Nations Serves U.S. Security Interests," address before the Council on Foreign Relations Conference on Cooperative Security and the United Nations," June 11, 1993, *US Department of State Dispatch* 4, no. 26 (June 28, 1993): 461.

49. For the term "cruise missile hegemony," see William Wohlforth, "The Stability of a Unipolar World," *International Security* 24, no. 1 (Summer 1999): 40. For "immaculate coercion," see Barton Gellman, "Allies Facing the Limits of Air Power," *Washington Post*, March 28, 1999.

50. Russell A. Burgos, "Origins of Regime Change: 'Ideapolitik' on the Long Road to Baghdad, 1993–2000," *Security Studies* 17, no. 2 (April 2008): 251–53.

51. Daalder and Destler, *In the Shadow of the Oval Office*, 231.

52. For Clinton's quote, see George C. Herring, *From Colony to Superpower: U.S. Foreign Relations Since 1776* (Oxford: Oxford University Press, 2008), 929.

53. Josef Joffe sees this as part of a wider pattern in Clinton's approach to grand strategy. See "Clinton's World: Purpose, Policy and Weltanschauung," *Washington Quarterly* 24, no. 1 (Winter 2001), 147.

54. Clinton, "A National Security Strategy for a Global Age," December 2000, 35, 67.

55. Christopher Preble, *The Power Problem: How American Military Dominance Makes Us Less Safe, Less Prosperous and Less Free* (Ithaca, NY: Cornell University Press, 2009), 5.

56. William Kristol and Robert Kagan, "Toward a Neo-Reaganite Foreign Policy," *Foreign Affairs* (July–August 1996): 31.

57. Clinton, "A New Covenant for American Security."

58. For an overall discussion of the decline of assertive multilateralism, see Jennifer Sterling-Folker, "Between a Rock and a Hard Place: Assertive Multilateralism and Post–Cold War U.S. Foreign Policy Making," in *After the End: Making U.S. Foreign Policy in the Post–Cold War World*, ed. James M. Scott (Durham, NC: Duke University Press, 1998), 277–304; and Ramesh Thakur, "UN Peace Operations and U.S. Unilateralism and Multilateralism," in *Unilateralism and U.S. Foreign Policy: International Perspectives*, ed. David M. Malone and Yuen Foong Khong (Boulder, CO: Lynne Reinner, 2003), 153–79. See also the debate surrounding Presidential Review Directive-13 (PRD-13), available at http://www.fas.org/irp/offdocs/pdd13.htm.

59. Albright, "A Strong United Nations Serves U.S. Security Interests," 461–63.

60. William Jefferson Clinton, "Remarks to the 48th Session of the United Nations General Assembly in New York City," September 27, 1993, available at http://www.presidency.ucsb.edu/ws/index.php?pid=47119#axzz1PpxWAZEf.

61. Clinton, "A National Security Strategy of Engagement and Enlargement," July 1994, p. 13. See also pp. 6 and 10.

62. Anthony Lake, "From Containment to Enlargement," remarks at Johns Hopkins School of Advanced International Studies, September 21, 1993, available at http://www.mtholyoke.edu/acad/intrel/lakedoc.html.

63. For the strategies that include both engagement and enlargement, see the documents produced in 1994, 1995, and 1996. The National Security Strategies 1997 and 1998 talked about the

imperative of engagement and the strategies of 1999 and 2000 talked about the strategy of engagement, but not one of these four mentioned any strategy of enlargement.

64. Clinton, "A National Security Strategy of Engagement and Enlargement," July 1994, 18–19. See also p. 2.

65. On these core liberal ideas, see Michael Mandelbaum, *The Ideas That Conquered the World: Peace, Democracy, and Free Markets in the Twenty-First Century* (New York: Public Affairs, 2002).

66. For an insider account of the Kosovo campaign that is relatively positive with regard to its goals and the advantages and disadvantages of conducting a campaign in a coalition environment, see Wesley A. Clark, *Waging Modern War: Bosnia, Kosovo and the Future of Conflict* (New York: Public Affairs, 2001).

67. Edward Mansfield and Jack Snyder, *Electing to Fight: Why Emerging Democracies Go to War* (Cambridge, MA: MIT Press, 2005).

68. William Jefferson Clinton "A National Security Strategy for a New Century," December 1999, p. 3.

69. Clinton "A National Security Strategy for a New Century," October 1998, p. 1.

70. Joffe, "Clinton's World," 149–53. See also Chollet and Goldgeier, *America between the Wars*, 29–43.

71. Daalder and Destler, *In the Shadow of the Oval Office*, 205–6. For a contemporaneous call to make foreign economic policy an even bigger part of U.S. foreign policy, see Jeffrey Garten, "Business and Foreign Policy," *Foreign Affairs* 76, no. 3 (May–June 1997): 67–79.

72. Chollet and Goldgeier, *America between the Wars*, 157–69.

73. Clinton, "A National Security Strategy of Engagement and Enlargement," July 1994, p. 1.

74. Clinton, "A National Security Strategy for a New Century," October 1998, p. iii.

75. Clinton, "A National Security Strategy For a Global Age," December 2000, p. 31.

76. Quoted in Brands, *From Berlin to Baghdad*, 202. For Brands's overall account of the Clinton administration's foreign policy, including the greater personal role played by the president in his second term, see pp. 101–262.

77. For this argument, see G. John Ikenberry, *After Victory: Institutions, Strategic Restraint, and the Rebuilding of Order after Major Wars* (Princeton, NJ: Princeton University Press, 2001).

78. Richard N. Haass, "The Squandered Presidency: Demanding More from the Commander in Chief," *Foreign Affairs* 79, no. 3 (May–June 2000): 136.

79. Joffe, "Clinton's World," 149.

7. The Rise and Fall of the War on Terror in U.S. Grand Strategy

1. Ian Shapiro argues that Bush's post-9/11 foreign policy represented "one of the most dramatic sea changes in U.S. national security policy ever," in *Containment: Rebuilding a Strategy against Global Terrorism* (Princeton, NJ: Princeton University Press, 2007), 1. Similarly, Ivo H. Daalder and James M. Lindsay talk about what they see as Bush's revolutionary foreign policy in their *America Unbound: The Bush Revolution in Foreign Policy* (Washington, DC: Brookings Institution Press, 2003). Stanley Hoffmann (with Frédéric Bozo) also stresses changes in U.S. foreign policy under Bush, in *Gulliver Unbound: America's Imperial Temptation and the War in Iraq* (New York: Rowman and Littlefield, 2004). For an account that stresses continuity, see John Lewis Gaddis, *Surprise, Security and the American Experience* (Cambridge, MA: Harvard University Press, 2004). For an analysis that stresses continuity as well as change, see Melvyn P. Leffler, "9/11 and American Foreign Policy," *Diplomatic History* 29, no. 3 (June 2005): 395–413; and Leffler, "9/11 in Retrospect: George W. Bush's Grand Strategy, Reconsidered," *Foreign Affairs* 90, no. 5 (September–October 2011): 33–44.

2. Quoted in Bob Woodward, *State of Denial: Bush at War, Part III* (New York: Simon and Schuster, 2006), 6. See also p. 3.

3. Quoted in Hendrick Hertzberg, "Manifesto," *New Yorker*, October 14–21, 2002: 63.

4. Condoleezza Rice, "Promoting the National Interest," *Foreign Affairs* 79, no. 1 (January–February 2000): 46–47; for the overall discussion on China and Russia, see pp. 54–60.

5. Quoted in Anne E. Kornblut, "Campaign Trail a Trip of the Tongue: Bush Bedeviled by Spoken Word," *Boston Globe*, January 23, 2000.

6. George W. Bush, "A Distinctly American Internationalism," remarks at the Ronald Reagan Presidential Library," November 19, 1999, available at http://www.mtholyoke.edu/acad/intrel/bush/wspeech.htm.

7. Ivo H. Daalder and I. M. Destler, *In the Shadow of the Oval Office: Profiles of the National Security Advisers and the Presidents They Served—From JFK to George W. Bush* (New York: Simon and Schuster, 2009), 244–49, 262–65. For Clarke's account of his experiences in the Clinton and Bush administration as the chief counterterrorism officer, see Richard Clarke, *Against All Enemies: Inside America's War on Terror* (New York: Free Press, 2004), 24–32. For an overview of many of the memoirs written by administration officials, see Melvyn P. Leffler, "The Foreign Policies of the George W. Bush Administration: Memoirs, History, Legacy," *Diplomatic History* 37, no. 2 (April 2013): 190–216.

8. Ron Suskind, *The One Percent Doctrine: Deep Inside America's Pursuit of Its Enemies* (New York: Simon and Schuster, 2006), 2.

9. Derek Chollet and James Goldgeier, *America between the Wars: From 11/9 to 9/11, The Misunderstood Years between the Fall of the Berlin Wall and the Start of the War on Terror* (New York: Public Affairs, 2008), 267, 310.

10. Rice, "Promoting the National Interest," 48.

11. For a largely negative assessment of the Bush administration's approach to international treaties, see Antonio Chayes, "How American Treaty Behavior Threatens National Security," *International Security* 33, no. 1 (Summer 2008): 45–81.

12. Rice, "Promoting the National Interest," 47–48.

13. Bush, "A Distinctly American Internationalism."

14. "Second Presidential Debate," October 11, 2000, available at http://www.pbs.org/newshour/bb/election/2000debates/2ndebate2.html.

15. Bush, "A Distinctly American Internationalism."

16. Rice, "Promoting the National Interest," 46, 60–61.

17. Ibid., 52–53.

18. Josef Joffe, "Of Hubs, Spokes, and Public Goods," *National Interest* (Fall 2002): 17. See also Stephen Walt, "Beyond Bin Laden: Reshaping U.S. Foreign Policy," *International Security* 26, no. 3 (Winter 2001–2): 56, 64.

19. Dick Cheney with Liz Cheney, *In My Time: A Personal and Political Memoir* (New York: Threshold Editions, 2011), 10.

20. George W. Bush "The National Security Strategy of the United States of America," September 2002, p. 1. This and all the National Security Strategy documents cited in this chapter are available at http://nssarchive.us/.

21. Ibid., v. For an argument that this vastly inflated the threat that terrorism posed, see John Mueller and Mark G. Stewart, "The Terrorism Delusion: America's Overwrought Response to September 11," *International Security* 37, no. 1 (Summer 2012): 81–110.

22. Bush, "The National Security Strategy of the United States of America," September 2002, pp. iv, 1. See also p. 13.

23. Ibid., v.

24. Stephen D. Biddle, *American Grand Strategy after 9/11: An Assessment* (Carlisle, PA: Strategic Studies Institute, April 2005), 5–6.

25. Bush, "The National Security Strategy of the United States of America," September 2002, p. 5.

26. Greenville Byford, "The Wrong War," *Foreign Affairs* 81, no. 4 (July–August 2002): 34.

27. Donald K. Steinberg, "Foreign Policy Post-September 11: Learning the Right Lessons," February 27, 2003, available at http://2001-2009.state.gov/s/p/rem/2003/18762.htm.

28. Donald Rumsfeld, "Opening Statement before the Senate Armed Services Committee," August 3, 2006, available at http://www.defense.gov/speeches/speech.aspx?speechid=1030.

29. "Second Presidential Debate," October 11, 2000.

30. Bush, "The National Security Strategy of the United States of America," September 2002, pp. iv, v, 3.

31. Robert Draper, *Dead Certain: The Presidency of George W. Bush* (New York: Free Press, 2007), 287.

32. George W. Bush, "President Holds Prime Time News Conference," October 11, 2001, available at http://georgewbush-whitehouse.archives.gov/news/releases/2001/10/20011011 -7.html.

33. Bush, "The National Security Strategy of the United States of America," September 2002, p. 31.

34. Ibid., 21-23.

35. George W. Bush, *Decision Points* (New York: Crown, 2010), 205.

36. Bush, "The National Security Strategy of the United States of America," September 2002, p. 5.

37. Rice, "Promoting the National Interest," 53.

38. Charles Krauthammer, "The Neoconservative Convergence," *Commentary* 120, no. 1 (July-August 2005): 26.

39. Quoted in Bob Woodward, *The War Within: A Secret White House History 2006-2008* (New York: Simon and Schuster, 2009), 27.

40. Scott McClellan, *What Happened: Inside the Bush White House and Washington's Culture of Deception* (New York: Public Affairs, 2008), 128-29. Overall, see 126-33, 195-96.

41. Anatol Lieven, *America Right or Wrong: An Anatomy of American Nationalism* (New York: Oxford University Press, 2005), 2.

42. On the role of neoliberalism as opposed to neoconservatism in the run-up to the war in Iraq, see Tony Smith, *A Pact With the Devil: Washington's Bid for World Supremacy and the Betrayal of the American Promise* (New York: Routledge, 2007).

43. G. John Ikenberry, "American Grand Strategy in the Age of Terror," *Survival* 43, no. 4 (Winter 2001-2): 28.

44. On the Bush administration's institution building efforts involving the great powers, see Daniel Drezner, "The New, New World Order," *Foreign Affairs* 86, no. 2 (March-April 2007): 34-46.

45. G. John Ikenberry, "Woodrow Wilson, the Bush Administration, and the Future of Liberal Internationalism," in *The Crisis of American Foreign Policy: Wilsonianism in the Twenty-First Century*, ed. G. John Ikenberry, Thomas J. Knock, Anne-Marie Slaughter, and Tony Smith (Princeton, NJ: Princeton University Press, 2009), 7-8.

46. Bush, "The National Security Strategy of the United States of America," September 2002, pp. vi, 25, 31.

47. William Jefferson Clinton, "A National Security Strategy for a Global Age," December 2000, p. 1; and Bush, "The National Security Strategy of the United States of America," September 2002, p. 1. This omission of any mention of allies in President Bush's formulation is noted in Anna Kasten Nelson, "Continuity and Change in the Age of Unlimited Power," *Diplomatic History* 29, no. 3 (June 2005): 437-39.

48. For an argument about how the rise of unipolarity led the United States more toward unilateralism, see Charles A. Kupchan and Peter L. Trubowitz, "Dead Center: The Demise of Liberal Internationalism in the United States," *International Security* 32, no. 2 (Fall 2007): 7-44.

49. Bush, "The National Security Strategy of the United States of America," September 2002, pp. 29-30.

50. Colin Powell, "A Strategy of Partnerships," *Foreign Affairs* 83, no. 1 (January-February 2004): 28.

51. Adam Quinn, "'The Deal': The Balance of Power, Military Strength and Liberal Internationalism in the Bush National Security Strategy," *International Studies Perspectives* 9 (2008): 40-56.

52. Richard N. Haass, "Defining U.S. Foreign Policy in a Post-Post-Cold War World," April 22, 2002, available at http://2001-2009.state.gov/s/p/rem/9632.htm; and Thom Shanker, "White House Says the U.S. Is Not a Loner, Just Choosy," *New York Times*, July 31, 2001.

53. Quoted in Bob Woodward, *Bush at War* (New York: Simon and Schuster, 2002), 341.

54. Robert Kagan, "The September 12 Paradigm: America, the World, and George W. Bush," *Foreign Affairs* 87, no. 5 (September-October 2008): 25-39.

55. G. John Ikenberry, *Liberal Leviathan: The Origins, Crisis, and Transformation of the American World Order* (Princeton, NJ: Princeton University Press, 2011), 8.

56. "Transcript of Secretary of Defense Rumsfeld at Town Hall Meeting at Nellis Air Force Base," Las Vegas, Nevada, February 20, 2002, available at http://www.defenselink.mil/Speeches/Speech.aspx?SpeechID=193. For a similar sentiment from Vice President Cheney, see Cheney, *In My Time*, 331. See also Charles Krauthammer, "The Unipolar Moment Revisited," *National Interest* 70 (Winter 2002–3): 5–17.

57. On such debates, see Robert Kagan, "America's Crisis of Legitimacy," *Foreign Affairs* 83, no. 2 (March–April 2004): 65–87.

58. Sarah Kreps, "When Does the Mission Determine the Coalition? The Logic of Multilateral Intervention and the Case of Afghanistan," *Security Studies* 17 (2008): 531–67.

59. Bill Keller, "Why Colin Powell Should Go" *New York Times*, March 22, 2003, available at http://www.nytimes.com/2003/03/22/opinion/why-colin-powell-should-go.html?pagewanted=all&src=pm.

60. Bradley Graham, *By His Own Rules: The Ambitions, Successes, and Ultimate Failures of Donald Rumsfeld* (New York: Public Affairs, 2009), 508–9.

61. Donald H. Rumsfeld, "The National Defense Strategy of the United States of America," March 2005, p. 5.

62. Quoted in Michael H. Hunt, *The American Ascendancy: How the United States Gained and Wielded Global Dominance* (Chapel Hill: University of North Carolina Press, 2007), 294.

63. On the AIDS initiative as a whole, see Bush, *Decision Points*, 336–37.

64. See David E. Sanger, *The Inheritance: The World Obama Confronts and the Challenges to American Power* (New York: Three Rivers Press, 2009), 113–14.

65. Ahmad Rashid, *Descent into Chaos: The U.S. and the Disaster in Pakistan, Afghanistan, and Central Asia* (New York: Penguin Books, 2008), 354; and Seth G. Jones, *In the Graveyard of Empires: America's War in Afghanistan* (New York: Norton, 2009), xxiv.

66. Bush, *Decision Points*, 211.

67. Graham, *By His Own Rules*, 670.

68. Quoted in Walter LaFeber, "The Bush Doctrine," *Diplomatic History* 26, no. 3 (Fall 2002): 545–50.

69. George W. Bush, "Address to a Joint Session of Congress and the American People," September 20, 2011, available at http://georgewbush-whitehouse.archives.gov/news/releases/2001/09/20010920-8.html.

70. For a discussion of the effect of these lessons from 9/11 on the Bush administration's decision to go to war in Iraq, see Christopher Hemmer, "The Lessons of September 11th, Iraq and the American Pendulum," *Political Science Quarterly* 122, no. 2 (Summer 2007): 207–38.

71. Rice, "Promoting the National Interest," 46, 60–61.

72. "President Delivers 'State of the Union,'" January 29, 2002, available at http://georgewbush-whitehouse.archives.gov/news/releases/2002/01/20020129-11.html.

73. "President Delivers 'State of the Union,'" January 28, 2003, available at http://georgewbush-whitehouse.archives.gov/news/releases/2003/01/20030128-19.html.

74. Bush, *Decision Points*, 262. For his application of this lesson to the Iraq case, see pp. 224, 229 and 252–53.

75. Cheney, *In My Time*, 344.

76. Woodward, *Bush at War*, 350.

77. John Newhouse, *Imperial America: The Bush Assault on the New World Order* (New York, Knopf, 2003), 47.

78. Quoted in Suskind, *The One Percent Doctrine*, 62.

79. Marc Trachtenberg, "Preventive War and U.S. Foreign Policy," *Security Studies* 16, no. 1 (January–March 2007): 1–31.

80. "President Bush Outlines Iraqi Threat, Remarks by the President on Iraq," October 7, 2002, available at http://georgewbush-whitehouse.archives.gov/news/releases/2002/10/20021007-8.html.

81. "President Bush Meets with Prime Minister Blair," January 31, 2003, available at http://georgewbush-whitehouse.archives.gov/news/releases/2003/01/20030131-23.html.

82. Richard Hofstadter, "The Paranoid Style in American Politics," in *The Fear of Conspiracy: Images of Un-American Subversion from the Revolution to the Present*, ed. David Brion Davis (Ithaca, NY: Cornell University Press, 1971), 2–9.

83. Ibid., 8.

84. See Senate Select Committee on Intelligence, "Report on the U.S. Intelligence Community's Prewar Intelligence Assessments on Iraq," July 9, 2004, pp. 31, 363, available at http://www.intelligence.senate.gov/108301.pdf.

85. See Rajiv Chandrasekaran, *Imperial Life in the Emerald City: Inside Iraq's Green Zone* (New York: Knopf, 2006), 287, 5.

86. Woodward, *State of Denial*, xiii.

87. For an extended treatment of the Bush–Rumsfeld relationship and the problems this caused regarding U.S. decision making during the Iraq War, see Stephen Benedict Dyson, *Leaders in Conflict: Bush and Rumsfeld in Iraq* (Manchester: Manchester University Press, 2014).

88. "It's Hawk vs. Hawk in the Bush Administration," *Washington Post*, October 27, 2002.

89. Graham, *By His Own Rules*, 313, 336–37, 407, 456. See also Fred Kaplan, *Daydream Believers: How a Few Grand Ideas Wrecked American Power* (Hoboken, NJ: John Wiley, 2008), 153.

90. David Von Drehle, "Wrestling With History: Sometimes You Have to Fight the War You Have, Not the War You Wish You Had," *Washington Post Magazine*, November 13, 2005.

91. Eliot A. Cohen, "A Tale of Two Secretaries," *Foreign Affairs* 81, no. 3 (May 2002): 33.

92. These quotes come from Graham, *By His Own Rules*, 670–73.

93. For accounts of the decision for the surge from a largely White House perspective, see Woodward, *The War Within*. For a perspective largely from the new military commanders in Iraq, see Thomas E. Ricks, *The Gamble: General Petraeus and the American Military Adventure in Iraq* (New York: Penguin Books, 2009), 88–104. For the president's own account, see Bush, *Decision Points*, 355–94.

94. Condoleezza Rice, "Rethinking the National Interest: American Realism for a New World," *Foreign Affairs* 87, no. 4 (July–August 2008): 2–26.

95. Cf. Rice, "Promoting the National Interest," 47–48, with Rice, "Rethinking the National Interest," 3.

96. Rice, "Rethinking the National Interest," 7.

97. Cf. Rice, "Promoting the National Interest," 47–48, with Rice, "Rethinking the National Interest," 5–6, 18.

98. Elizabeth Sherwood Randall, "Alliances and American National Security," *Letort Papers* (Carlisle, PA: U.S. Army War College, 2006), vii, 9.

99. Rice, "Rethinking the National Interest," 21, 10, 14. For a balanced assessment of the Bush administration's democratization strategy in the Middle East, including its intended and unintended effects, see Bruce Gilley, "Did Bush Democratize the Middle East? The Effects of External and Internal Linkages," *Political Science Quarterly* 128, no. 4 (2013–14): 653–85.

100. Rice, "Rethinking the National Interest," 23.

101. Ibid., 23–26.

102. Ibid., 26.

103. Ibid., 24.

104. David C. Hendrickson, "The Curious Case of American Hegemony: Imperial Aspirations and National Decline," *World Policy Journal* 22, no. 2 (Summer 2005): 14.

8. "Don't Do Stupid Stuff"

1. John Dickerson, "In a Tight Spot: For Obama, Being President Is Like Parallel Parking," *Slate* May 14, 2009. In the article Dickerson is paraphrasing rather than quoting the president directly, available at http://ww.slate.com/articles/news_and_politics/politics/2009/05/in_a_tight_spot.html. I was directed to this quote by Sarah Kreps, "American Grand Strategy after Iraq," *Orbis* (Fall 2009), 632.

2. Barack Obama, "National Security Strategy," May 2010, p. 7.

3. Ibid., 17.

4. "Remarks by Vice President Biden at 45th Munich Conference on Security Policy," February 7, 2009, available at http://www.whitehouse.gov/the-press-office/remarks-vice-president -biden-45th-munich-conference-security-policy; and "Remarks by the President at the United States Naval Academy Commencement," May 22, 2009, available at http://www.whitehouse .gov/the-press-office/remarks-president-us-naval-academy-commencement.

5. For President Obama's most explicit discussion of his evolving counterterrorism polices, see "Remarks by the President at the National Defense University," May 23, 2013, available at http://www.whitehouse.gov/the-press-office/2013/05/23/remarks-president-national -defense-university.

6. "Remarks by John O. Brennan, Assistant to the President for Homeland Security and Counterterrorism—As Prepared for Delivery 'A New Approach to Safeguarding Americans,'" August 6, 2009, available at http://www.whitehouse.gov/the-press-office/remarks-john -brennan-center-strategic-and-international-studies.

7. Obama, "National Security Strategy," May 2010, p. 20. See also "Remarks by the President at the National Defense University," May 23, 3013.

8. "Remarks by the President on National Security," May 21, 2009, available at http://www .whitehouse.gov/the-press-office/remarks-president-national-security-5-21-09.

9. On legal debates and their resolution inside the Obama White House, see Daniel Klaidman, *Kill or Capture: The War on Terror and the Soul of the Obama Presidency* (Boston: Houghton Mifflin Harcourt, 2012); James Mann, *The Obamians: The Struggle inside the White House to Redefine American Power* (New York: Viking, 2012), 100–116; and Jo Becker and Scott Shane, "Secret 'Kill List' Proves a Test of Obama's Principles and Will," *New York Times*, May 29, 2012, available at http://www.nytimes.com/2012/05/29/world/obamas-leadership-in-war-on-al-qaeda .html?ref=ameasureofchange. With al-Qaeda weakened and the United States pulling the bulk of its forces out of Afghanistan, President Obama promised that the number of drone strikes would decline in his second term. See "Remarks by the President at the National Defense University," May 23, 2013.

10. "Statement by the President," San Jose, June 7, 2013, available at http://www.whitehouse .gov/the-press-office/2013/06/07/statement-president.

11. On the challenges and changes to the legal regime of the War on Terror during the Bush presidency, see Barton Gellman, *Angler: The Cheney Vice Presidency* (New York: Penguin Press, 2008), 299–326, 344–58.

12. George W. Bush, "The National Security Strategy of the United States of America," September 2002, p. 15.

13. "Remarks by the President at the United States Military Academy Commencement Ceremony," May 28, 2014, available at http://www.whitehouse.gov/the-press-office/2014/05/28 /remarks-president-west-point-academy-commencement-ceremony.

14. Obama, "National Security Strategy," May 2010, p. 23.

15. David E. Sanger, *Confront and Conceal: Obama's Secret Wars and Surprising Use of American Power* (New York: Crown 2012), ix–xx, 188–209.

16. "Remarks by the President at AIPAC Policy Conference," March 4, 2012, available at http://www.whitehouse.gov/the-press-office/2012/03/04/remarks-president-aipac-policy -conference-0. For similar statements on Iran from the president, see his remarks on July 1, 2010, November 2, 2010, May 22, 2011, and March 5, 2012.

17. "CJCS Interview with Fareed Zakaria," February 14, 2012, available at http://www.jcs .mil/speech.aspx?ID=1684#.

18. Jeffrey Goldberg, "Obama to Iran and Israel: 'As President of the United States, I Don't Bluff,'" *Atlantic*, March 2, 2012, available at http://www.theatlantic.com/international/archive /2012/03/obama-to-iran-and-israel-as-president-of-the-united-states-i-dont-bluff/253875/.

19. Barack Obama, *The Audacity of Hope: Thoughts on Reclaiming the American Dream* (New York: Three Rivers Press, 2006), 303.

20. Barack Obama, "Remarks in Chicago: 'A New Beginning,'" October 2, 2007, available at http://www.presidency.ucsb.edu/ws/index.php?pid=77015#axzz1y9syj5fc. For an account of the decision-making process inside the Obama White House, see Jonathan Alter, *The Promise: President Obama, Year One* (New York: Simon and Schuster, 2010). Obama's secretary of defense

similarly saw Obama as demonstrating "a lack of passion," but being "the most deliberative president I worked for." Robert M. Gates, *Duty: Memoirs of a Secretary at War* (New York: Knopf, 2014), 298–99.

21. Quoted in David Remnick, "Going the Distance: On and off the Road with Barack Obama," *New Yorker*, January 27, 2014, available at http://www.newyorker.com/reporting /2014/01/27/140127fa_fact_remnick?currentPage=all.

22. For a compilation of White House officials who have used the phrase, see Mike Allen, "'Don't Do Stupid Sh—' (Stuff)," *Politico*, June 1, 2014, available at http://www.politico.com /story/2014/06/dont-do-stupid-shit-president-obama-white-house-107293.html. This phrase got the most attention when Secretary of State Clinton, after leaving office, criticized it as being an insufficient "organizing principle" for a great power. See Jeffrey Goldberg, "Hillary Clinton: 'Failure' to Help Syrian Rebels Led to the Rise of ISIS," *Atlantic*, August 10, 2014, available at http://www.theatlantic.com/international/archive/2014/08/hillary-clinton-failure-to-help -syrian-rebels-led-to-the-rise-of-isis/375832/?single_page=true.

23. For early assessments of President Obama's foreign policy, see Martin Indyk, Kenneth G. Lieberthal, and Michael E. O'Hanlon, *Bending History? Barack Obama's Foreign Policy* (Washington, DC: Brookings Institution Press, 2012); Mann, *The Obamians*; Henry R. Nau, "The Jigsaw Puzzle and the Chessboard: The Making and Unmaking of Foreign Policy in the Age of Obama," *Commentary* 133, no. 5 (May 2012): 13–26; Daniel W. Drezner, "Does Obama Have a Grand Strategy? Why We Need New Doctrines in Uncertain Times," *Foreign Affairs* 90, no. 4 (July–August 2011): 57–68; Leslie H. Gelb, "The Elusive Obama Doctrine," *National Interest* 121 (September–October 2012): 18–28, and see the contributions of various analysts to "America Self-Contained? A Symposium" *American Interest* 9, no. 5 (May–June 2014): 7–49.

24. The first quote comes from Barack Obama, "Responsibly Ending the War in Iraq, February 27, 2009, available at http://www.whitehouse.gov/the-press-office/remarks-president -barack-obama-ndash-responsibly-ending-war-iraq; the second from "Remarks of President Barack Obama at Student Roundtable," April 7, 2009, available at http://www.whitehouse.gov /the-press-office/remarks-president-barack-obama-student-roundtable-istanbul. For similar comments, see his statements on April 17, 2009, and the statement of Secretary of State Hillary Clinton on July 15, 2009.

25. William Jefferson Clinton, "A National Security Strategy of Engagement and Enlargement," February 1996, p. 1. James Mann argues that the single term that best describes the Obama administration's foreign policy is "rebalancing." See his *The Obamians*, 340.

26. Bush, "The National Security Strategy of the United States of America," September 2002, p. v.

27. Barack Obama, "Remarks by the President at the Acceptance of the Nobel Peace Prize," December 10, 2009, available at http://www.whitehouse.gov/the-press-office/remarks-presi dent-acceptance-nobel-peace-prize.

28. Obama, "National Security Strategy," May 2010, pp. 8, 23.

29. Barack Obama, "Remarks to the Chicago Council on Global Affairs," April 23, 2007, available at http://www.presidency.ucsb.edu/ws/index.php?pid=77043#axzz1y9syj5fc.

30. Barack Obama, "Remarks by the President on a New Beginning," June 4, 2009, available at http://www.whitehouse.gov/the-press-office/remarks-president-cairo-university-6-04-09.

31. James Jones, "Remarks by National Security Advisor Jones at 45th Munich Conference on Security Policy," February 9, 2009, available at http://www.whitehouse.gov/the-press-office /remarks-national-security-adviser-jones-45th-munich-conference-security-policy.

32. Obama, "National Security Strategy," May 2010, p. 1.

33. For the pivot or rebalancing to Asia, see Department of Defense, "Sustaining U.S. Global Leadership: Priorities for the 21st Century," January 5, 2012, and its "Defense Budget Priorities and Choices," January 2012. See also, Hillary Clinton, "America's Pacific Century," *Foreign Policy* 189 (November 2011): 56–63.

34. Department of Defense, "Sustaining U.S. Global Leadership," 2.

35. Department of Defense, "Sustaining U.S. Global Leadership," 1–6.

36. George W. Bush, "The National Security Strategy of the United States of America," March 2006, pp. 47–48.

37. "Press Conference by the President," April 19, 2009, available at http://www.whitehouse .gov/the-press-office/press-conference-president-trinidad-and-tobago-4192009. The second principle he mentioned focused on the role of U.S. values in its foreign policy, an issue that will be dealt with below. David Sanger also makes multilateralism a key part of the Obama Doctrine, see his *Confront and Conceal*, xiv–xv.

38. Obama, "Remarks to the Chicago Council on Global Affairs," April 23, 2007.

39. The phrase was first used by Ryan Lizza in the context of discussing Obama's foreign policy; see "The Consequentialist: How the Arab Spring Remade Obama's Foreign Policy," *New Yorker*, May 2, 2011, available at http://www.newyorker.com/reporting/2011/05/02/110502fa _fact_lizza?currentPage=all.

40. Obama, "National Security Strategy" May 2010, p. 1.

41. Ibid., 22.

42. "Remarks by the President at the United States Military Academy Commencement Ceremony," May 28, 2014.

43. Bush, "The National Security Strategy of the United States of America," September 2002, pp. 1, 29.

44. Obama, "National Security Strategy," May 2010, pp. ii, 2, 9, 34.

45. "News Conference by President Obama," April 2, 2009, available at http://www.white house.gov/the-press-office/news-conference-president-obama-40209.

46. "Foreign Policy Address at the Council on Foreign Relations," July 15, 2009, available at http://www.state.gov/secretary/rm/2009a/july/126071.htm.

47. "News Conference by President Obama," April 4, 2009, available at http://www .whitehouse.gov/the-press-office/news-conference-president-obama-4042009.

48. Obama, "National Security Strategy," May 2010, p. ii.

49. For an early assessment on how the Obama administration is handling such issues, see Stephen Schlesinger, "Bosom Buddies? Ban and Obama's Curious Relations," *World Policy Journal* (Spring 2010): 87–95. For a discussion of how the post–Cold War environment has made it harder both domestically and internationally for the Obama administration to pursue multilateralism successfully, see David Skidmore, "The Obama Presidency and US Foreign Policy: Where's the Multilateralism?" *International Studies Perspectives* 13 (2012): 43–64.

50. Drezner, "Does Obama Have a Grand Strategy?," 65.

51. For one example of its use and of Obama's identification of this quote as one of his favorites, see "Interview of the President by Yonit Levi, Israeli TV," July 7, 2010, available at http:// www.whitehouse.gov/the-press-office/interview-president-yonit-levi-israeli-tv.

52. Barack Obama, "Inaugural Address," January 21, 2009, available at http://www.white house.gov/briefing-room/Speeches-and-Remarks/2009/01?page=1.

53. Barack Obama, "Remarks by the President on National Security," May 21, 2009, available at http://www.whitehouse.gov/the-press-office/remarks-president-national-security-5-21-09.

54. Barack Obama, "Remarks by the President at United States Military Academy at West Point Commencement," May 22, 2010, available at http://www.whitehouse.gov/the-press-office /remarks-president-united-states-military-academy-west-point-commencement.

55. Obama, "Remarks by the President at the Acceptance of the Nobel Peace Prize."

56. Obama, "Remarks by the President at United States Military Academy at West Point Commencement."

57. Mann, *The Obamians*, 196–99.

58. Barack Obama, "Statement by the President on Cuba Policy Changes" December 17, 2014, available at http://www.whitehouse.gov/the-press-office/2014/12/17/statement-president -cuba-policy-changes.

59. Barack Obama, "Remarks by the President at a DNC Event," August 11, 2011, available at http://www.whitehouse.gov/the-press-office/2011/08/11/remarks-president-dnc-event.

60. Many of Obama's partisan critics have accused him of not believing in U.S. exceptionalism, primarily based on a truncated reading of his response to a question during an early press conference (News Conference by President Obama," April 4, 2009); however, such a reading can only be sustained by ignoring huge parts of his rhetoric, which is filled with a discussion of U.S. values and his conception of the mission of the United States to help spread those values. For

an example of this argument from a serious student of U.S. foreign policy, and one who is not a partisan critic, see Josef Joffe, "Who is this Guy?" *American Interest* (Winter 2010): 18; and Joffe, "America Self-Contained?" *American Interest* 9, no. 5 (May–June 2014): 7–9.

61. Obama, *The Audacity of Hope*, 316, 321.

62. Barack Obama, "Remarks in Clinton, Iowa: 'Turning the Page in Iraq,'" September 12, 2007, available at http://www.presidency.ucsb.edu/ws/index.php?pid=77011#axzz1y9syj5fc.

63. Obama, "Remarks in Chicago: 'A New Beginning.'"

64. Barack Obama, "Address to Joint Session of Congress," February 24, 2009, available at http://www.whitehouse.gov/the-press-office/remarks-president-barack-obama-address -joint-session-congress.

65. For examples, see "Remarks by the President on National Security," May 21, 2009; "Remarks by the President at United States Military Academy at West Point Commencement," May 22, 2010; "Remarks by the President at Independence Day Celebration," July 4, 2010, available at http://www.whitehouse.gov/the-press-office/remarks-president-independence-day -celebration; and "Remarks by the President at the Pentagon Memorial," September 11, 2010, available at http://www.whitehouse.gov/the-press-office/2010/09/11/remarks-president-pentagon -memorial.

66. Barack Obama, "Remarks by the President to the Ghanaian Parliament," July 11, 2009, available at http://www.whitehouse.gov/the-press-office/remarks-president-ghanaian-par liament.

67. Obama, "National Security Strategy," May 2010, pp. 5, 35.

68. Barack Obama, "Remarks by President Obama in Address to the United Nations General Assembly," September 24, 2014, available at http://www.whitehouse.gov/the-press-office /2014/09/24/remarks-president-obama-address-united-nations-general-assembly.

69. Barack Obama, "Statement by the President [on the] Report of the Senate Select Committee on Intelligence" December 9, 2014, available at http://www.whitehouse.gov/the-press -office/2014/12/09/statement-president-report-senate-select-committee-intelligence.

70. Barack Obama, "Remarks by the President in Address to the Nation on the Way Forward in Afghanistan and Pakistan," December 1, 2009, available at http://www.whitehouse .gov/the-press-office/remarks-president-address-nation-way-forward-afghanistan-and -pakistan.

71. Barack Obama, "Remarks by President Barack Obama at Town Hall Meeting with Future Chinese Leaders," November 16, 2009, available at http://www.whitehouse.gov/the-press -office/remarks-president-barack-obama-town-hall-meeting-with-future-chinese-leaders.

72. Obama, "Remarks by the President on a New Beginning."

73. See Barack Obama, "Press Conference by the President," June 23, 2009, available at http://www.whitehouse.gov/the-press-office/press-conference-president-6-23-09; "Remarks By President Obama and Chancellor Merkel of Germany in Joint Press Availability," June 26, 2009, available at http://www.whitehouse.gov/the-press-office/remarks-president-obama-and -chancellor-merkel-germany-joint-press-availability; and "Remarks of President Obama Marking Nowruz," March 20, 2010, available at http://www.whitehouse.gov/the-press-office/remarks -president-obama-marking-nowruz.

74. For a critical assessment of the Obama administration's response to the Arab Spring, which he sees as characterized by disengagement and an emphasis on counterterrorism, see Vali Nasr, *The Dispensable Nation: American Foreign Policy in Retreat* (New York: Doubleday, 2013), 159–83.

75. Barack Obama, "Remarks by the President in Address to the Nation on Libya," March 28, 2011, available at http://www.whitehouse.gov/the-press-office/2011/03/28/remarks-presi dent-address-nation-libya. See also his "Remarks by the President on Libya," March 19, 2011, available at http://www.whitehouse.gov/the-press-office/2011/03/19/remarks-president-libya; and "Remarks by the President on the Middle East and North Africa," May 19, 2011, available at http://www.whitehouse.gov/the-press-office/2011/05/19/remarks-president-middle-east -and-north-africa.

76. Also known as ISIS or ISIL as acronyms for the Islamic State in Iraq and Syria/the Levant.

77. Barack Obama, "Statement by the President," August 7, 2014, available at http://www .whitehouse.gov/the-press-office/2014/08/07/statement-president.

78. Barack Obama, "Statement by the President on ISIL," September 10, 2014, available at http://www.whitehouse.gov/the-press-office/2014/09/10/statement-president-isil-1.

79. Obama, "National Security Strategy," May 2010, p. 9.

80. Thomas L. Friedman and Michael Mandelbaum, *That Used to Be Us: How America Fell Behind in the World It Invented and How We Can Come Back* (New York: Farrar, Strauss and Giroux, 2011), 159–60. See also Mandelbaum, *The Frugal Superpower: America's Global Leadership in a Cash-Strapped Era* (New York: Public Affairs, 2010). For a historically informed discussion of U.S. deficit spending, see Robert D. Hormats, *The Price of Liberty: Paying for America's Wars* (New York: Times Books, 2007). For a more optimistic assessment of what the United States can continue to afford, see Robert J. Lieber, *Power and Willpower in the American Future: Why The United States Is Not Destined to Decline* (Cambridge: Cambridge University Press, 2012).

81. See the Rolling Stones song, "Before They Make Me Run," on the album *Some Girls*.

Conclusion

1. Reinhold Niebuhr, *The Irony of American History* (New York: Scribner's, 1952), 133.

2. Colin Dueck, *Hard Line: The Republican Party and U.S. Foreign Policy since World War II* (Princeton, NJ: Princeton University Press, 2010), 229.

3. For similar approaches to the definition of multilateralism, see Benjamin Miller, "Explaining Changes in US Grand Strategy: 9/11, the Rise of Offensive Liberalism, and the War in Iraq," *Security Studies* 19 (2010): 32; Sarah Kreps, "When Does the Mission Determine the Coalition? The Logic of Multilateral Intervention and the Case of Afghanistan," *Security Studies* 17 (2008): 531–67; and Sarah Kreps, "Multilateral Military Interventions: Theory and Practice," *Political Science Quarterly* 123, no. 4 (2008–9): 590.

4. Michael Hirsh, *At War with Ourselves: Why America Is Squandering Its Chance to Build a Better World* (Oxford: Oxford University Press, 2003), 240–41.

5. Daniel W. Drezner, "Does Obama Have a Grand Strategy? Why We Need New Doctrines in Uncertain Times," *Foreign Affairs* 90, no. 4 (July–August 2011): 65.

6. Joseph S. Nye Jr., *The Paradox of American Power: Why the World's Only Superpower Can't Go It Alone* (New York: Oxford University Press, 2002), 110. See also Nina Hachigian and Mona Sutphen, "Strategic Collaboration: How the United States Can Thrive as Other Powers Rise," *Washington Quarterly* 31, no. 4 (Autumn 2008): 43–57. The need for the United States to take the interests of others into account because of fiscal deficits is a major theme of Stephen S. Cohen and J. Bradford DeLong, *The End of Influence: What Happens When Other Countries Have the Money* (New York: Basic Books, 2010), 7.

7. Richard Haass, *The Opportunity: America's Moment to Alter History's Course* (New York: Public Affairs, 2005), 20.

8. Steve Weber and Bruce Jentleson call this "mutuality," see their *The End of Arrogance: America in the Global Competition of Ideas* (Cambridge, MA: Harvard University Press, 2010), 104.

9. Charles Krauthammer, "The Lonely Superpower," *New Republic* 205, no. 5 (July 29, 1991): 26.

10. The term "multi-multilateralism" is from Francis Fukuyama, *America at the Crossroads: Democracy, Power, and the Neoconservative Legacy* (New Haven, CT: Yale University Press, 2006), 158, 163. The term "à la carte" multilateralism is from Haass, *The Opportunity*, 178. On the latter, see also Stewart Patrick, "Prix Fixe and à la Carte: Avoiding False Multilateral Choices," *Washington Quarterly* 32, no. 4 (October 2009): 77–95. On the coalition of the relevant, see Naazneen Barma, Ely Ratner, and Steven Weber, "The Mythical Liberal Order," *National Interest* 124 (March–April 2013): 56–67.

11. For examples of calls for the United States to pursue an activist grand strategy, which in many cases includes an energetic commitment to the spread of U.S. values, see Robert Kagan, *The World America Made* (New York: Knopf, 2012); Peter Feaver, "American Grand Strategy at the Crossroads: Leading from the Front, Leading from Behind, or Not Leading at All," in *America's Path: Grand Strategy for the Next Administration*, ed. Robert Fontaine and Kristin M. Lord (Washington, DC: Center for New American Security, May 2012), 59–70; Henry R. Nau, "Conser-

vative Internationalism," *Policy Review* 150 (August–September 2008): 3–44; Niall Ferguson, *Colossus: The Price of America's Empire* (New York: Penguin Press, 2004); Walter Russell Mead, *Power, Terror, Peace and War: America's Grand Strategy in a World at Risk* (New York: Vintage Books, 2005), 165–213; Robert E. Kagan and William Kristol, eds., *Present Dangers: Crisis and Opportunity in American Foreign and Defense* Policy (San Francisco: Encounter Books, 2000); Charles Krauthammer, *Democratic Realism: An American Foreign Policy for a Unipolar World* (Washington: AEI Press, 2004), 1–19; and David Frum and Richard Perle, *An End to Evil: How to Win the War on Terror* (New York: Random House, 2003).

12. For similar discussions of the relationship between the power of the United States and its tendencies toward crusading, see Miller, "Explaining Changes in American Grand Strategy"; and Michael C. Desch, "America's Liberal Illiberalism: The Ideological Origins of Overreaction in U.S. Foreign Policy," *International Security* 32, no. 3 (Winter 2007–8): 7–43.

13. For an excellent summary of much of this literature, which comes to the relatively pessimistic conclusion that none offers a sound guide for policy, see James F. Miskel, "Grand Strategies for Dealing with Other States in the New, New World Order," *Naval War College Review* 58, no. 1 (Winter 2005): 63–75. On the concept of geopolitical pivots and the Global Balkans, see Zbigniew Brzezinski, *The Grand Chessboard: American Primacy and Its Geostrategic Imperatives* (New York: Basic Books, 1997), 40–48, 123–50, and his *The Choice: Global Domination or Global Leadership* (New York: Basic Books, 2004), 42, 79, 226. On pivotal states, see Robert Chase, Emily Hill, and Paul M. Kennedy, eds,. *The Pivotal States: A New Framework for US Policy in the Developing World* (New York: Norton, 1998). On the core versus the gap, see Thomas P. M. Barnett, *The Pentagon's New Map* (New York: Putnam's, 2004).

14. Anne-Marie Slaughter, "America's Edge: Power in the Networked Century," *Foreign Affairs* 88, no. 1 (January–February 2009): 96, 106. For an argument that the United States inflates the threats it is currently facing, largely for domestic political reasons, see Micah Zenko and Michael A. Cohen, "Clear and Present Safety: The United States Is More Secure Than Washington Thinks," *Foreign Affairs* 91, no. 2 (March–April 2012): 79–93.

15. See Frank Ahrens, "The Reluctant Warrior," *Washington Post*, February 24, 1998, available at http://www.washingtonpost.com/wp-srv/inatl/longterm/iraq/keyplayers/berger022498.htm.

16. See Josef Joffe, "The Default Power: The False Prophecy of America's Decline," *Foreign Affairs* 88, no. 5 (September–October 2009): 21–35. For the argument that the United States gains economically from playing such a role, see Carla Norrlof, *America's Global Advantage: US Hegemony and International Cooperation* (Cambridge: Cambridge University Press, 2010).

17. For calls for a grand strategy of offshore balancing, see Christopher Layne, *The Peace of Illusions: American Grand Strategy from 1940 to the Present* (Ithaca, NY: Cornell University Press, 2006). See also John Mearsheimer, "Imperial by Design," *National Interest* 111 (January–February 2011): 16–34; and Stephen M. Walt, "The End of the American Era," *National Interest* 116 (November–December 2011): 6–16. For similar calls for restraint and greater isolationism, see Christopher A. Preble, *The Power Problem: How American Military Dominance Makes Us Less Safe, Less Prosperous, and Less Free* (Ithaca, NY: Cornell University Press, 2009); Barry Posen, "Pull Back: The Case for a Less Activist Foreign Policy," *Foreign Affairs* 92, no. 1 (January–February 2013): 116–28; Barry Posen, *Restraint: A New Foundation for U.S. Grand Strategy* (Ithaca, NY: Cornell University Press, 2014); Eugene Gholz, Daryl S. Press, and Harvey M. Sapolsky, "Come Home America: The Strategy of Restraint in the Face of Temptation," *International Security* 21, no. 4 (Spring 1997): 5–48; and Eric A. Nordlinger, *Isolationism Reconfigured: American Foreign Policy for a New Century* (Princeton, NJ: Princeton University Press, 1995).

18. Thus, the argument here is more consistent with the concepts of "forward," "selective," or "deep engagement" rather than offshore balancing. For a defense of forward engagement, see Michèle Flournoy and Janine Davidson, "Obama's New Global Posture: The Logic of U.S. Foreign Deployments," *Foreign Affairs* 91, no. 4 (July–August 2012): 54–63. On selective engagement, see Robert J. Art, *A Grand Strategy for America* (Ithaca, NY: Cornell University Press, 2003), as well as his "Selective Engagement in The Era of Austerity," in Fontaine and Lord, *America's Path*, 15–27. On deep engagement, see Stephen Brooks, G. John Ikenberry, and William C. Wohlforth, "Don't Come Home America: The Case against Retrenchment," *International Security* 37, no. 3 (Winter 2012–13): 7–51.

19. Bradley A. Thayer, "In Defense of Primacy," *National Interest* 86 (November–December 2006): 34–35.

20. G. John Ikenberry, "Liberal Order Building," in *To Lead the World: American Strategy after the Bush Doctrine*, ed. Melvyn P. Leffler and Jeffery W. Legro (Oxford: Oxford University Press, 2008), 106.

21. For a full exposition of the logic of making institution building a key part of future U.S. grand strategy, see G. John Ikenberry, *Liberal Leviathan: The Origins, Crisis, and Transformation of the American World Order* (Princeton, NJ: Princeton University Press, 2011). For related arguments, see also Charles A. Kupchan, *No One's World: The West, the Rising Rest, and the Coming Global Turn* (New York: Oxford University Press, 2012); Stephen B. Brooks and William C. Wohlforth, *World out of Balance: International Relations Theory and the Challenge of American Primacy* (Princeton, NJ: Princeton University Press, 2008), 214–18; Michael Mandelbaum, *The Case for Goliath: How America Acts as the World's Government in the Twenty-First Century* (New York: Public Affairs, 2005); *Forging a World of Liberty under Law: U.S. National Security in the 21st Century*, Final Report of the Princeton Project on National Security, Woodrow Wilson School of Public Affairs, G. John Ikenberry and Anne-Marie Slaughter, codirectors, September 27, 2006; Charles A. Kupchan, *The End of the American Era: US Foreign Policy and the Geopolitics of the 21st Century* (New York: Knopf, 2002); and Peter Beinart, *The Good Fight: Why Liberals and Only Liberals Can Win the War on Terror and Make America Great Again* (New York: HarperCollins, 2006).

22. For an excellent discussion of examples of threat inflation regarding the potential rise of great power competitors to the United States see Josef Joffe, *The Myth of America's Decline: Politics, Economics and a Half Century of False Prophecies* (New York: Norton, 2014).

23. For the original quote, see Ron Suskind, *The Price of Loyalty: George W. Bush, the White House, and the Education of Paul O'Neill* (New York: Simon and Schuster, 2004), 291. For Cheney's elaboration on this quote, see Dick Cheney with Liz Cheney, *In My Time: A Personal and Political Memoir* (New York: Threshold Editions, 2011), 310–11.

24. Aaron L. Friedberg, *A Contest for Supremacy: China, America and the Struggle for Mastery in Asia* (New York: Norton, 2011), 2–6.

25. For a more direct entrant in the Kennan sweepstakes based on an earlier version of the framework developed in this book, see Christopher Hemmer, "Grand Strategy for the Next Administration," *Orbis* 51, no. 3 (Summer 2007): 447–60.

26. Quoted in Walter Russell Mead, *Special Providence: American Foreign Policy and How it Changed the World* (New York: Knopf, 2001), 39. This quote is also paraphrased by Samuel Huntington to close his *The Common Defense: Strategic Programs in National Politics* (New York: Columbia University Press, 1961), 447.

Index